CONTENTS

edited by R. Funck · Karlsruhe papers in regional science 1 · a pion publication

recent developments in regional science

Pion Limited, 207 Brondesbury Park, London NW2 5JN

ISBN 0 85086 034 2

Set on IBM 72 Composers by Pion Limited, London.
Printed in Great Britain by J.W.Arrowsmith Limited, Bristol.

Preface

This volume contains some of the papers which were presented, or which were developed from the authors' lectures, at the Advanced Studies Institute on *Recent Developments in Regional Science,* held in Karlsruhe, Germany, July 20 to August 14, 1970 at the Institut für Regionalwissenschaft der Universität Karlsruhe in cooperation with the Regional Science Association and the Gesellschaft für Regionalforschung (German Speaking Section, R.S.A.).

Thus, although not all of the lecturers nor all of the topics which were on the program are represented here, the volume gives a good impression of what was being worked at during the Karlsruhe summer. The reader who is interested to learn in more detail about some of the organizational aspects of the Institute may refer to the brief proceedings also included in the volume.

This book is the first of a series which is intended to be published annually. Subsequent volumes will display cross sections of the work performed at future Advanced Studies Institutes, or will record, possibly at varying intervals, other scientific events on the European continent, or report on results of the most recent research efforts in areas of special interest to regional scientists.

Hence it is expected that the series will provide a platform where the mutual exchange of ideas, between regional scientists of different backgrounds and different linguistic origins, takes place. One special goal will be to present some of the results of the theoretical and empirical research, which is being done in the German Speaking Section of the Regional Science Association, to the broad international public of experts interested in the economic, geographic, mathematical, planning, sociological, statistical, and administrative aspects of regional, urban, and environmental problems.

R.F.

Recent Developments in Regional Science
Proceedings of the Advanced Studies Institute at Karlsruhe, July 20 to August 14, 1970

1. *Program*

The purposes of the Institute were to

(1) provide information on recent contributions of various disciplines to the sample of analytical methods used in regional science, and

(2) provide a platform to discuss, in a multidisciplinary approach, the usefulness of these methods from the point of view of their applicability to problems of regional policy and regional planning.

From these goals the following principles were derived, in order to specify the topics to be discussed at the Institute and the ways of having them presented to the participants:

(a) since the participants had different backgrounds, adequate basic information had to be provided in order to enable everybody to achieve a critical view of the various problems arising along the frontier of scientific development;

(b) the new methods selected for discussion had to be of multidisciplinary interest, in the sense that they might be applicable in more than one of the disciplines in regional science;

(c) along with the presentation of theoretical material, there had to be a study of practical questions of regional policy and regional planning to which the theories might be relevant.

The major organizational problems were to develop an Institute's schedule, to invite lecturers, and to select participants according to these principles. The directors of the Institute were supported by the three members of the Advisory Board in their efforts to solve these problems. Fourteen lecturers were on the Institute's teaching staff; between four and six of them were available for lecturing, discussions, and informal conversation at any given point in time during the period of the Institute. A regional science library had been especially compiled for the use of the participants from the stacks of the University Library, the Institut für Regionalwissenschaft, and the Department of Economics, as well as from private sources. A small organizational staff of graduate students and members of the Institut für Regionalwissenschaft der Universität Karlsruhe was responsible for the technical details connected with the academic activities and with the problems of accommodation, leisure activities, etc.

The scientific materials were presented and discussed during a total time period of about 150 hours in the following ways:

(1) series of lectures and discussions (about 65% of the time budget)

(2) seminars for groups of participants with special interests (about 15%)

(3) single lectures on selected topics (about 10%)

(4) special seminars initiated by participants (about 10%).

In order to allow for an optimal level of scientific communication among Institute members, the total number of participants was restricted to about 35. Invitations were distributed to regional scientists all over the world, with an emphasis on residents of Western Europe. Out of a number of about 70 applicants, 36 scholars were admitted as participants. Since two had to revoke their application on short notice, the total number of participants, including the three members of the organization staff, was 37. The decisions on admission to the Institute were based on the following criteria:

(a) Adequate scientific qualification to ensure a high degree of receptive achievement and of active participation in the Institute's academic activities. Examination of this criterion was based on the applicant's vitae and list of publications, as well as on a letter of recommendation to be provided to the Advisory Board.

(b) A well balanced interdisciplinary spectrum of participants in order to guarantee that as many different aspects of the Institute's topics as possible would be considered in the discussions.

Actually the backgrounds of the participants were as follows:

Regional economics	17 participants
City and regional planning	13 participants
Human and regional geography	6 participants
City and regional sociology	1 participant.

(c) Together with a balanced international spectrum of participants, a special research stimulus had to be achieved for the host institutions, the University of Karlsruhe and the german speaking section of the Regional Science Association. Thus the share of participants from Germany was set at a rather high level. The actual figures were:

Participants from	Western Europe except Germany	11
	Germany except Karlsruhe	9
	Karlsruhe (including organizational staff)	8
	Eastern Europe	2
	Africa	1
	America	5
	Asia	1

At the end of the four week period an anonymous form for teacher and program evaluation was distributed and returned by most of the participants. The program and organization of the Institute, as well as the didactic and scientific performance of many—thought not all—of the lecturers, was very highly valued in most responses. Virtually all participants and members of the teaching staff stated that by attending the Institute they had greatly improved their understanding of regional problems, and recommended that more Advanced Studies Institutes in Regional Science be held in the future.

Among the most valuable recommendations for the organizing of future Institutes were the following (omitting those which were contradictory among participants): reduction of the Institute's period to three weeks; reduction of the portion of the time budget spent on receptive activities (lectures), and expansion of the time budget available for seminars, including seminar preparation, in order to increase active participation; accentuation of technological, environmental, and social aspects of regional planning. All of these recommendations are being followed in the preparation of the Second Advanced Studies Institute in Regional Science which will be held in Karlsruhe in 1972.

D.B. and R.F.

2. *Lectures and teaching staff*
* Member of Advisory Board

W. Alonso, University of California, Berkeley, California, USA.
Location Theory, 10 hours

M. J. Beckmann, Brown University, Providence, Rhode Island, USA, and Technische Universität München, Germany.
Selected Topics in Regional Science I, 6 hours

D. Bökemann, Universität Karlsruhe, Germany, Assistant Director.
Infrastructure Systems, 6 hours

*E. von Böventer, Universität München, Germany.
Selected Topics in Regional Science II, 6 hours

D. Boyce, University of Pennsylvania, Philadelphia, Pennsylvania, USA.
Metropolitan Transportation Problems, 8 hours

J. Dyckman, University of California, Berkeley, California, USA.
The Planning Process, 8 hours

W. Eichhorn, Universität Karlsruhe, Germany.
Mathematical Tools in Regional Analysis, 22 hours

R. Funck, Universität Karlsruhe, Germany, Scientific Director.
Multiregional Growth Models, 6 hours

B. Harris, University of Pennsylvania, Philadelphia, Pennsylvania, USA.
Urbanization and City Planning Models, 10 hours

W. Isard, University of Pennsylvania, Philadelphia, Pennsylvania, USA.
Future Developments in Regional Science, 6 hours

R. Jochimsen, Universität Kiel, Germany.
Strategies in Regional Politics, 2 hours

L. B. M. Mennes, Nederlandse Economische Hogeschool, Rotterdam, Netherlands.
Spatial Equilibrium Models, 10 hours

*J. Paelinck, Université de Namur, Belgium.
Methods of Regional Analysis, 20 hours

R. Thoss, Universität Mannheim, Germany.
Methods of Regional Forecasting, 4 hours

3. *Participants*

* Member of Advisory Board. † Member of Organizational Staff.

F. Allgayer, Augsburg, Germany.
D. Bjørnland, Oslo, Norway.
A. Boato, Trento, Italy.
U. Christiansen, Copenhagen, Denmark.
M. Daub, Berlin, Germany.
J. De Rooy, Easton, Pennsylvania, USA.
H. Diedrich, Hamburg, Germany.
D. Donkor, Kumasi, Ghana.
D. Fürst, Köln, Germany.
W. Gaebe, Karlsruhe, Germany.
S. Geisenberger, Freiburg, Germany.
R. B. Goodman, St. Louis, Missouri, USA.
†H. Hellmann, Karlsruhe, Germany.
R. Herz, Karlsruhe, Germany.
C. Jaumotte, Namur, Belgium.
R. Jensen, Oslo, Norway.
D. Keil, Wien, Austria.
H. -J. Klein, Karlsruhe, Germany.
Barbara Kreibich, München, Germany.
V. Kreibich, München, Germany.
†D. Kumpf, Karlsruhe, Germany.
R. Laulajainen, Tikkurila, Finland.
G. Lippert, München, Germany.
W. H. Long, University Park, Pennsylvania, USA.
I. Masser, Liverpool, England.
H. Schoof, Karlsruhe, Germany.
B. Sing, St. John's, Newfoundland, Canada.
A. Steiner, Karlsruhe, Germany.
I. Tekeli, Ankara, Turkey.
M. Termote, Kessel-Lo, Belgium.
*P. Treuner, Kiel, Germany.
A. Trigo de Abreu, Lisboa, Portugal.
A. Trumiç, Sarajevo, Yugoslavia.
A. Villani, Milano, Italy.
C. Werner, Laguna Beach, California, USA.
S. Zduniç, Zagreb, Yugoslavia.
†J. Zimmermann, Karlsruhe, Germany.

Linear and Non-linear Systems of Equations

W.EICHHORN, R.ERDMANN
Universität Karlsruhe

Introduction

The mathematical formulation of economic models often leads to the following particular problem: that of finding the real solutions of a real system of m equations in n unknowns (for example, see Alonso, 1964, pages 150, 151; Isard, 1968, pages 363-371). The methods employed to solve such a problem depend on the type of system, and generally one can only give approximate solutions. However, in some special cases an 'exact' solution is possible, the most important case of this kind being a linear system of equations. Before treating this favourable example, we wish to emphasize that usually one cannot say anything about the solution of a system of equations if only the number n of unknowns and the number m of equations are known. To illustrate this we give the following examples.

Examples

1. $m = n$

(a) $\begin{aligned} x_1 + x_2 &= 1 \\ x_1 + x_2 &= 0 \end{aligned}$ (no solution),

(b) $\cos x = 1$ (infinite number of solutions),

(c) $\begin{aligned} x_1 + x_2 &= 1 \\ 2x_1 - x_2 &= 1 \end{aligned}$ (a unique solution),

(d) $(x - a_1)(x - a_2) \ldots (x - a_k) = 0$ (k solutions).

2. $m < n$

(a) $x_1^2 + x_2^2 = -1$ (no solution),

(b) $\cos(x_1 x_2) = 0$ (infinite number of solutions),

(c) $x_1^2 + x_2^2 = 0$ (a unique solution)

(d) $[(x_1 - 1)^2 + (x_2 - 1)^2][(x_1 - 2)^2 + (x_2 - 2)^2] \ldots [(x_1 - k)^2 + (x_2 - k)^2] = 0$ (k solutions).

3. $n < m$

(a) $\begin{aligned} x_1 + x_2 &= 1 \\ 2x_1 + x_2 &= 0 \\ 3x_1 - 2x_2 &= 2 \end{aligned}$ (no solution),

(b) $$\begin{aligned} \cos x &= 0 \\ 1-\sin x &= 0 \end{aligned} \qquad \text{(infinite number of solutions),}$$

(c) $$\begin{aligned} x-a &= 0 \\ x^3-a^3 &= 0 \end{aligned} \qquad \text{(a unique solution),}$$

(d) $$\begin{aligned} (x-1)(x-2)\,\dots\,(x-k) &= 0 \\ \cos\left[\frac{\pi}{2}(2x+1)\right] &= 0 \end{aligned} \qquad (k \text{ solutions}).$$

1 Vector spaces and matrices

We denote real n-dimensional vectors by

$$\mathbf{a} = \begin{pmatrix} a_1 \\ a_2 \\ \cdot \\ \cdot \\ \cdot \\ a_n \end{pmatrix}$$

where the components a_i of $\mathbf{a}$ are real numbers, that is $a_i \in \mathcal{R}$.

We assume the reader to be familiar with the definition ofaddition and subtraction of vectors, multiplication of a vector by a scalar, and the scalar product of two vectors $\mathbf{a}$ and $\mathbf{b}$, which we denote by $\mathbf{a}^T\mathbf{b}$, where $\mathbf{a}^T = (a_1, a_2, \dots, a_n)$.

A *real vector space* is a set V of real vectors (of the same dimension) with the following property: if $\mathbf{v}_1, \mathbf{v}_2 \in V$ then $\lambda\mathbf{v}_1 + \mu\mathbf{v}_2 \in V$ for all $\lambda, \mu \in \mathcal{R}$.

Examples

1. The set $\mathcal{R}^n$, that is the set of all n-dimensional real vectors, is a real vector space.
2. Let $\mathbf{v}_1, \mathbf{v}_2, \dots, \mathbf{v}_n$ be given vectors of the same dimension. The set

$$\left\{ \sum_{j=1}^{k} \lambda_j \mathbf{v}_j \,\middle|\, \lambda_j \in \mathcal{R}, \qquad j = 1, 2, \dots, k \right\}^{(1)}$$

is a vector space. It is called the *vector space spanned by the vectors* $\mathbf{v}_1, \mathbf{v}_2, \dots, \mathbf{v}_k$.

A set of vectors $\mathbf{a}_1, \mathbf{a}_2, \dots, \mathbf{a}_s$, $\mathbf{a}_i \in \mathcal{R}^n$, $(i = 1, \dots, s)$, is called *linearly independent* if

$$\sum_{j=1}^{s} \lambda_j \mathbf{a}_j = \mathbf{0} \qquad [\mathbf{0} = (0, 0, \dots, 0)^T, \text{ the zero vector, } \lambda_i \in \mathcal{R}],$$

implies $\lambda_i = 0$ where $i = 1, 2, \dots, s$. Otherwise the set $\{\mathbf{a}_1, \dots, \mathbf{a}_s\}$ is called *linearly dependent*.

(1) This symbol means: the set of all vectors which are representable in the form $\lambda_1\mathbf{v}_1 + \lambda_2\mathbf{v}_2 + \dots + \lambda_k\mathbf{v}_k$ with $\lambda_1, \lambda_2, \dots, \lambda_k \in \mathcal{R}$.

Examples

1. The vectors $\begin{pmatrix}3\\4\end{pmatrix}$ and $\begin{pmatrix}2\\1\end{pmatrix}$ are linearly independent in $\mathcal{R}^2$.

2. The vectors $\mathbf{a}_1 = (1, 3, 1)^T$, $\mathbf{a}_2 = (4, 2, 1)^T$, $\mathbf{a}_3 = (2, 0, \frac{1}{5})^T$ are linearly dependent in R^3 since $2\mathbf{a}_1 + (-3)\mathbf{a}_2 + 5\mathbf{a}_3 = \mathbf{0}$.

Let V be a real vector space. A set $\{\mathbf{b}_1, \mathbf{b}_2, ..., \mathbf{b}_s\}$ of vectors of V is called a *basis of V* if

(1) the set $\{\mathbf{b}_1, \mathbf{b}_2, ..., \mathbf{b}_s\}$ is linearly independent, and

(2) for any $\mathbf{v} \in V$ there exist real numbers $\lambda_1, ..., \lambda_s$ with the property that

$$\mathbf{v} = \lambda_1\mathbf{b}_1 + \lambda_2\mathbf{b}_2 + ... + \lambda_s\mathbf{b}_s .$$

One can prove that the λ's in (2) are uniquely defined, that every vector space V has infinitely many bases, and that each basis of V contains the same number of vectors. This number is called the *dimension of V*.

Examples

1. The space $\mathcal{R}^n$ has dimension n, for the unit vectors

$$\mathbf{e}_1 = (1, 0, ..., 0)^T, \qquad \mathbf{e}_2 = (0, 1, 0, ..., 0)^T, \; ..., \; \mathbf{e}_n = (0, ..., 0, 1)^T$$

form a basis of the $\mathcal{R}^n$.

2. If the vectors $\mathbf{v}_1, \mathbf{v}_2, ..., \mathbf{v}_k$ are linearly independent then the space spanned by the $\mathbf{v}_i$ $(i = 1, 2, ..., k)$, is a k-dimensional vector space and $\{\mathbf{v}_1, \mathbf{v}_2, ..., \mathbf{v}_k\}$ is a basis of this space.

We suppose the reader to be familiar with the notion $(a_{\mu\nu}) = A(\mu = 1, ..., m,\; \nu = 1, ..., n)$ for a matrix A of order $m \times n$. If we denote the column vectors of A by

$$\mathbf{a}_1, \mathbf{a}_2, ..., \mathbf{a}_n ;\; \mathbf{a}_i = (a_{1i}, ..., a_{mi})^T \quad (i = 1, 2, ..., n)$$

we sometimes write $A = (\mathbf{a}_1, \mathbf{a}_2, ..., \mathbf{a}_n)$. The transpose of A, that is, the matrix

$$\begin{pmatrix}\mathbf{a}_1^T\\ \cdot\\ \cdot\\ \cdot\\ \mathbf{a}_n^T\end{pmatrix},$$

is denoted by A^T. The product of two matrices $A = (a_{\mu\nu})$ and $B = (b_{\rho\tau})$, where A is of the order $m \times n$ and B of order $n \times k$, is defined to be a matrix of order $m \times k$ whose element $\lambda\nu$ is

$$\mathbf{a}_\lambda^T \mathbf{b}_\nu = \sum_{\mu=1}^{n} a_{\lambda\mu} b_{\mu\nu}$$

[$\mathbf{a}_\lambda^T$ is the λth row vector of A, and $\mathbf{b}_\nu$ is the νth column vector of B].

2 Linear systems of equations

A system of m equations in n unknowns $x_1, ..., x_n$ of the following kind

$$\begin{array}{l} a_{11}x_1+a_{12}x_2+ ... +a_{1n}x_n = b_1 \\ a_{21}x_1+a_{22}x_2+ ... +a_{2n}x_n = b_2 \\ \cdots \cdots \cdots \cdots \cdots \cdots \\ a_{m1}x_1+a_{m2}x_2+ ... +a_{mn}x_n = b_m \end{array} \qquad (a_{\mu\nu}, b_i \in \mathbb{R}) \qquad (1)$$

is called a *linear system of equations.* If $b_1 = b_2 = ... = b_m = 0$, system (1) is called *homogeneous*; otherwise *inhomogeneous*. Writing

$$\mathbf{x} = \begin{pmatrix} x_1 \\ x_2 \\ \cdot \\ \cdot \\ \cdot \\ x_n \end{pmatrix}, \quad \mathbf{b} = \begin{pmatrix} b_1 \\ b_2 \\ \cdot \\ \cdot \\ \cdot \\ b_m \end{pmatrix}, \quad \mathbf{A} = \begin{pmatrix} a_{11} & a_{12} & \cdots & a_{1n} \\ a_{21} & a_{22} & \cdots & a_{2n} \\ \cdot & \cdot & & \cdot \\ \cdot & \cdot & & \cdot \\ \cdot & \cdot & & \cdot \\ a_{m1} & a_{m2} & \cdots & a_{mn} \end{pmatrix},$$

and using the above definitions we may write system (1) in the following way:

$$A\mathbf{x} = \mathbf{b} . \qquad (1')$$

If we denote by $\mathbf{a}_1, \mathbf{a}_2, ..., \mathbf{a}_n$ the n column vectors of A, we may also write

$$\mathbf{a}_1 x_1+\mathbf{a}_2 x_2+ ... +\mathbf{a}_n x_n = \mathbf{b} \qquad (1'')$$

instead of equations (1) or (1′).

We now ask for the conditions under which system (1) is solvable. In other words: when do real numbers $x_1, x_2, ..., x_n$ exist which satisfy system (1)? A vector $\mathbf{x}$ of such numbers is called a *solution vector* of (1).

The following definitions are necessary for this problem:

Definition. Let $A = (a_{\mu\nu})$ be a real matrix of order $m \times n$. The *row-rank of A* is the maximal number of linearly independent row vectors of A. The *column-rank of A* is the maximal number of linearly independent column vectors of A.

Theorem 1: Let $A = (a_{\mu\nu})$ be a real matrix of order $m \times n$. Then

$$\text{row-rank of } A = \text{column-rank of } A \leqslant \min(m, n) .$$

Because of Theorem 1 we may simply speak of the *rank of A*. We shall denote it by r. The following yields a simple method for evaluating the rank of a given matrix A.

Theorem 2: The rank r of a matrix is not changed if one transforms it by the following operations:

(a) interchange any two rows (respectively columns),

(b) multiply a row (respectively column) by a real number $a \neq 0$, or

(c) add a row (respectively column) which has been multiplied by a real number to another row (respectively column).

Proof. The rank r of A equals the dimension of the vector space spanned by the row (respectively column) vectors of A, and this space remains fixed under the operations (a), (b), and (c).

By Theorem 2, A may be transformed until it reaches the form

$$\begin{pmatrix} 1 & 0 & \cdots & 0 & c_{1,r+1} & c_{1,r+2} & \cdots & c_{1n} \\ 0 & 1 & 0 \cdots & 0 & c_{2,r+1} & c_{2,r+2} & \cdots & c_{2n} \\ \vdots & & \ddots & \vdots & \vdots & \vdots & & \vdots \\ \vdots & & & 0 & \vdots & \vdots & & \vdots \\ 0 & \cdots & 0 & 1 & c_{r,r+1} & c_{r,r+2} & \cdots & c_{rn} \\ 0 & \cdots & \cdots & 0 & \cdots & \cdots & \cdots & 0 \\ \vdots & & & \vdots & & & & \vdots \\ 0 & \cdots & \cdots & 0 & \cdots & \cdots & \cdots & 0 \end{pmatrix}. \qquad (2)$$

Example

We transform the matrix

$$\begin{pmatrix} 3 & 4 & 2 \\ 1 & 3 & 7 \\ 7 & 11 & 11 \\ -2 & -1 & 5 \end{pmatrix} \xrightarrow{\text{by (a)}} \begin{pmatrix} 1 & 3 & 7 \\ 3 & 4 & 2 \\ 7 & 11 & 11 \\ -2 & -1 & 5 \end{pmatrix} \xrightarrow{\text{by (c)}} \begin{pmatrix} 1 & 3 & 7 \\ 0 & -5 & -19 \\ 0 & -10 & -38 \\ 0 & 5 & 19 \end{pmatrix}$$

$$\xrightarrow{\text{by (b)}} \begin{pmatrix} 1 & 3 & 7 \\ 0 & 1 & \frac{19}{5} \\ 0 & -10 & -38 \\ 0 & 5 & 19 \end{pmatrix} \xrightarrow{\text{by (c)}} \begin{pmatrix} 1 & 0 & -\frac{22}{5} \\ 0 & 1 & \frac{19}{5} \\ 0 & 0 & 0 \\ 0 & 0 & 0 \end{pmatrix}.$$

The rank of the matrix (2) is obviously equal to the number of 1's.

By Theorem 2 this is also the rank of the matrix A. In the example the rank is 2.

Now we are in a position to give a necessary and sufficient condition for the existence of a solution vector $\mathbf{x}$ of system (1).

Theorem 3: The linear system $A\mathbf{x} = \mathbf{b}$ of m equations in n unknowns is solvable if, and only if, the rank of A equals the rank of

$$\begin{pmatrix} a_{11} & a_{12} & \cdots & a_{1n} & b_1 \\ a_{21} & a_{22} & \cdots & a_{2n} & b_2 \\ \vdots & \vdots & & \vdots & \vdots \\ a_{m1} & a_{m2} & \cdots & a_{mn} & b_m \end{pmatrix} =: B\,.^{(2)}$$

(2) We write $A =: B$, if B is defined by A.

Proof. We have to show (a) that from rank of A = rank of B follows the solvability of system (1) and conversely, (b) that from "system (1) is solvable" follows rank of A = rank of B.

(a) Let U be the vector space spanned by the column vectors $\mathbf{a}_1, \mathbf{a}_2, ..., \mathbf{a}_n$ of A, V the space spanned by these vectors and by the vector $\mathbf{b}$. Then $U \subseteq V$ and $\dim U = \dim V = r$, therefore $U = V$. It follows that $\mathbf{b} \in V\ (= U)$ is representable in the form of equation (1″), which means that system (1) is solvable.

(b) If there exist $x_1, x_2, ..., x_n \in \mathbb{R}$ with equation (1″), then $\mathbf{b} \in V \subseteq U$, and therefore $U = V$ which implies rank of $A = \dim U = \dim V =$ rank of B.

We now suppose that system (1) is solvable, and we try to find all solutions. To understand the solution method we need

Theorem 4:

(a) Let S be the set of all solution vectors of the homogeneous linear system $A\mathbf{x} = \mathbf{0}$. Then S is a vector space.

(b) Let $\mathbf{x}_o$ be an arbitrary solution vector of the linear system $A\mathbf{x} = \mathbf{b}\ (\neq \mathbf{0})$ and let S be the solution set of the homogeneous system $A\mathbf{x} = \mathbf{0}$ belonging to system (1). Then the set of all solution vectors of $A\mathbf{x} = \mathbf{b}$ is $\{\mathbf{x}_o + \mathbf{s} \mid \mathbf{s} \in S\} = : \mathbf{x}_o + S$.

Proof. (a) If $\mathbf{x}_1, \mathbf{x}_2 \in S$ then $\lambda\mathbf{x}_1 + \mu\mathbf{x}_2 \in S$ for all real numbers λ, μ, since

$$A(\lambda\mathbf{x}_1 + \mu\mathbf{x}_2) = \lambda A\mathbf{x}_1 + \mu A\mathbf{x}_2 = \mathbf{0} + \mathbf{0} = \mathbf{0}\,.$$

(b) If $\mathbf{x} = \mathbf{x}_o + \mathbf{s}$ for $\mathbf{s} \in S$ then

$$A\mathbf{x} = A(\mathbf{x}_o + \mathbf{s}) = A\mathbf{x}_o + A\mathbf{s} = \mathbf{b} + \mathbf{0} = \mathbf{b}\,.$$

Therefore $\mathbf{x}_o + S$ is contained in the solution set of $A\mathbf{x} = \mathbf{b}$. If $\mathbf{x}$ lies in the solution set of $A\mathbf{x} = \mathbf{b}$ then $\mathbf{x} - \mathbf{x}_o \in S$ because

$$A(\mathbf{x} - \mathbf{x}_o) = A\mathbf{x} - A\mathbf{x}_o = \mathbf{b} - \mathbf{b} = \mathbf{0}\,.$$

Therefore $\mathbf{x} = \mathbf{x}_o + \mathbf{s}$ with $\mathbf{s} \in S$, that is, the solution set of $A\mathbf{x} = \mathbf{b}$ is contained in $\mathbf{x}_o + S$.

Now it is clear what we do in order to solve system (1). We need to compute both a basis for the vector space S of Theorem 4 and a particular solution vector $\mathbf{x}_o$ of system (1), with $\mathbf{b} \neq \mathbf{0}$. Let us start with the homogeneous case.

Theorem 5: Let $A\mathbf{x} = \mathbf{0}$ be a real homogeneous linear system of equations. The solution set S of this system is not changed if A is transformed by the operations (a), (b), (c) defined in Theorem 2.

Proof. Trivial.

Let r be the rank of A. Transforming A suitably by (a), (b), (c) reduces it to the form (2)[3]. The new system

$$\begin{array}{l} x_1 + c_{1,r+1}x_{r+1} + c_{1,r+2}x_{r+2} + \dots\dots + c_{1n}x_n = 0 \\ x_2 + c_{2,r+1}x_{r+1} + c_{2,r+2}x_{r+2} + \dots\dots + c_{2n}x_n = 0 \\ \vdots \\ x_r + c_{r,r+1}x_{r+1} + c_{r,r+2}x_{r+2} + \dots\dots + c_{rn}x_n = 0 \end{array} \qquad (2')$$

which has the same solution set as $A\mathbf{x} = \mathbf{0}$ by Theorem 5, can be solved easily. One may choose arbitrary values for the unknowns $x_{r+1}, x_{r+2}, \dots, x_n$, and then determine the remaining ones uniquely from system (2′). If one takes each of the $x_{r+1}, x_{r+2}, \dots, x_n$ terms in turn to be equal to unity, the remainder being zero, the following set of particular solution vectors are obtained:

$$\mathbf{x}_1 = \begin{pmatrix} -c_{1,r+1} \\ -c_{2,r+1} \\ \cdot \\ \cdot \\ \cdot \\ -c_{r,r+1} \\ 1 \\ 0 \\ \cdot \\ \cdot \\ 0 \end{pmatrix}, \quad \mathbf{x}_2 = \begin{pmatrix} -c_{1,r+2} \\ -c_{2,r+2} \\ \cdot \\ \cdot \\ \cdot \\ -c_{r,r+2} \\ 0 \\ 1 \\ 0 \\ \cdot \\ 0 \end{pmatrix}, \dots, \quad \mathbf{x}_{n-r} = \begin{pmatrix} -c_{1n} \\ -c_{2n} \\ \cdot \\ \cdot \\ \cdot \\ -c_{rn} \\ 0 \\ \cdot \\ \cdot \\ 0 \\ 1 \end{pmatrix}.$$

These vectors form a basis of the solution set S mentioned above. We formulate this result as follows.

Theorem 6: Let $A\mathbf{x} = \mathbf{0}$ be a homogeneous linear system of equations. The solution set S of this system is a vector space of dimension $n-r$, where n is the number of unknowns and r is the rank of A.

Remark 1: If the rank of A is n, then the dimension of S is 0. That is, system (1) with $\mathbf{b} = \mathbf{0}$ has the vector $\mathbf{x} = \mathbf{0}$ as its only solution, the so-called *trivial solution*. If the rank of $A < n$, then system (1) has solution vectors $\mathbf{x} \neq \mathbf{0}$.

Remark 2: If $m < n$ in system (1) with $\mathbf{b} = \mathbf{0}$, then system (1) has non-trivial solution vectors, since the rank of $A \leqslant \min(m,n) = m < n$ (see Theorem 1 and Remark 1).

[3] If one changes two columns of A in order to get matrix (2) one has a renumbering of the unknowns. See the example on p.12.

Remark 3: System (1) is uniquely solvable if, and only if,

rank of $A = n =$ rank of B (see Theorem 3).

Proof. By Remark 1 the homogeneous system $A\mathbf{x} = \mathbf{0}$ belonging to system (1) has only the trivial solution $\mathbf{x} = \mathbf{0}$. On the other hand, system (1) is solvable by Theorem 3 and its solution set is

$$\mathbf{x}_o + S = \mathbf{x}_o + \mathbf{0} = \mathbf{x}_o$$

by Theorem 4 (b), where $\mathbf{x}_o$ solves $A\mathbf{x} = \mathbf{b}$ $(\mathbf{b} \neq \mathbf{0})$.

Remark 4: In the case $m = n =$ rank of A [= rank of B], we may compute the unique solution vector $\mathbf{x}_o$ of system (1) by evaluating the so-called *inverse of* A. This is a matrix, denoted by A^{-1}, of order $n \times n$ with the property that

$$AA^{-1} = A^{-1}A = \begin{pmatrix} 1 & 0 & \cdot & \cdot & \cdot & 0 \\ 0 & 1 & \cdot & \cdot & \cdot & 0 \\ \cdot & & & \cdot & & \cdot \\ \cdot & & & & \cdot & \cdot \\ \cdot & & & & \cdot & 0 \\ 0 & \cdot & \cdot & \cdot & 0 & 1 \end{pmatrix} = : I_n .$$

The last matrix is called the *identity matrix* of order $n \times n$. Let $A = (a_{\mu\nu})$ have rank n; $\mu = 1, 2, ..., n$; $\nu = 1, 2, ..., n$.

In order to get A^{-1}, we first form the matrix

$$\begin{pmatrix} a_{11} & a_{12} & \cdot & \cdot & \cdot & a_{1n} & 1 & 0 & \cdot & \cdot & \cdot & \cdot & 0 \\ a_{21} & a_{22} & \cdot & \cdot & \cdot & a_{2n} & 0 & 1 & 0 & \cdot & \cdot & \cdot & 0 \\ \cdot & \cdot & & & & \cdot & \cdot & & \cdot & & & & \cdot \\ \cdot & \cdot & & & & \cdot & \cdot & & & \cdot & & & \cdot \\ \cdot & \cdot & & & & \cdot & \cdot & & & & & \cdot & 0 \\ a_{n1} & a_{n2} & \cdot & \cdot & \cdot & a_{nn} & 0 & \cdot & \cdot & \cdot & \cdot & 0 & 1 \end{pmatrix} . \qquad (*)$$

Transforming (*) by the row-operations (a), (b), (c), defined in Theorem 2, until (*) is reduced to the form

$$\begin{pmatrix} 1 & 0 & \cdot & \cdot & \cdot & 0 & a'_{11} & a'_{12} & \cdot & \cdot & \cdot & a'_{1n} \\ 0 & 1 & \cdot & \cdot & \cdot & 0 & a'_{21} & a'_{22} & \cdot & \cdot & \cdot & a'_{2n} \\ \cdot & & \cdot & & & \cdot & \cdot & \cdot & & & & \cdot \\ \cdot & & & \cdot & & \cdot & \cdot & \cdot & & & & \cdot \\ \cdot & & & & \cdot & 0 & \cdot & \cdot & & & & \cdot \\ 0 & \cdot & \cdot & \cdot & 0 & 1 & a'_{n1} & a'_{n2} & \cdot & \cdot & \cdot & a'_{nn} \end{pmatrix} ,$$

we have

$$A^{-1} = \begin{pmatrix} a'_{11} & a'_{12} & \cdot & \cdot & \cdot & \cdot & a'_{1n} \\ a'_{21} & a'_{22} & \cdot & \cdot & \cdot & \cdot & a'_{2n} \\ \cdot & \cdot & & & & & \cdot \\ \cdot & \cdot & & & & & \cdot \\ \cdot & \cdot & & & & & \cdot \\ a'_{n1} & a'_{n2} & \cdot & \cdot & \cdot & \cdot & a'_{nn} \end{pmatrix}.$$

A^{-1}, if it exists, is uniquely determined by A. We now come back to the linear system (1) with A of order $n \times n$ and rank of $A = n$. The unique solution $\mathbf{x}_o$ of system (1) is then given by

$$\mathbf{x}_o = A^{-1}\mathbf{b}\,.$$

Proof. We multiply system (1) from the left by A^{-1} and use the associative law of the matrix product and the property $I_n B = B$ for each matrix B of order $n \times k$. This gives

$$A^{-1}\mathbf{b} = A^{-1}(A\mathbf{x}_o) = (A^{-1}A)\mathbf{x}_o = I_n\mathbf{x}_o = \mathbf{x}_o\,.$$

Remark 5: In the case $m = n =$ rank of A, the unique solution vector $\mathbf{x}_o$ of system (1) can be obtained in still another way. We first introduce the notion of the determinant of a matrix A of order $x \times n$.

Let $A = (a_{\mu\nu})$ be a matrix of order $n \times n$. Let $\pi = [\pi(1), \pi(2), ..., \pi(n)]$ be a *permutation* of the numbers 1, 2, ..., n (that is, any arrangement of the numbers 1, ..., n). If $\pi(i) > \pi(j)$ when $i < j$, $i, j \in \{1, ..., n\}$, we call this an *inversion of* π. Let $N(\pi)$ denote the number of inversions of π and let sign $\pi := (-1)^{N(\pi)}$ denote the *sign of* π.

Then the *determinant of* A is the real number

$$\det A = \sum_{\pi} \operatorname{sign} \pi \cdot a_{1\pi(1)} \cdot a_{2\pi(2)} \cdot \ldots \cdot a_{n\pi(n)}\,,$$

where the sum is taken over all permutations π of $(1, 2, ..., n)$.

Example:

$$n = 2, \ A = \begin{pmatrix} a_{11} & a_{12} \\ a_{21} & a_{22} \end{pmatrix}.$$

We have two permutations of (1, 2), namely $\pi_1 = (1, 2)$ and $\pi_2 = (2, 1)$. The numbers of their inversions are $N(\pi_1) = 0$ and $N(\pi_2) = 1$. Therefore

$$\det A = (-1)^0 a_{11}a_{22} + (-1)^1 a_{12}a_{21} = a_{11}a_{22} - a_{12}a_{21}\,.$$

It would be troublesome to evaluate determinants of matrices for which n is large by use of this definition. The following proposition yields a more convenient method to evaluate a determinant.

Proposition 1: The determinant of a matrix A of order $n \times n$ is not changed if A is transformed by operation (c) defined in Theorem 2.

Thus in order to evaluate the determinant of A we transform it by this operation until the matrix is reduced to the 'triangular' form

$$A' = \begin{pmatrix} a'_{11} & a'_{12} & \cdots & a'_{1n} \\ 0 & a'_{22} & \cdots & a'_{2n} \\ \cdot & 0 & & \cdot \\ \cdot & \cdot & & \cdot \\ \cdot & \cdot & & \cdot \\ 0 & 0 & \cdots & a'_{nn} \end{pmatrix},$$

where $a'_{ij} = 0$ for $i > j$. If $\pi \neq (1, 2, ..., n)$, we have $a'_{1\pi(1)} a'_{2\pi(2)} \dots a'_{n\pi(n)} = 0$, since there exists at least one $i \in \{1, 2, ..., n\}$ with $i > \pi(i)$ and thus $a'_{i\pi(i)} = 0$ for that i. Therefore, applying the definition of the determinant to A', we see by proposition 1 that

$$\det A = \det A' = a'_{11} a'_{12} \dots a'_{nn} \,.$$

Example:

$$A = \begin{pmatrix} 1 & 4 & 6 & 2 \\ -1 & 2 & 0 & -4 \\ 8 & -4 & 2 & -1 \\ -1 & 2 & 3 & -5 \end{pmatrix} \to \begin{pmatrix} 1 & 4 & 6 & 2 \\ 0 & 6 & 6 & -2 \\ 0 & -36 & -46 & -17 \\ 0 & 6 & 9 & -3 \end{pmatrix} \to$$

$$\begin{pmatrix} 1 & 4 & 6 & 2 \\ 0 & 6 & 6 & -2 \\ 0 & 0 & -10 & -29 \\ 0 & 6 & 9 & -3 \end{pmatrix} \to \begin{pmatrix} 1 & 4 & 6 & 2 \\ 0 & 6 & 6 & -2 \\ 0 & 0 & -10 & -29 \\ 0 & 0 & 3 & -1 \end{pmatrix} \to$$

$$\begin{pmatrix} 1 & 4 & 6 & 2 \\ 0 & 6 & 6 & -2 \\ 0 & 0 & -10 & -29 \\ 0 & 0 & 0 & -\frac{97}{10} \end{pmatrix} = A'$$

$$\det A = \det A' = 1 \times 6 \times (-10) \times (-\tfrac{97}{10}) = 582 \,.$$

From Theorem 2 and the process described above we easily conclude

Proposition 2: Let A be a matrix of order $n \times n$. The following assertions are equivalent:

(a) rank of $A = n$

(b) $\det A \neq 0$.

We now state without proof the famous rule of Cramer, which expresses the solution of certain special linear systems of equations in terms of ratios of determinants.

Theorem (Cramer's rule):
Let $A\mathbf{x} = \mathbf{b}$ be a linear system of n equations in n unknowns. If $\det A \neq 0$, this system has a unique solution vector $\mathbf{x}_o$ whose components $x_{o1}, x_{o2}, \ldots, x_{on}$ are given by

$$x_{oi} = \frac{\det A_i}{\det A}, \qquad (i = 1, \ldots, n),$$

where A_i is the matrix obtained from A by replacing the column vector

$$\mathbf{a}_i = \begin{pmatrix} a_{1i} \\ a_{2i} \\ \cdot \\ \cdot \\ \cdot \\ a_{ni} \end{pmatrix} \text{ of } A \text{ by } \begin{pmatrix} b_1 \\ b_2 \\ \cdot \\ \cdot \\ \cdot \\ b_n \end{pmatrix} = \mathbf{b}\,.$$

Remark 6: One can now solve the general case of system (1) ($\mathbf{b} \neq \mathbf{0}$) without first solving the homogeneous system belonging to it and without resolving the problem of the existence of a solution vector of system (1). This emerges automatically.

We transform the matrix

$$\begin{pmatrix} a_{11} & \cdots & a_{1n} & b_1 \\ \cdot & & \cdot & \cdot \\ \cdot & & \cdot & \cdot \\ \cdot & & \cdot & \cdot \\ a_{m1} & \cdots & a_{mn} & b_m \end{pmatrix}$$

by the operations (a), (b), (c) defined in Theorem 2[(4)] until we attain the form

$$\begin{pmatrix} 1 & 0 & \cdots & 0 & c_{1,r+1} & \cdots & c_{1n} & d_1 \\ 0 & 1 & \cdots & 0 & c_{2,r+1} & \cdots & c_{2n} & d_2 \\ \cdot & & \cdot & \cdot & \cdot & & \cdot & \cdot \\ \cdot & & & \cdot & \cdot & & \cdot & \cdot \\ \cdot & & & \cdot & \cdot & & \cdot & \cdot \\ 0 & \cdots & & 1 & c_{r,r+1} & \cdots & c_{rn} & d_r \\ 0 & \cdots & & 0 & 0 & \cdots & 0 & d_{r+1} \\ \cdot & & & \cdot & \cdot & & \cdot & \cdot \\ \cdot & & & \cdot & \cdot & & \cdot & \cdot \\ \cdot & & & \cdot & \cdot & & \cdot & \cdot \\ 0 & \cdots & & 0 & 0 & \cdots & 0 & d_m \end{pmatrix}.$$

If $d_{r+1} = d_{r+2} = \ldots = d_m = 0$, system (1) is solvable, since the condition of Theorem 3 is then fulfilled. In this case one obtains the general

(4) Here we must *not* exchange the last column with another column! See the footnote (3) on p.7.

solution of system (1) in the form

$$\mathbf{x} = \mathbf{x}_o + \lambda_1 \mathbf{x}_1 + \lambda_2 \mathbf{x}_2 + \ldots + \lambda_{n-r} \mathbf{x}_{n-r} ,$$

where $\lambda_1, \lambda_2, \ldots, \lambda_{n-r} \in \mathcal{R}$ and $\{\mathbf{x}_1, \mathbf{x}_2, \ldots, \mathbf{x}_{n-r}\}$ is a basis of S (see p.3). Obviously $\mathbf{x}_o = (d_1, d_2, \ldots, d_r, 0, \ldots, 0)^T$ is a particular solution vector of $A\mathbf{x} = \mathbf{b}$ ($\mathbf{b} \neq \mathbf{0}$) [see Theorem 4 (b)].

Example:
Suppose the following system is given.

$$\begin{aligned} x_1 + 2x_2 - x_3 + 4x_5 &= 2 \\ x_1 + 4x_2 - 5x_3 + x_4 + 3x_5 &= 1 \\ 3x_1 + 2x_2 + 5x_3 + 2x_4 + 2x_5 &= 12 \\ 2x_1 - 2x_2 + 10x_3 + x_4 - x_5 &= 11 . \end{aligned}$$

We transform the matrix B defined in Theorem 3 (without exchanging the last column).

$$\begin{pmatrix} 1 & 2 & -1 & 0 & 4 & 2 \\ 1 & 4 & -5 & 1 & 3 & 1 \\ 3 & 2 & 5 & 2 & 2 & 12 \\ 2 & -2 & 10 & 1 & -1 & 11 \end{pmatrix} \xrightarrow{\text{by (c)}} \begin{pmatrix} 1 & 0 & 3 & -1 & 5 & 3 \\ 0 & 1 & -2 & \frac{1}{2} & -\frac{1}{2} & -\frac{1}{2} \\ 0 & 0 & 0 & 4 & -12 & 4 \\ 0 & 0 & 0 & 0 & 0 & 0 \end{pmatrix}$$

$$\xrightarrow[\text{by (a)}]{(*)} \begin{pmatrix} 1 & 0 & -1 & 3 & 5 & 3 \\ 0 & 1 & \frac{1}{2} & -2 & -\frac{1}{2} & -\frac{1}{2} \\ 0 & 0 & 4 & 0 & -12 & 4 \\ 0 & 0 & 0 & 0 & 0 & 0 \end{pmatrix} \xrightarrow[\text{by (c)}]{\text{by (b)}} \begin{pmatrix} 1 & 0 & 0 & 3 & 2 & 4 \\ 0 & 1 & 0 & -2 & 1 & -1 \\ 0 & 0 & 1 & 0 & -3 & 1 \\ 0 & 0 & 0 & 0 & 0 & 0 \end{pmatrix}$$

We see that the given system is solvable since $d_4 = 0$ and $r = 3$. From the last matrix, we have the preliminary solution

$$\mathbf{x}'_o = (4 \quad -1 \quad 1 \quad 0 \quad 0)^T, \qquad \mathbf{x}'_1 = (-3 \quad 2 \quad 0 \quad 1 \quad 0)^T,$$
$$\mathbf{x}'_2 = (-2 \quad -1 \quad 3 \quad 0 \quad 1)^T .$$

The $'$ indicates that we have not allowed for the renumbering of the unknowns which has occurred. This took place when the unknowns x_3 and x_4 were interchanged. [See (*).] In order to restore the original numbering we have to exchange the third and the fourth component of the vectors $\mathbf{x}_o, \mathbf{x}_1, \mathbf{x}_2$. Then the general solution appears in the form

$$\mathbf{x} = (4 \quad -1 \quad 0 \quad 1 \quad 0)^T + \lambda_1(-3 \quad 2 \quad 1 \quad 0 \quad 0)^T + \lambda_2(-2 \quad -1 \quad 0 \quad 3 \quad 1)^T$$

with $\lambda_1, \lambda_2 \in \mathcal{R}$.

3 Nonlinear systems of equations

3.1 *One equation in one unknown*

Let f: $x \in D \subseteq \mathcal{R} \to f(x) \in \mathcal{R}$ (D domain of f) be a not necessarily linear real function. We would like to find those x's which are mapped on zero by function f, that is, we want to find the *roots* of the equation

$$f(x) = 0 . \tag{3}$$

Remark: The determination of the x's which are mapped on a real constant $a \neq 0$ by f is the same problem as finding the x's for which $\Phi(x) = 0$, where $\Phi(x) = f(x) - a$.

3.1.1 *Newton's method*

If the function f is of a special kind we may solve equation (3) by iteration.

***Theorem** 7:* Let f be a real function of the real variable x with domain D. Let f be twice differentiable in D. Let $x_o \in D$ be such that $f(x_o) \times f'(x_o) \neq 0$. Assume that the interval

$$J_o : \left[x_o, x_o - 2\frac{f(x_o)}{f'(x_o)} \right] \text{ lies in } D \text{ and that}$$

$$\max_{x \in J_o} |f''(x)| \leqslant \tfrac{1}{2} \frac{|f'(x_o)|^2}{|f(x_o)|} .$$

Form the sequence $\{x_\nu\}$ by the formula

$$x_{\nu+1} = x_\nu - \frac{f(x_\nu)}{f'(x_\nu)} \qquad (\nu = 0, 1, 2, ...) .$$

Then all x_ν lie in J_o, $\lim_{\nu \to \infty} x_\nu = \zeta$ exists, $f(\zeta) = 0$ and $f(\xi) \neq 0$ for $\xi \in J_o \setminus \{\zeta\}$.

If $\zeta \neq x_o - 2\dfrac{f(x_o)}{f'(x_o)}$, ζ is a simple root of equation (3).

For a proof of this see Ostrowski (1966).

The shape of the most familiar type of a function f which satisfies the conditions of Theorem 7 is shown in figure 1.

For this function we have: $f(a) \times f(b) < 0$, $f'(x) < 0$, $f''(x) > 0$ for all x lying in the interval $[a, b]$. Graphically, the sequence $\{x_\nu\}$ of the theorem can be easily understood. $x_{\nu+1}$ is just the intersection of the tangent to f at the point x_ν, with the x-axis (see figure 2).

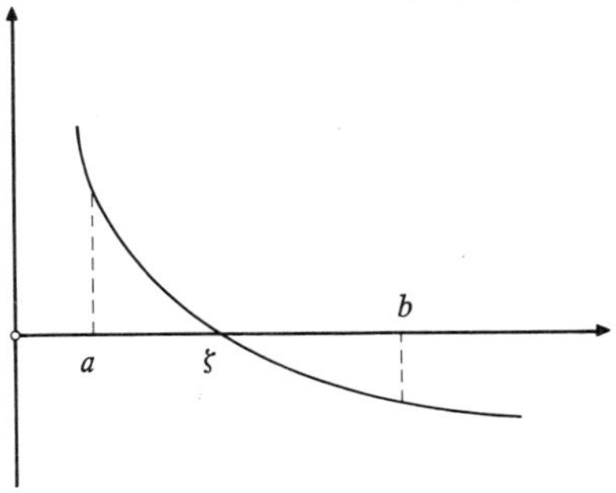

Figure 1.

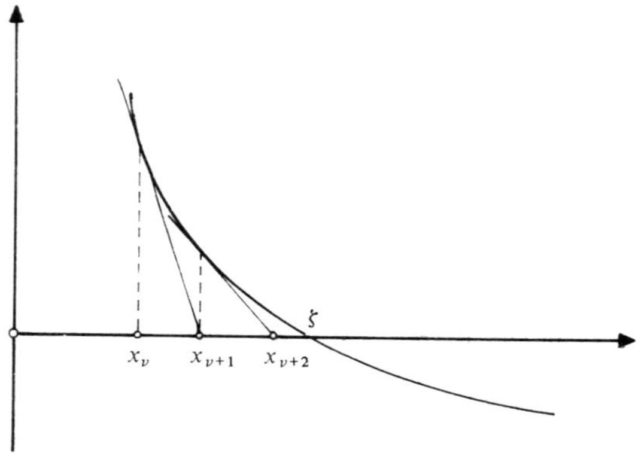

Figure 2.

3.1.2 *Solution by iteration*
Write equation (3) in the form

$$x = x - f(x) . \tag{3'}$$

Theorem 8: Let ζ be a root of equation (3) [respectively (3′)] and let the function f be differentiable in an ϵ-neighbourhood $N = \{x \mid |x - \zeta| < \epsilon; \epsilon > 0\}$ of ζ. If $|1 - f'(x)| < 1$ for all x lying in N, then the series $x_1 \in N,\ x_2 = x_1 - f(x_1),\ x_3 = x_2 - f(x_2), \ldots$ converges to ζ.

Proof: See section 3.2.2, Remark 2, p.18.

3.2 *m equations in n unknowns*
Let $\mathbf{f}\colon\ \mathbf{x} \in D \subseteq \mathbb{R}^n \rightarrow \mathbf{f}(\mathbf{x}) \in \mathbb{R}^m$ be a function (not necessarily linear) with domain in $\mathbb{R}^n$ and the range in $\mathbb{R}^m$. We should like to find all vectors $\mathbf{x}$ with the property that

$$f(x) = \mathbf{0} \in \mathbb{R}^m .$$

In components, this means

$$\begin{aligned} f_1(x_1, \ldots, x_n) &= 0 \\ f_2(x_1, \ldots, x_n) &= 0 \\ &\ \ \vdots \\ f_m(x_1, \ldots, x_n) &= 0 \end{aligned} \tag{4}$$

As mentioned in the introduction, no unified theory exists from which it is possible to say for every case of a system like (4) how all the solutions may be found. We shall consider two special cases of system (4), namely 3.2.1: where $m = n = 2$ and 3.2.2: where $m = n$, with some imposed conditions on the function f.

3.2.1 *Graphical solution of system (4) in the case* $m = n = 2$

Let

$$\begin{aligned} f_1(x_1,x_2) &= 0 \\ f_2(x_1,x_2) &= 0 \end{aligned} \tag{4'}$$

be the given system. One constructs the sets—usually simple loci of course—

$$S_1 = \{(x_1,x_2)\,|\,f_1(x_1,x_2) = 0\}\,, \qquad S_2 = \{(x_1,x_2)\,|\,f_2(x_1,x_2) = 0\}$$

in the (x_1, x_2)-plane. The points lying in the intersection $S_1 \cap S_2$ are the solutions of equations (4′).

Examples:

(a) $x_1^2+x_2^2-1 = 0$
$\quad x_1-x_2 = 0\,.$

Two solution points exist:

$$(x_1,x_2) = \left(\frac{\sqrt{2}}{2}, \frac{\sqrt{2}}{2}\right) \quad \text{and} \quad (x_1,x_2) = -\left(\frac{\sqrt{2}}{2}, \frac{\sqrt{2}}{2}\right).$$

See figure 3(a).

(b) $x_1^2+x_2^2-1 = 0$
$\quad x_1-x_2+2 = 0\,.$

There is no solution. See figure 3(b).

(c) $x_1^2+x_2^2-1 = 0$
$\quad x_1-x_2+\sqrt{2} = 0\,.$

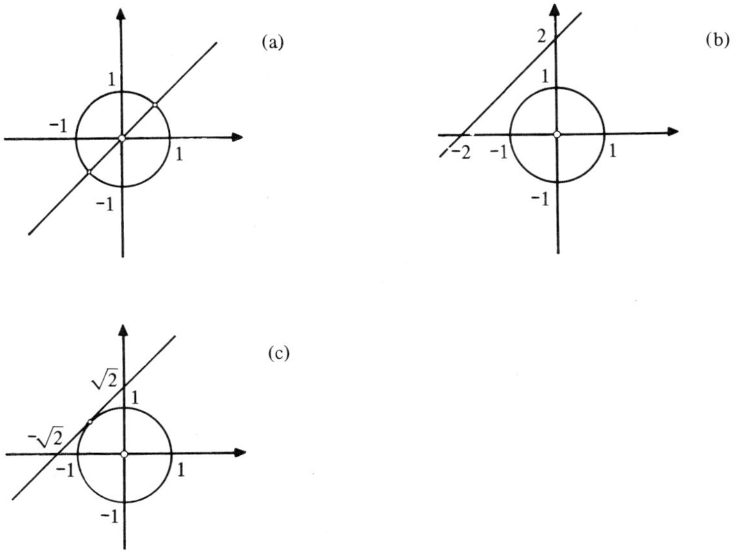

Figure 3.

Here we have the unique solution point

$$(x_1, x_2) = \left(-\frac{\sqrt{2}}{2}, \frac{\sqrt{2}}{2}\right).$$

See figure 3(c).

3.2.2 *The case* $m = n$
Write system (4) in the following form:

$$\mathbf{x} = \mathbf{x} - \mathbf{f}(\mathbf{x}) \,. \tag{4''}$$

Denoting by F the function

$$F\colon\ \mathbf{x} \in D \subseteq \mathbb{R}^n \to \mathbf{x} - \mathbf{f}(\mathbf{x}) \in \mathbb{R}^n \,,$$

our problem is now to find the *fixed points of* F, that is vectors $\mathbf{x}_o \in \mathbb{R}^n$ with the property

$$F(\mathbf{x}_o) = \mathbf{x}_o \,, \tag{4'''}$$

or without brackets, $F\mathbf{x}_o = \mathbf{x}_o$. Denoting by $|\mathbf{x}|$ the *length* of $\mathbf{x} = (x_1, x_2, ..., x_n)^T$, defined by

$$|\mathbf{x}|: = (\mathbf{x}^T\mathbf{x})^{1/2} = \left(\sum_{i=1}^{n} x_i^2\right)^{1/2},$$

we may formulate conditions under which a unique fixed point $\mathbf{x}_o$ of a function $T\colon\ D \subseteq \mathbb{R}^n \to \mathbb{R}^n$ exists. This is a special case of Banach's famous fixed-point theorem.

***Theorem** 9:* If there exists an ϵ-neighbourhood $N\colon = \{x \mid |\mathbf{x} - \mathbf{a}| < \epsilon; \epsilon > 0\}$ of a point $\mathbf{a}$ in the domain D of a function $T\colon\ D \subseteq \mathbb{R}^n \to \mathbb{R}^n$ such that $N \subseteq D$ and $|T\mathbf{x} - T\mathbf{y}| \leqslant \alpha|\mathbf{x} - \mathbf{y}|$ for all $\mathbf{x}, \mathbf{y} \in N$, and $|\mathbf{a} - T\mathbf{a}| < (1-\alpha)\epsilon$, where α is a constant with $0 \leqslant \alpha < 1$, then the series $\mathbf{a} = \mathbf{x}_1 \in N \subseteq D$, $\mathbf{x}_2 = T\mathbf{x}_1$, $\mathbf{x}_3 = T\mathbf{x}_2$, ... converges to a fixed point $\mathbf{x}_o \in N$ of T. $\mathbf{x}_o$ is unique in N.

Proof: We show the convergence of the sequence $\mathbf{x}_1, \mathbf{x}_2 = T\mathbf{x}_1, ...$ We have:

$$|\mathbf{x}_3 - \mathbf{x}_2| = |T\mathbf{x}_2 - T\mathbf{x}_1| \leqslant \alpha|\mathbf{x}_2 - \mathbf{x}_1|$$
$$|\mathbf{x}_4 - \mathbf{x}_3| = |T\mathbf{x}_3 - T\mathbf{x}_2| \leqslant \alpha|\mathbf{x}_3 - \mathbf{x}_2| \leqslant \alpha^2|\mathbf{x}_2 - \mathbf{x}_1|$$

since all the x_ν lie in N, which will be shown later.
It follows that for all $n \geqslant 2$

$$|\mathbf{x}_{n+1} - \mathbf{x}_n| \leqslant \alpha^{n-1}|\mathbf{x}_2 - \mathbf{x}_1|$$

holds. Therefore for $m > n \geqslant 2$:

$$|\mathbf{x}_n - \mathbf{x}_m| \leqslant |\mathbf{x}_n - \mathbf{x}_{n+1}| + |\mathbf{x}_{n+1} - \mathbf{x}_{n+2}| + ... + |\mathbf{x}_{m-1} - \mathbf{x}_m|$$
$$\leqslant \alpha^{n-1}|\mathbf{x}_2 - \mathbf{x}_1| + \alpha^n|\mathbf{x}_2 - \mathbf{x}_1| + ... + \alpha^{m-2}|\mathbf{x}_2 - \mathbf{x}_1|$$
$$\leqslant \sum_{\nu=n-1}^{\infty} \alpha^\nu|\mathbf{x}_2 - \mathbf{x}_1| = \alpha^{n-1}|\mathbf{x}_2 - \mathbf{x}_1|\sum_{\nu=0}^{\infty} \alpha^\nu = \frac{\alpha^{n-1}}{1-\alpha}|\mathbf{x}_2 - \mathbf{x}_1| \,.$$

Since $0 \leqslant \alpha < 1$ we can conclude that $\lim_{n \to \infty} |\mathbf{x}_n - \mathbf{x}_m| = 0$ (for $m > n$) and this implies that $\lim_{\nu \to \infty} \mathbf{x}_\nu$ exists. Let $\mathbf{x}_o$ be the limit. Then because

$$|\mathbf{x}_o - T\mathbf{x}_o| \leqslant |\mathbf{x}_o - \mathbf{x}_n| + |\mathbf{x}_n - T\mathbf{x}_o| = |\mathbf{x}_o - \mathbf{x}_n| + |T\mathbf{x}_{n-1} - T\mathbf{x}_o|$$
$$\leqslant \tfrac{1}{2}\epsilon + \alpha|\mathbf{x}_{n-1} - \mathbf{x}_o| < \tfrac{1}{2}\epsilon + \tfrac{1}{2}\epsilon\alpha = \tfrac{1}{2}\epsilon(1+\alpha)$$

for sufficiently large n, we have $\mathbf{x}_o = T\mathbf{x}_o$, that is $\mathbf{x}_o$ is a fixed point of T.

We now show that there is only one fixed point of T in N. Assume that there exists $\mathbf{x}_o, \mathbf{y}_o \in N$ with $T\mathbf{x}_o = \mathbf{x}_o$, $T\mathbf{y}_o = \mathbf{y}_o$, and $\mathbf{x}_o \neq \mathbf{y}_o$. Then

$$|\mathbf{x}_o - \mathbf{y}_o| = |T\mathbf{x}_o - T\mathbf{y}_o| \leqslant \alpha|\mathbf{x}_o - \mathbf{y}_o|$$

and therefore $1 \leqslant \alpha$, QED.

Finally, we complete the proof by proving the property employed above that all $\mathbf{x}_\nu$ lie in N.

Suppose that $\mathbf{x}_1 = \mathbf{a}$, $\mathbf{x}_2 = T\mathbf{x}_1, \ldots, \mathbf{x}_k = T\mathbf{x}_{k-1}$ lie in N. We show that $\mathbf{x}_{k+1}$ lies in N, from which the result follows by induction.

$$\begin{aligned} |\mathbf{x}_3 - \mathbf{x}_2| &\leqslant \alpha|\mathbf{x}_2 - \mathbf{x}_1| = \alpha|T\mathbf{a} - \mathbf{a}| \leqslant \alpha(1-\alpha)\epsilon \\ |\mathbf{x}_4 - \mathbf{x}_3| &\leqslant \alpha|\mathbf{x}_3 - \mathbf{x}_2| \leqslant \alpha^2(1-\alpha)\epsilon \\ |\mathbf{x}_k - \mathbf{x}_{k-1}| &\leqslant \alpha^{k-2}(1-\alpha)\epsilon\ . \end{aligned}$$

Hence

$$|\mathbf{x}_{k+1} - \mathbf{x}_k| = |T\mathbf{x}_k - T\mathbf{x}_{k-1}| \leqslant \alpha|\mathbf{x}_k - \mathbf{x}_{k-1}| < \alpha^{k-1}(1-\alpha)\epsilon$$

and

$$|\mathbf{x}_{k+1} - \mathbf{a}| \leqslant |\mathbf{x}_2 - \mathbf{a}| + |\mathbf{x}_3 - \mathbf{x}_2| + \ldots + |\mathbf{x}_{k+1} - \mathbf{x}_k|$$
$$\leqslant (1-\alpha)\epsilon + \alpha(1-\alpha)\epsilon + \ldots + \alpha^{k-1}(1-\alpha)\epsilon$$
$$= (1-\alpha)\epsilon\frac{1-\alpha^k}{1-\alpha} = \epsilon(1-\alpha^k) < \epsilon, \text{ since } 0 \leqslant \alpha < 1.$$

This shows that $\mathbf{x}_{k+1}$ indeed lies in N.

Remark 1: If we take the function F defined above instead of T in Theorem 9 and if F satisfies the conditions of Theorem 9, that is $|\mathbf{x} - \mathbf{f}(\mathbf{x}) - \mathbf{y} + \mathbf{f}(\mathbf{y})| \leqslant \alpha|\mathbf{x} - \mathbf{y}|$ for all $\mathbf{x}, \mathbf{y}$ in a suitable ϵ-neighbourhood N of a point $\mathbf{a} \in D \subseteq \mathbb{R}^n$ and $|F\mathbf{a} - \mathbf{a}| < (1-\alpha)\epsilon$ or $|\mathbf{f}(\mathbf{a})| \leqslant (1-\alpha)\epsilon$, then we can get a root of the function $\mathbf{f}$ as the limit of the sequence $\mathbf{a} = \mathbf{x}_1$, $\mathbf{x}_2 = \mathbf{x}_1 - \mathbf{f}(\mathbf{x}_1)$, $\mathbf{x}_3 = \mathbf{x}_2 - \mathbf{f}(\mathbf{x}_2)$, ...

Remark 2: The statements of Theorem 8 are also a special case of Banach's fixed-point theorem because the conditions of Theorem 9 are satisfied by the functions which were considered there.

Proof: For the function T of Theorem 9, we take again
$F\colon x \in \mathcal{R} \to x - \mathrm{f}(x)$.

Since $1 - \mathrm{f}'(x) = \mathrm{d}[x - \mathrm{f}(x)]/\mathrm{d}x$, we have

$$\left| \frac{\mathrm{d}[x - \mathrm{f}(x)]}{\mathrm{d}x} \right| < 1 \quad \text{for all } x \in N.$$

Therefore, if N is taken small enough

$$\left| \frac{x - \mathrm{f}(x) - [y - \mathrm{f}(y)]}{x - y} \right| < 1 \quad \text{or} \quad \left| \frac{F(x) - F(y)}{x - y} \right| < 1 \quad \text{for all } x, y \in N.$$

This implies $|F(x) - F(y)| \leqslant \alpha |x - y|$ for a suitable constant α, $0 \leqslant \alpha < 1$.

From the continuity of function f it follows that

$$|F(x_1) - x_1| = |\mathrm{f}(x_1)| < (1 - \alpha)\epsilon \,,$$

where 2ϵ is the length of N, which has to be taken suitably.

Remark 3: Theorem 7 can be proved in a similar way to Theorem 9. If we put

$$h_\nu = -\frac{\mathrm{f}(x_\nu)}{\mathrm{f}'(x_\nu)} \,,$$

the sequence x_ν defined in Theorem 7 can be written $x_{\nu+1} = x_\nu + h_\nu$.

It can be shown that $|h_\nu| < (\frac{1}{2})^\nu |h_0|$ (see Ostrowski, 1966, pp.61 ff.). If we set

$$G\colon x \in D \subseteq \mathcal{R} \to x - \frac{\mathrm{f}(x)}{\mathrm{f}'(x)} \,, \quad x \in J_\mathrm{o} \subseteq D$$

we can now repeat the proof of Theorem 9, with G instead of T, in order to show that there exists a unique fixed point ζ of G in J_0. Clearly one has to show that $\mathrm{f}'(x) \neq 0$ for $x \in J_\mathrm{o}$ is a consequence of the assumptions of Theorem 7. We have $G(\zeta) = \zeta$ or

$$\zeta - \frac{\mathrm{f}(\zeta)}{\mathrm{f}'(\zeta)} = \zeta \,.$$

This implies $\mathrm{f}(\zeta) = 0$.

References

Alonso, W., 1964, *Location and Land Use* (Harvard University Press, Cambridge, Mass.).
Isard, W., 1968, *Methods of Regional Analysis* (MIT Press, New York).
Ostrowski, A., 1966, *Solution of Equations and Systems of Equations* (Academic Press, New York).

Linear Systems of Difference Equations

W.EICHHORN, F.STEHLING
Universität Karlsruhe

Introduction

The methods of solving *single* linear difference equations are well-known and described in many excellent books (see Goldberg, 1958; Allen, 1964; Yamane, 1962; Baumol, 1970; and Levy and Lessman, 1959). In the following an introduction to the theory of *systems* of linear difference equations will be given. In particular, many economic models require the study and solution of not one, but a number of simultaneous difference equations. Such simultaneous sets arise because the economic variables (for example, income, consumption, production, input, output, different kinds of investment, imports, exports, taxes, and so on) are connected with one another by several equations, especially in the more realistic models (for example, see the models of Goodwin, 1949, 1950; Chipman, 1950; Paelinck, in this volume; Krelle *et al.*, 1969; Hansen, 1967). Of course, one may ask: why are the variables in these models linked only by *linear* equations? Two of the reasons are:

1 the models are only first attempts to describe economic reality; and
2 whereas a full theory of solutions of systems of linear difference equations exists, this is not the case for nonlinear systems.

1 General definitions

Let Z be the set of all integers, that is:

$$Z = \{0, \pm 1, \pm 2, \pm 3, ...\}.$$

Let t_0 be a fixed element of Z and

$$Z_0 = \{t_0, t_0 + 1, t_0 + 2, ...\}. \tag{1.1}$$

Let F_0 be the set of all functions f which map Z_0 into $\mathcal{R}$, the set of all real numbers, that is:

$$F_0 = \{f | f(t) \in \mathcal{R} \text{ for } t \in Z_0\}. \tag{1.2}$$

Denote $Z \times \mathcal{R}^{n+1}$ the set of all $(n+2)$-tuples with the first component in Z and the other $n+1$ in $\mathcal{R}$, that is:

$$Z \times \mathcal{R}^{n+1} = \{(t, y_0, y_1, y_2, ..., y_n) | t \in Z,\ y_i \in \mathcal{R} \quad (i = 0, 1, ..., n)\}.$$

Now let a function H be given with the property that

$$H:\ \mathbf{x} = (t, y_0, y_1, y_2, \ldots, y_n) \in Z \times \mathbb{R}^{n+1} \rightarrow H(\mathbf{x}) \in \mathbb{R}.^{(1)} \tag{1.3}$$

Definition: With the above notations an identity of the form

$$H[t, f(t), f(t+1), f(t+2), \ldots, f(t+n)] = 0\,, \tag{1.4}$$

with $f \in F_0$, which holds for all $t \in Z_0$, is called a (single) *difference equation.*

Equation (1.4) is said to be of the nth order if, and only if, H depends at least on $y_0 = f(t)$, and $y_n = f(t+n)$. Each function $f \in F_0$ is called a *solution* of equation (1.4) on Z_0, if and only if f satisfies equation (1.4) for all $t \in Z_0$.

Remark: Instead of $f(t), f(t+1), \ldots$, one often finds the notation $f_t, f_{t+1}, \ldots$, employed.

Example: The equation

$$t^2 + f(t)^2 + f(t+1) - f(t+1)f(t+3) = 0 \tag{1.5}$$

is a difference equation of order 3, where clearly the defining function H is

$$H:\ \mathbf{x} = (t, y_0, y_1, y_2, y_3) \rightarrow t^2 + y_0^2 + y_1 - y_1 y_3\,.$$

Definition: Let n be any integer with $n \geqslant 1$. An equation is called a *linear difference equation* if, and only if, it is of the form

$$a_0(t)f(t) + a_1(t)f(t+1) + \ldots + a_n(t)f(t+n) = g(t)\,, \tag{1.6}$$

where g, $a_i \in F_0$ $(i = 0, 1, \ldots, n)$ are given functions, and at least two of the a_i's are not identically zero.

Remark: Clearly from the above definitions it follows that equation (1.6) is of nth order if, and only if, $a_0(t) \not\equiv 0$,$^{(2)}$ and $a_n(t) \not\equiv 0$.

Example:

$$tf(t) + 2f(t+1) + (t+1)^2 f(t+2) = \sin t \tag{1.7}$$

is a linear difference equation (of the second order) with $g(t) = \sin t$, $a_0(t) = t$, $a_1(t) = 2$, and $a_2(t) = (t+1)^2$. The difference equation (1.5) is not linear because of the terms $f(t)^2$ and $f(t+1)f(t+3)$.

Remark: It may happen that a difference equation has no solution for some initial values, for example, the difference equation

$$f(t) + (t-1)f(t+1) = 0\,, \tag{1.8}$$

has no solution which satisfies the initial condition $f(0) = 1$.

(1) Where $H:\ \mathbf{x} \rightarrow H(\mathbf{x}) \in \mathbb{R}$ means: the function H maps $\mathbf{x}$ on the element $H(\mathbf{x})$ of $\mathbb{R}$.
(2) $a_0(t) \not\equiv 0$ means: there exists at least one t $(= t^* \in Z_0)$ for which $a_0(t^*) \neq 0$.

Definition: The linear difference equation (1.6) is called *homogeneous* if $g(t) \equiv 0$ [that is $g(t) = 0$ for all $t \in Z_0$]. Otherwise, it is called *inhomogeneous.*

Example:

$$tf(t)+2f(t+1)+(t+1)^2f(t+2) = 0$$

is a linear homogeneous difference equation of order 2, and as it is the same as equation (1.8) except for the term $g(t) = \sin t$, it is called the *homogeneous difference equation associated with equation* (1.8). Analogously, for the inhomogeneous equation

$$f(t)-(3t+1)f(t+2) = 2\,, \tag{1.9}$$

the associated homogeneous difference equation is

$$f(t)-(3t+1)f(t+2) = 0\,. \tag{1.9.1}$$

2 Systems of linear difference equations of order 1 with constant coefficients

Some economic models take the form of a system of linear difference equations of order 1 (for example, see Paelinck, in this volume). We consider the theory of such systems in this section.

Suppose the real numbers

$$a'_{ij} \qquad (i = 1, 2, ..., k; \quad j = 0, 1, 2, ..., k)\,,$$

and

$$g'_i \qquad (i = 1, 2, ..., k)$$

are given. These are fixed, and do not depend on t. A system of simultaneous linear difference equations of order 1

$$\begin{aligned} a'_{10}f_1(t+1) &= a'_{11}f_1(t)+a'_{12}f_2(t)+ ... +a'_{1k}f_k(t)+g'_1 \\ a'_{20}f_2(t+1) &= a'_{21}f_1(t)+a'_{22}f_2(t)+ ... +a'_{2k}f_k(t)+g'_2 \\ &\;\cdot \\ &\;\cdot \\ &\;\cdot \\ a'_{k0}f_k(t+1) &= a'_{k1}f_1(t)+a'_{k2}f_2(t)+ ... +a'_{kk}f_k(t)+g'_k\,, \end{aligned} \tag{2.1'}$$

where $f_i \in F_0$ $(i = 1, 2, ..., k)$, is called a *linear system of difference equations of order 1 with constant coefficients and constant inhomogeneity* (that is, the g'_i). It is called homogeneous if $g'_i = 0$ $(i = 1, 2, ..., k)$ and otherwise inhomogeneous.

On the assumption that if $a'_{i0} = 0$ for any $i \in \{1, 2, ..., k\}$, then $a'_{ii} \neq 0$, one can use the ith equation to solve for $f_i(t)$. Inserting this into the other equations reduces equation (2.1′) to a system of $k-1$ equations for the remaining $k-1$ functions. Let us suppose that all such simplifications have already been made, so that equation (2.1′) can be brought into the form

$$\begin{aligned} f_1(t+1) &= a_{11}f_1(t)+a_{12}f_2(t)+\ldots+a_{1n}f_n(t)+g_1 \\ f_2(t+1) &= a_{21}f_1(t)+a_{22}f_2(t)+\ldots+a_{2n}f_n(t)+g_2 \\ &\;\vdots \\ f_n(t+1) &= a_{n1}f_1(t)+a_{n2}f_2(t)+\ldots+a_{nn}f_n(t)+g_n\,. \end{aligned} \qquad (2.1)$$

In matrix notation (see the preceding article in this book of Eichhorn and Erdmann) equation (2.1) becomes

$$\mathbf{f}(t+1) = A\mathbf{f}(t)+\mathbf{g}\,, \qquad (2.2)$$

where

$$A = \begin{pmatrix} a_{11} & a_{12} & \cdots & a_{1n} \\ a_{21} & a_{22} & \cdots & a_{2n} \\ \cdot & & & \\ \cdot & & & \\ \cdot & & & \\ a_{n1} & a_{n2} & \cdots & a_{nn} \end{pmatrix}, \qquad \mathbf{f}(t) = \begin{pmatrix} f_1(t) \\ f_2(t) \\ \cdot \\ \cdot \\ \cdot \\ f_n(t) \end{pmatrix}, \qquad \mathbf{g} = \begin{pmatrix} g_1 \\ g_2 \\ \cdot \\ \cdot \\ \cdot \\ g_n \end{pmatrix}.$$

Each vector-valued function

$$\mathbf{f}\colon t \in Z_0 \to \mathbf{f}(t)\,,$$

which satisfies equation (2.2) for all $t \in Z_0$, is called a solution of equation (2.2) equal to equation (2.1) on Z_0.

Theorem 1: Let $c_1, c_2, \ldots, c_n$ be arbitrary real numbers. Let us denote the vector $(c_1, c_2, \ldots, c_n)$ by $\mathbf{f}_0'$.[3] The only solution of equation (2.2) which has the initial value

$$\mathbf{f}'(t_0) = (c_1, c_2, \ldots, c_n) = \mathbf{f}_0' \qquad (2.3)$$

is

$$\mathbf{f}(t) = A^{t-t_0}\mathbf{f}_0 + \sum_{\nu=t_0}^{t-1} A^{\nu-t_0}\mathbf{g} \qquad (t > t_0)\,. \qquad (2.4)$$

Proof: Define $\mathbf{f}(t_0)$ as $\mathbf{f}_0$. With this initial value one gets from equation (2.2) for $t = t_0$,

$$\mathbf{f}(t_0+1) = A\mathbf{f}(t_0)+\mathbf{g} = A\mathbf{f}_0+\mathbf{g}\,. \qquad (2.4.1)$$

If we consider equation (2.2) for $t = t_0+1$ and use equation (2.4.1), then

$$\mathbf{f}(t_0+2) = A\mathbf{f}(t_0+1)+\mathbf{g} = AA\mathbf{f}_0+A\mathbf{g}+\mathbf{g} = A^2\mathbf{f}_0+(A+1)\mathbf{g}\,.$$

(3) $\mathbf{f}_0'$ means $\mathbf{f}_0$ written as a row vector.

The same procedure gives

$$\mathbf{f}(t_0+3) = A^3\mathbf{f}_0+(A^2+A+1)\mathbf{g}\,,$$

and generally, by induction, for each $\kappa > 0$,

$$\mathbf{f}(t_0+\kappa) = A^\kappa\mathbf{f}_0+\sum_{\nu=0}^{\kappa-1} A^\nu\mathbf{g}\,.$$

Setting $\kappa = t-t_0$, one gets

$$\mathbf{f}(t) = A^{t-t_0}\mathbf{f}_0+\sum_{\nu=t_0}^{t-1} A^{\nu-t_0}\mathbf{g} \qquad (t > t_0)\,.$$

This completes the proof of the theorem, as one sees that $\mathbf{f}(t)$ is uniquely determined by $\mathbf{f}_0$.

If the matrix $(1-A)$ has an inverse, then from

$$(1+A+A^2+\ldots+A^{t-t_0-1})(1-A) = 1-A^{t-t_0}\,,$$

follows

$$1+A+A^2+\ldots+A^{t-t_0-1} = (1-A^{t-t_0})(1-A)^{-1}\,.$$

In this case one can express formula (2.4) as

$$\begin{aligned}\mathbf{f}(t) &= A^{t-t_0}\mathbf{f}_0+\sum_{\nu=t_0}^{t-1} A^{\nu-t_0}\mathbf{g}\\ &= A^{t-t_0}\mathbf{f}_0+(1-A^{t-t_0})(1-A)^{-1}\mathbf{g}\,.\end{aligned} \tag{2.4'}$$

A necessary and sufficient condition for the existence of $(1-A)^{-1}$ is that

$$\det|1-A| \neq 0\,.^{(4)}$$

Remark: Formula (2.4) is the solution of the first-order system (with $\mathbf{g} = \mathbf{0}$ and $t_0 = 0$) in section 2 of Paelinck's article in this volume.

It is often of interest to examine the behaviour of the solution of equation (2.4) for large t; that is, to ask what happens with equation (2.4) if $t \to \infty$? For this purpose, we recall some results from linear algebra.

If A is a square matrix, then the roots of the characteristic polynomial of A, that is the roots of the polynomial

$$\det|A-\lambda 1|\,,$$

are called the *eigenvalues* of A.

For example, if

$$A = \begin{pmatrix} 2 & -1\\ -1 & 0\end{pmatrix},$$

(4) See Eichhorn and Erdmann in this volume.

then

$$A - \lambda 1 = \begin{pmatrix} 2 & -1 \\ -1 & 0 \end{pmatrix} - \begin{pmatrix} \lambda & 0 \\ 0 & \lambda \end{pmatrix} = \begin{pmatrix} 2-\lambda & -1 \\ -1 & -\lambda \end{pmatrix},$$

and

$$\det|A - \lambda 1| = -\lambda(2-\lambda) - 1 = \lambda^2 - 2\lambda - 1 \text{ .}^{(5)}$$

Thus $\det|A - \lambda 1| = 0$, if and only if

$$\lambda = \lambda_1 = 1 + \sqrt{2} \text{ ,}$$

or

$$\lambda = \lambda_2 = 1 - \sqrt{2} \text{ ,}$$

and the eigenvalues of A are $1+\sqrt{2}$ and $1-\sqrt{2}$. It is a result of linear algebra that A^t converges to the zero-matrix, denoted by 0, as $t \to \infty$, if all eigenvalues of A are smaller absolutely than 1. Then

$$\lim_{t \to \infty} \sum_{\nu=0}^{t-1} A^{\nu} =: \sum_{\nu=0}^{\infty} A^{\nu} = (1-A)^{-1} \text{ .}^{(6)} \tag{2.5}$$

In other words, if all eigenvalues of A are smaller absolutely than 1, $(1-A)$ has an inverse. Some sufficient conditions are known for which the eigenvalues of a matrix A have this property (see Kantorowitsch and Akilov, 1964). Now we can say what happens to equation (2.4) for large t values. From equations (2.4) and (2.5), under the condition that all eigenvalues of A are less than unity in absolute value, it follows that

$$\lim_{t \to \infty} \mathbf{f}(t) = \left(\lim_{t \to \infty} A^{t-t_0}\right) \mathbf{f}_0 + \left(\lim_{t \to \infty} \sum_{\nu = t_0}^{t-1} A^{\nu - t_0}\right) \mathbf{g}$$

$$= 0\mathbf{f}_0 + \sum_{\nu=0}^{\infty} A^{\nu}\mathbf{g} = (1-A)^{-1}\mathbf{g} \text{ .} \tag{2.6}$$

It is noteworthy that the limit (2.6) is independent of the initial value $\mathbf{f}_0$.

If some of the eigenvalues (or even one of them) have absolute values greater than or equal to 1, nothing can be generally said about convergence.

Example: Suppose the given system is

$$\begin{aligned} f_1(t+1) &= \tfrac{1}{2}f_1(t) + \tfrac{1}{4}f_2(t) + 1 \text{ ,} \\ f_2(t+1) &= \tfrac{1}{4}f_1(t) + \tfrac{1}{2}f_2(t) + 2 \text{ .} \end{aligned} \tag{2.7'}$$

A solution $\mathbf{f}' = (f_1, f_2)$ is sought which, by choosing $t_0 = 0$, has the initial value

$$\mathbf{f}(0)' = [f_1(0), f_2(0)] = (0, 1) \text{ .} \tag{2.8}$$

(5) See Eichhorn and Erdmann in this volume.

(6) We write $A =: B$ or $B := A$, if B is defined by A.

In matrix notation, the problem to be solved is

$$\mathbf{f}(t+1) = A\mathbf{f}(t)+\mathbf{g}\,, \tag{2.7}$$

with the initial condition (2.8), where

$$A = \begin{pmatrix} \frac{1}{2} & \frac{1}{4} \\ \frac{1}{4} & \frac{1}{2} \end{pmatrix}, \qquad \mathbf{g} = \begin{pmatrix} 1 \\ 2 \end{pmatrix}, \qquad \mathbf{f}(t) = \begin{pmatrix} f_1(t) \\ f_2(t) \end{pmatrix}.$$

Solution: Since

$$\det|1-A| = \det\begin{vmatrix} \frac{1}{2} & -\frac{1}{4} \\ -\frac{1}{4} & \frac{1}{2} \end{vmatrix} = \tfrac{3}{16} \neq 0\,,$$

formula (2.4′) can be used and, using $t_0 = 0$, the solution is obtained

$$\mathbf{f}(t) = A^t\mathbf{f}_0+(1-A^t)(1-A)^{-1}\mathbf{g}\,.$$

Furthermore

$$(1-A)^{-1} = \begin{pmatrix} \frac{8}{3} & \frac{4}{3} \\ \frac{4}{3} & \frac{8}{3} \end{pmatrix},$$

and therefore

$$(1-A)^{-1}\mathbf{g} = \begin{pmatrix} \frac{8}{3} & \frac{4}{3} \\ \frac{4}{3} & \frac{8}{3} \end{pmatrix}\begin{pmatrix} 1 \\ 2 \end{pmatrix} = \begin{pmatrix} \frac{8}{3}+\frac{8}{3} \\ \frac{4}{3}+\frac{16}{3} \end{pmatrix} = \begin{pmatrix} \frac{16}{3} \\ \frac{20}{3} \end{pmatrix}.$$

Thus

$$\mathbf{f}(t) = A^t\begin{pmatrix} 0 \\ 1 \end{pmatrix}+(1-A^t)\begin{pmatrix} \frac{16}{3} \\ \frac{20}{3} \end{pmatrix}, \tag{2.9}$$

and it only remains to calculate A^t for each $t > 1$ (see Goldberg, 1958, pp.229–233). To examine the behaviour of the solution (2.9) for large values of t, the eigenvalues of A must be calculated:

$$\det|A-\lambda 1| = \det\begin{vmatrix} \frac{1}{2}-\lambda & \frac{1}{4} \\ \frac{1}{4} & \frac{1}{2}-\lambda \end{vmatrix} = \lambda^2-\lambda+\tfrac{3}{16}\,.$$

The roots of

$$\lambda^2-\lambda+\tfrac{3}{16} = 0$$

are

$$\lambda_1 = \tfrac{1}{4}\,, \qquad \text{and } \lambda_2 = \tfrac{3}{4}\,.$$

Thus, the eigenvalues of A are both smaller than 1 and therefore A^t converges to the zero-matrix and from equation (2.9) it follows

$$\mathbf{f}(t) \to \mathbf{0}+(1-0)\begin{pmatrix} \frac{16}{3} \\ \frac{20}{3} \end{pmatrix} = \begin{pmatrix} \frac{16}{3} \\ \frac{20}{3} \end{pmatrix} \quad (t\to\infty)\,. \tag{2.10}$$

Formulae analogous to equation (2.4) exist if, in the system (2.1) [= equation (2.2)], the a_{ij} and g_i are not constants but functions of t:

$$\begin{aligned} a_{ij}&: t \in Z_0 \to a_{ij}(t) \in \mathcal{R}\,, \\ g_i&: t \in Z_0 \to g_i(t) \in \mathcal{R}\,, \end{aligned} \qquad (i = 1, 2, ..., n) \text{ and } (j = 1, 2, ..., n)\,.$$

It can be proved by induction in this case that the only solution of equation (2.2) which satisfies the given initial condition,

$$(c_1, c_2, ..., c_n) = \mathbf{f}'_0 = \mathbf{f}(t_0)' ,$$

is (for $\kappa > 0$),

$$\mathbf{f}(t_0+\kappa) = \prod_{\nu=\kappa-1}^{0} A(t_0+\nu)\mathbf{f}(t_0) + \sum_{\nu=0}^{\kappa-1} \sum_{\mu=\kappa-1}^{\nu+1} A(t_0+\mu)\mathbf{g}(t_0+\nu) , \tag{2.11}$$

where

$$\prod_{\nu=\kappa-1}^{0} A(t_0+\nu) := A(t_0+\kappa-1)A(t_0+\kappa-2) \ldots A(t_0+1)A(t_0) ,$$

and

$$\prod_{\nu=\kappa-1}^{\kappa} A(t_0+\nu) := 1 .$$

3 Systems of linear difference equations of order 2 with constant coefficients

Since it cannot be expected that realistic economic models will include only difference equations of the first order, in this section we give a method for solving linear systems of the second order, from which the general case will follow. Such a system of order two is of the form

$$\mathbf{f}(t+1) = A\mathbf{f}(t) + B\mathbf{f}(t-1) + \mathbf{g} , \tag{3.1}$$

where

$$A = \begin{pmatrix} a_{11} & a_{12} & \cdots & a_{1n} \\ a_{21} & a_{22} & \cdots & a_{2n} \\ \cdot & \cdot & & \cdot \\ \cdot & \cdot & & \cdot \\ \cdot & \cdot & & \cdot \\ a_{n1} & a_{n2} & \cdots & a_{nn} \end{pmatrix} , \qquad B = \begin{pmatrix} b_{11} & b_{12} & \cdots & b_{1n} \\ b_{21} & b_{22} & \cdots & b_{2n} \\ \cdot & \cdot & & \cdot \\ \cdot & \cdot & & \cdot \\ \cdot & \cdot & & \cdot \\ b_{n1} & b_{n2} & \cdots & b_{nn} \end{pmatrix} ,$$

$$a_{ij} \in \mathbb{R}; \quad b_{ij} \in \mathbb{R}; \qquad (i, j = 1, 2, ..., n) ,$$

and **f** and **g** are defined as in section 2. One can reduce the system (3.1), of order two, to a system of order one by setting

$$\mathbf{h}(t) := \mathbf{f}(t-1) , \tag{3.2}$$

that is

$$\mathbf{h}(t)' = [h_1(t), h_2(t), ..., h_n(t)] := [f_1(t-1), f_2(t-1), ..., f_n(t-1)] .$$

One gets, by substituting equation (3.2) into equation (3.1), the two systems of order one

$$\begin{aligned} \mathbf{f}(t+1) &= A\mathbf{f}(t) + B\mathbf{h}(t) + \mathbf{g} , \\ \mathbf{h}(t+1) &= 1\mathbf{f}(t) . \end{aligned} \tag{3.3}$$

To solve the two systems (3.3) simultaneously, it is convenient to define a new vector $\mathbf{v}$ ($\in \mathbb{R}^{2n}$) having the components

$$\begin{aligned}\mathbf{v}(t)' &= [v_1(t), v_2(t), ..., v_n(t), v_{n+1}(t), v_{n+2}(t), ..., v_{2n}(t)] \\ :&= [f_1(t), f_2(t), ..., f_n(t), h_1(t), h_2(t), ..., h_n(t)]\,,\end{aligned} \tag{3.4}$$

and

$$\tilde{\mathbf{g}}' := (g_1, g_2, ..., g_n, 0, 0, ..., 0)\,. \tag{3.5}$$

In this notation, equation (3.3) becomes

$$\mathbf{v}(t+1) = C\mathbf{v}(t) + \tilde{\mathbf{g}}\,, \tag{3.6}$$

where $\mathbf{v}$ and $\tilde{\mathbf{g}}$ are defined above and

$$C = \begin{pmatrix} a_{11} & a_{12} & \cdots & a_{1n} & b_{11} & b_{12} & \cdots & b_{1n} \\ a_{21} & a_{22} & \cdots & a_{2n} & b_{21} & b_{22} & \cdots & b_{2n} \\ \cdot & \cdot & & \cdot & \cdot & \cdot & & \cdot \\ \cdot & \cdot & & \cdot & \cdot & \cdot & & \cdot \\ \cdot & \cdot & & \cdot & \cdot & \cdot & & \cdot \\ a_{n1} & a_{n2} & \cdots & a_{nn} & b_{n1} & b_{n2} & \cdots & b_{nn} \\ 1 & 0 & \cdots & 0 & 0 & 0 & \cdots & 0 \\ 0 & 1 & 0 \cdots & 0 & 0 & 0 & \cdots & 0 \\ \cdot & 0 & \ddots & \cdot & \cdot & \cdot & & \cdot \\ \cdot & & \ddots & \cdot & \cdot & \cdot & & \cdot \\ \cdot & & \cdots & 0 & \cdot & \cdot & & \cdot \\ 0 & 0 & \cdots 0 & 1 & 0 & \cdots & \cdots & 0 \end{pmatrix} = \left(\begin{array}{c|c} A & B \\ \hline 1 & 0 \end{array}\right).$$

Since systems of difference equations of the type (3.6) have already been solved in section 2, the solution of equation (3.6) can be taken immediately from formula (2.4), viz

$$\mathbf{v}(t) = C^{t-t_0}\mathbf{v}_0 + \left(\sum_{\nu=t_0}^{t-1} C^{\nu-t_0}\right)\tilde{\mathbf{g}} \qquad (t > t_0)\,, \tag{3.7}$$

where $\mathbf{v}_0$ is determined uniquely by the initial values at $t = t_0$, and $t = t_0 + 1$, which we assume to be given:

$$\begin{aligned}\mathbf{v}_0 &= \mathbf{v}(t_0+1) \\ &= [f_1(t_0+1), ..., f_n(t_0+1), h_1(t_0+1), ..., h_n(t_0+1)] \\ &= [f_1(t_0+1), ..., f_n(t_0+1), f_1(t_0), f_2(t_0), ..., f_n(t_0)]\,.\end{aligned}$$

The reader will easily see that this method of reducing a system of difference equations of order two to a system of order one can be immediately extended to systems of arbitrarily higher (but finite) order.

4 Linear systems of difference equations of first and higher order with non-constant coefficients

If in equation (2.2) the elements of the matrix A and the components of the vector $\mathbf{g}$ are not constants but functions of t, one cannot use formula

(2.4) to arrive at a solution. Analogously, if in the second-order system (3.1) the elements of the matrices A and B, and the components of the vector $\mathbf{g}$, are not constant but functions of t, equation (3.7) does not give a solution for equation (3.1). However, there are other methods of solving systems of the type (2.2) or (3.1) which will now be discussed.

Let the functions

$$a_{ij} \in F_0 \qquad (i,j = 1,2,\ldots,n)\,,$$
$$g_i \in F_0 \qquad (i = 1,2,\ldots,n)\,,$$

be given.

We consider the finding of all solutions of the first-order system

$$\mathbf{f}(t+1) = A(t)\mathbf{f}(t)+\mathbf{g}(t)\,, \tag{4.1}$$

where

$$A(t) = \begin{pmatrix} a_{11}(t), & a_{12}(t), & \ldots, & a_{1n}(t) \\ a_{21}(t), & a_{22}(t), & \ldots, & a_{2n}(t) \\ \cdot & & & \\ \cdot & & & \\ \cdot & & & \\ a_{n1}(t), & a_{n2}(t), & \ldots, & a_{nn}(t) \end{pmatrix}, \qquad \mathbf{f}(t) = \begin{pmatrix} f_1(t) \\ f_2(t) \\ \cdot \\ \cdot \\ \cdot \\ f_n(t) \end{pmatrix},$$

$$\mathbf{g}(t) = \begin{pmatrix} g_1(t) \\ g_2(t) \\ \cdot \\ \cdot \\ \cdot \\ g_n(t) \end{pmatrix}.$$

Implicit in Theorem 1 of section 2 is the following statement:

Theorem 2: Let $c_1, c_2, \ldots, c_n$ be arbitrary real numbers. There exists one, and only one, solution $\mathbf{f} = (f_1, f_2, \ldots, f_n)'$ with $f_i \in F_0$ $(i = 1,2,\ldots,n)$ of system (4.1) for which

$$\mathbf{f}(t_0) = (c_1, c_2, \ldots, c_n)' = : \mathbf{f}_0\,. \tag{4.2}$$

Proof: Evaluating system (4.1) for $t = t_0$ gives

$$\mathbf{f}(t_0+1) = A(t_0)\mathbf{f}(t_0)+\mathbf{g}(t_0)\,,$$
$$= A(t_0)\mathbf{f}_0+\mathbf{g}(t_0)\,, \text{ from equation (4.2)}\,. \tag{4.3}$$

Thus if $\mathbf{f}(t_0)$ is given it can be seen that $\mathbf{f}(t_0+1)$ is uniquely determined. In the same way, $f(t_0+2)$ can be uniquely determined by considering equation (4.1) for $t = t_0+1$ and substituting from equation (4.3), and so on for successive solutions.

Let us consider the homogeneous system associated with equation (4.1), that is,

$$\mathbf{f}(t_0+1) = A(t)\mathbf{f}(t_0)\,. \tag{4.4}$$

***Theorem** 3:* Let $\mathbf{f}^1$ and $\mathbf{f}^2$ be solutions of the homogeneous system (4.4) belonging to system (4.1). Then the functions

$$c_1\mathbf{f}^1 + c_2\mathbf{f}^2 \qquad (c_1, c_2 \in \mathcal{R} \text{ arbitrary constants})$$

are solutions of system (4.4), too.

Proof: It has to be shown that

$$c_1\mathbf{f}^1(t+1) + c_2\mathbf{f}^2(t+1) = A(t)[c_1\mathbf{f}^1(t) + c_2\mathbf{f}^2(t)] ,$$

or

$$c_1\mathbf{f}^1(t+1) + c_2\mathbf{f}^2(t+1) - A(t)[c_1\mathbf{f}^1(t) + c_2\mathbf{f}^2(t)] = \mathbf{0} . \tag{4.5}$$

The left-hand side of equation (4.5) equals

$$c_1[\mathbf{f}^1(t+1) - A(t)\mathbf{f}^1(t)] + c_2[\mathbf{f}^2(t+1) - A(t)\mathbf{f}^2(t)] = c_1\mathbf{0} + c_2\mathbf{0} = \mathbf{0} ,$$

since $\mathbf{f}^1$ and $\mathbf{f}^2$ are solutions of system (4.4) by assumption. This proves the theorem.

***Theorem** 4:* Let $\mathbf{f}^*$ be any *particular* solution of the inhomogeneous system (4.1) that is corresponding to any particular initial condition $\mathbf{f}_0$. Then the following statements are true.

a. If $\mathbf{h}$ is an *arbitrary* solution of the homogeneous system (4.4) belonging to system (4.1), then

$$\mathbf{f}^* + \mathbf{h} = (f_1^* + h_1, f_2^* + h_2, ..., f_n^* + h_n)'$$

is also a solution of the inhomogeneous system (4.1).

b. On the other hand, *each* solution $\mathbf{f} = (f_1, f_2, ..., f_n)'$ of the inhomogeneous system (4.1) can be represented as

$$\mathbf{f} = \mathbf{f}^* + \mathbf{h} ,$$

where $\mathbf{h}$ is a suitably chosen solution of the homogeneous system (4.4) belonging to system (4.1).

Proof: a. By assumption

$$\mathbf{f}^*(t+1) = A(t)\mathbf{f}^*(t) + \mathbf{g}(t)$$

$$\mathbf{h}(t+1) = A(t)\mathbf{h}(t) .$$

Since the two equations are valid for all $t \in Z_0$, one obtains by addition:

$$\mathbf{f}^*(t+1) + \mathbf{h}(t+1) = A(t)[\mathbf{f}^*(t) + \mathbf{h}(t)] + \mathbf{g}(t) ,$$

which means that $\mathbf{f}^* + \mathbf{h}$ is a solution of system (4.1), as asserted.

b. By assumption, $\mathbf{f}^*$ and $\mathbf{f}$ satisfy equation (4.1).

$$\mathbf{f}(t+1) = A(t)\mathbf{f}(t) + \mathbf{g}(t) , \tag{4.5.1}$$

$$\mathbf{f}^*(t+1) = A(t)\mathbf{f}^*(t) + \mathbf{g}(t) . \tag{4.5.2}$$

To prove the assertion, a solution $\mathbf{h}$ of the homogeneous system (4.4) must be found which has the property that $\mathbf{f} = \mathbf{f}^* + \mathbf{h}$; in other words, it must be proved that $\mathbf{f} - \mathbf{f}^* = \mathbf{h}$ is a solution of the homogeneous system.

Subtraction of equation (4.5.2) from (4.5.1) gives, for all $t \in Z_0$,

$$\mathbf{f}(t+1) - \mathbf{f}^*(t+1) = A(t)[f(t) - f^*(t)] \, .$$

Hence, $\mathbf{f} - \mathbf{f}^*$ is a solution, say $\mathbf{h}$, of the homogeneous system, and the proof of the theorem is completed.

The three theorems show how the problem of finding the only solution of system (4.1) which satisfies a given initial condition $\mathbf{f}_0$ may be simplified. From Theorem 2 it follows that there is one, and only one, solution of equation (4.1) which corresponds to $\mathbf{f}_0$. First, one determines *all* solutions $\mathbf{h}$ of the homogeneous system (4.4) belonging to system (4.1). Since the functions of inhomogeneity g_i may be very complicated, this is much easier in most cases than determining all solutions of the inhomogeneous system (4.1). Second, one then finds any single solution $\mathbf{f}^*$ of the inhomogeneous system (4.1). Probably $\mathbf{f}^*$ will not satisfy the initial condition; but from Theorem 4 one knows that the solution $\mathbf{f}$, which satisfies the initial condition, can be represented by the sum of $\mathbf{f}^*$ and a suitably chosen solution $\mathbf{h}$ of the homogeneous system. $\mathbf{h}$ is uniquely determined by the initial conditions.

One can easily show that these results can be extended to the case of systems of difference equations of arbitrary (but finite) order. The corresponding theorems will be formulated without proofs (which are closely analogous to the proofs above).

Let the functions

$$\begin{aligned} &a_{ijk} \in F_0 \quad (i = 1, 2, ..., m; \quad j, k = 1, 2, ..., n) \, , \\ &g_i \in F_0 \quad (i = 1, 2, ..., n) \end{aligned} \tag{4.6}$$

be given. Consider the mth order system of n simultaneous difference equations

$$\mathbf{f}(t+1) = A_1(t)\mathbf{f}(t) + A_2(t)\mathbf{f}(t-1) + ... + A_m(t)\mathbf{f}(t-m+1) + \mathbf{g}(t) \tag{4.7}$$

where

$$A_i(t) = \begin{pmatrix} a_{i11}(t) & a_{i12}(t) & \dots & a_{i1n}(t) \\ a_{i21}(t) & a_{i22}(t) & \dots & a_{i2n}(t) \\ \cdot & & & \\ \cdot & & & \\ \cdot & & & \\ a_{in1}(t) & a_{in2}(t) & \dots & a_{inn}(t) \end{pmatrix}, \qquad \mathbf{f}(t) = \begin{pmatrix} f_1(t) \\ f_2(t) \\ \cdot \\ \cdot \\ \cdot \\ f_n(t) \end{pmatrix},$$

$$\mathbf{g}(t) = \begin{pmatrix} g_1(t) \\ g_2(t) \\ \cdot \\ \cdot \\ \cdot \\ g_n(t) \end{pmatrix},$$

and $i = 1, 2, ..., m$.

Theorem 5: Let

$$\begin{array}{l} c_{11}, c_{12}, \ldots, c_{1m} \\ c_{21}, c_{22}, \ldots, c_{2m} \\ \cdot \quad \cdot \quad \cdot \\ \cdot \quad \cdot \quad \cdot \\ \cdot \quad \cdot \quad \cdot \\ c_{n1}, c_{n2}, \ldots, c_{nm} \end{array}$$

be arbitrary real constants. There exists one and only one solution $\mathbf{f} = (f_1, f_2, \ldots, f_n)'$ with $f_i \in F_0$ $(i = 1, 2, \ldots, n)$ of system (4.7) for which

$$\mathbf{f}(t_0) = \begin{pmatrix} c_{11} \\ c_{21} \\ \cdot \\ \cdot \\ \cdot \\ c_{n1} \end{pmatrix} =: \mathbf{c}_1, \quad \mathbf{f}(t_0+1) = \begin{pmatrix} c_{12} \\ c_{22} \\ \cdot \\ \cdot \\ \cdot \\ c_{n2} \end{pmatrix} =: \mathbf{c}_2, \ldots,$$

$$\mathbf{f}(t_0+m-1) = \begin{pmatrix} c_{1m} \\ c_{2m} \\ \cdot \\ \cdot \\ \cdot \\ c_{nm} \end{pmatrix} =: \mathbf{c}_m .$$

With system (4.7), consider the associated homogeneous system

$$\mathbf{f}(t+1) = A_1(t)\mathbf{f}(t) + A_2(t)\mathbf{f}(t-1) + \ldots + A_m(t)\mathbf{f}(t-m+1) . \qquad (4.8)$$

Theorem 6: Let $\mathbf{h}^1$ and $\mathbf{h}^2$ be solutions of the homogeneous system (4.8). Then the function

$$c_1\mathbf{h}^1 + c_2\mathbf{h}^2 \qquad (c_1, c_2 \in \mathbb{R} \text{ arbitrary constants})$$

is also a solution of system (4.8).

Theorem 7: Let $\mathbf{f}^*$ be any *particular* solution of the inhomogeneous system (4.7). Then

a. if $\mathbf{h}$ is an *arbitrary* solution of the homogeneous system (4.8) belonging to system (4.7), $\mathbf{f}^* + \mathbf{h}$ is also a solution of the inhomogeneous system (4.7), and
b. on the other hand, *each* solution $\mathbf{f}$ of the inhomogeneous system (4.7) can be represented as

$$\mathbf{f} = \mathbf{f}^* + \mathbf{h} ,$$

where $\mathbf{h}$ is a suitably chosen solution of the homogeneous system (4.8) [7].

[7] For further study the reader is referred to the following list of references, especially to the books of Goldberg (1958), Miller (1968), and Yamane (1962).

References

Allen, R. G. D., 1964, *Mathematical Economics* (Macmillan, New York).
Baumol, W. J., 1970, *Economic Dynamics* (Macmillan, New York).
Chipman, J. S., 1950, "The multi-sector multiplier", *Econometrica,* **18**, 355-374.
Eichhorn, W., Erdmann, R., 1972, "Linear and nonlinear systems of equations", in this volume, pp. 1-18.
Goldberg, S., 1958, *Introduction to Difference Equations* (John Wiley, New York).
Goodwin, R. M., 1949, "The multiplier as matrix", *Economic Journal,* **59**, 537-555.
Goodwin, R. M., 1950, "Does the matrix multiplier oscillate?", *Economic Journal,* **60**, 764-770.
Hansen, G., 1967, *Ein ökonometrisches Modell für die Bundesrepublik 1951-1964* (Vandenhoeck and Ruprecht, Göttingen).
Kantorowitsch, L., Akilov, G., 1964, *Funktionalanalysis in normierten Räumen* (Akademie-Verlag, Berlin).
Krelle, W., Beckerhoff, D., Langer, H. G., Fuss, H., 1969, *Ein Prognosesystem für die Wirtschaftliche Entwicklung der BRD* (Anton Hain, Meisenheim).
Levy, H., Lessman, F., 1959, *Finite Difference Equations* (Pitman, London).
Miller, K., 1968, *Linear Difference Equations* (Benjamin, New York).
Paelinck, J., 1972, "Alternative methods for the study of urban dynamics", in this volume, pp. 33-49.
Yamane, T., 1962, *Mathematics for Economics* (Prentice-Hall, Englewood Cliffs, N.J.).

Alternative Methods for the Study of Urban Dynamics

J.H.P.PAELINCK
Netherlands Economic Institute and Netherlands School of Economics, Rotterdam

1 Introduction

Over the last twenty years the urban phenomenon has received considerable attention from different types of scholars, for example, planners, economists, and geographers. Mostly, urban studies have been limited to certain factual aspects: transportation flows, land use, urban blight, ghetto problems, etc. Hypotheses have been proposed to account for the empirical findings.

Urban statistics are now improving quickly, and the author believes that it will be possible, in the future, to be more ambitious concerning the scope of urban studies. In other words, urban econometrics could lead, in the years to come, to fully-fledged econometric models of the metropolis integrated in its region. What has been done on the national and regional levels could be repeated in the urban field.

The present article reviews experience of the study of urban (economic) dynamics. The main thesis is that a combination of methods is, and will be, necessary to fully understand the complexities of city life.

Three methods are described below: the use of theoretical models, the simulation of more complex systems, and urban econometric methods. Each of these can, and must, contribute in its own right to the study of urban phenomena over time.

How this is done will now be explained.

2 Theoretical models[1]

There should no longer be any confusion about the status of theoretical models: they are an intellectual tool, and allow us to derive *propositions* or *meaningful theorems* in any field of study. But these propositions have to be verified—or possibly contradicted—by the study of empirical material.

Theoretical urban models represent a consistent set of relationships among urban variables. They can be constructed by using coherently partial relations that have already been proposed in the literature.

(1) Further details can be found in Paelinck, 1970.

All the relations should be dimensionally correct. They can be of various types: equilibrium conditions, tendency towards equilibrium, reaction equations, functional relations, accounting identities, and definitional relations.

Let us take a simple example using elementary base–non base analysis. The variables are defined as follows:

P is the total population,
A is the total active population,
E_{i} are the basic urban activities,
E_{s} are the service activities,
E is the total employment.

The following relations can be defined:

$$\Delta' E_{\mathrm{i},t+1} = \alpha(A_t - E_t) + \alpha^* E_{\mathrm{i},t} , \tag{2.1}$$

$$\Delta' E_{\mathrm{s},t+1} = \beta(\beta^* P_t - E_{\mathrm{s},t}) + \beta^{**} E_{\mathrm{s},t} , \tag{2.2}$$

$$\Delta' A_{t+1} = \gamma \Delta' P_{t+1} + \gamma^* (E_t - A_t) , \tag{2.3}$$

$$\Delta' P_{t+1} = \delta(E_t - A_t) + \delta^* P_t , \tag{2.4}$$

$$E \equiv E_{\mathrm{i}} + E_{\mathrm{s}}, \qquad \forall t . \tag{2.5}$$

Equation (2.1) describes how basic activities are attracted by the available manpower; relation (2.2) shows how employment in service industries tends progressively to an equilibrium level ($\beta^* P_t$); equation (2.3) generates active population as a function of total population and of the pressure resulting from excess demand for manpower; relation (2.4) explains how population is attracted towards the city; equation (2.5) is an accounting identity. Autonomous rates of growth have been added; some of these parameters might be policy variables (for instance α^*, as an attractiveness parameter for basic activities).

The system can be rewritten in matrix notation as follows

$$\begin{bmatrix} 1 & 0 & 0 & 0 & 0 \\ -\gamma & 1 & 0 & 0 & 0 \\ 0 & 0 & 1 & -1 & -1 \\ 0 & 0 & 0 & 1 & 0 \\ 0 & 0 & 0 & 0 & 1 \end{bmatrix} \begin{bmatrix} P \\ A \\ E \\ E_{\mathrm{i}} \\ E_{\mathrm{s},t+1} \end{bmatrix} = \begin{bmatrix} 1+\delta^* & -\delta & \delta & 0 & 0 \\ -\gamma & 1-\gamma^* & \gamma^* & 0 & 0 \\ 0 & 0 & 0 & 0 & 0 \\ 0 & \alpha & -\alpha & 1+x^* & 0 \\ \beta\beta^* & 0 & 0 & 0 & 1-\beta+\beta^{**} \end{bmatrix} \begin{bmatrix} P \\ A \\ E \\ E_{\mathrm{i}} \\ E_{\mathrm{s}} \end{bmatrix}$$

or in condensed form

$$A\mathbf{x}_t = B\mathbf{x}_{t-1} ,$$

which can be rewritten as

$$\mathbf{x}_t = A^{-1}B\mathbf{x}_{t-1} = C\mathbf{x}_{t-1} .$$

It is well known that $\mathbf{x}_t$ can be expressed in terms of its initial values as

$$\mathbf{x}_t = C^t \mathbf{x}_0 ,$$

with the matrix C^t being given by

$$C^t = \alpha_0 1 + \alpha_1 C + \alpha_2 C^2 + \alpha_3 C^3 + \alpha_4 C^4 ,$$

and the α_i's being solutions of the system

$$\begin{bmatrix} 1 & \lambda_1 & \lambda_1^2 & \lambda_1^3 & \lambda_1^4 \\ 1 & \lambda_2 & \lambda_2^2 & \lambda_2^3 & \lambda_2^4 \\ 1 & \lambda_3 & \lambda_3^2 & \lambda_3^3 & \lambda_3^4 \\ 1 & \lambda_4 & \lambda_4^2 & \lambda_4^3 & \lambda_4^4 \\ 1 & \lambda_5 & \lambda_5^2 & \lambda_5^3 & \lambda_5^4 \end{bmatrix} \begin{bmatrix} \alpha_0 \\ \alpha_1 \\ \alpha_2 \\ \alpha_3 \\ \alpha_4 \end{bmatrix} = \begin{bmatrix} \lambda_1^t \\ \lambda_2^t \\ \lambda_3^t \\ \lambda_4^t \\ \lambda_5^t \end{bmatrix} ,$$

where the λ's are the eigenvalues of C.

In fact, C^t is a linear combination of the λ_i^t's, which means that the dynamics of the system are essentially a function of the values taken on by the characteristic roots. Cycling and alternating are possibilities in our systems.

From the study of the model given by equations (2.1) through to (2.5) the following propositions could be made:

(1) an urban economic system is a very susceptible one, in the sense that medium- and long-term cycles can easily set in;
(2) a high service–population ratio tends to stabilize the urban system;
(3) the intensity with which basic activities are attracted towards the metropolis tends to stabilize the city;
(4) external push effects contribute to stabilize the system.

It should not be forgotten that these propositions have been derived under very restrictive conditions: for example, no reference has been made to urban space; a large variety of typical urban relations have been neglected; relations were supposed to be reversible, etc. On the other hand, as the system gets larger and larger, theoretical study is hampered by the difficulty in deriving analytical expressions for the eigenvalues. At this point, simulation comes in as a check on the theory, and as a tool for further and broader investigation.

3 Urban simulation (2)

In a recent attempt to construct a more realistic model the following features were introduced:

—the distinction between resident and commuting workers,
—the attractiveness of the city;
—the integration of the city with its hinterland;
—expanding job opportunities;
—the pressure of urban activities on available land, and the extensibility of the city;
—four main activity sectors: industry, services, public government, and building;

(2) See, for further details, Jaumotte and Paelinck (1969).

—economic indicators: income *per capita*, city budget, and infrastructure expenditures.

The model was set up as follows[3]:

$$PIV_{t+1} \equiv A_{\mathrm{i},t+1}\pi_{\mathrm{i},t+1} + A_{\mathrm{s},t+1}\pi_{\mathrm{s},t+1} + A_{\mathrm{a},t+1}\pi_{\mathrm{a},t+1} + A_{\mathrm{c},t+1}\pi_{\mathrm{c},t+1} \,, \tag{3.1}$$

$$\Delta' A_{\mathrm{i},t+1} = a_2 A_{\mathrm{i},t} + b_2 \Delta' OE_{\mathrm{i},t+1} \,, \tag{3.2}$$

$$\Delta' A_{\mathrm{s},t+1} = a_3 A_{\mathrm{s},t} + b_3 \Delta' OE_{\mathrm{s},t+1} \,, \tag{3.3}$$

$$\Delta' A_{\mathrm{a},t+1} = a_4 A_{\mathrm{a},t} + b_4 \Delta' OE_{\mathrm{a},t+1} \,, \tag{3.4}$$

$$\Delta' A_{\mathrm{c},t+1} = a_5 A_{\mathrm{c},t} + b_5 \Delta' OE_{\mathrm{c},t+1} \,, \tag{3.5}$$

$$A_{t+1} \equiv A_{\mathrm{i},t+1} + A_{\mathrm{s},t+1} + A_{\mathrm{a},t+1} + A_{\mathrm{c},t+1} \,, \tag{3.6}$$

$$A_{\mathrm{v},t+1} \equiv A_{t+1} - A_{\mathrm{R},t+1} - A_{\mathrm{M},t+1} \,, \tag{3.7}$$

$$\Delta' A_{\mathrm{R},t+1} = a_8 \Delta' P_{\mathrm{R},t+1} + b_8 A_{\mathrm{R},t} \,, \tag{3.8}$$

$$\Delta' A_{\mathrm{M},t+1} = a_9 \Delta'(OE_{t+1} - A_{\mathrm{R},t+1})^{(4)} + b_9 \Delta' W_{\mathrm{i},t+1} + \underline{d_9} \Delta' Di_{t+1} \,, \tag{3.9}$$

$$\Delta' \pi_{\mathrm{i},t+1} = a_{10} \Delta'(DC_{t+1} - De_{t+1})^{(4)} + b_{10} \Delta' AF_{t+1} + c_{10} \pi_{\mathrm{i},t} \,, \tag{3.10}$$

$$\Delta' \pi_{\mathrm{s},t+1} = a_{11} \pi_{\mathrm{s},t} \,, \tag{3.11}$$

$$\Delta' \pi_{\mathrm{a},t+1} = a_{12} \pi_{\mathrm{a},t} \,, \tag{3.12}$$

$$\Delta' \pi_{\mathrm{c},t+1} = a_{13} \pi_{\mathrm{c},t} \,, \tag{3.13}$$

$$OE_{t+1} \equiv OE_{\mathrm{i},t+1} + OE_{\mathrm{s},t+1} + OE_{\mathrm{a},t+1} + OE_{\mathrm{c},t+1} \,, \tag{3.14}$$

$$OE_{\mathrm{i},t+1} \equiv OE_{\mathrm{ie},t+1} + OE_{\mathrm{id},t+1} \,, \tag{3.15}$$

$$\Delta' OE_{\mathrm{ie},t+1} = a_{16} OE_{\mathrm{ie},t} + b_{16} \Delta' De_{t+1} + \underline{c_{16}}(S_t - \bar{S}) \,, \tag{3.16}$$

$$\Delta' OE_{\mathrm{id},t+1} = a_{17} \Delta' OE_{\mathrm{ie},t+1} + b_{17} \Delta' V_{t+1} + \underline{c_{17}}(S_t - \bar{S}) \,, \tag{3.17}$$

$$\Delta' OE_{\mathrm{c},t+1} = a_{18} \Delta' P_{\mathrm{R},t+1} + b_{18} \Delta' A_{t+1} + d_{18} OE_{\mathrm{c},t} \,, \tag{3.18}$$

$$\Delta' OE_{\mathrm{s},t+1} = a_{19} \Delta' P_{\mathrm{R},t+1} + b_{19} \Delta' R_{t+1} + c_{19} OE_{\mathrm{s},t} + d_{19}(S_t - \bar{S}) + \gamma_{19}(\alpha P_{\mathrm{R},t} - OE_{\mathrm{s},t}) \,, \tag{3.19}$$

$$\Delta' OE_{\mathrm{a},t+1} = a_{20} \Delta' B_{t+1} + b_{20} \Delta' P_{\mathrm{R},t+1} + c_{20} OE_{\mathrm{a},t} \,, \tag{3.20}$$

$$\Delta' De_{t+1} = a_{21} \Delta' De_{t+1} + b_{21} De_t \,, \tag{3.21}$$

$$\Delta' W_{\mathrm{i},t+1} = a_{22} W_{\mathrm{i},t} + \underline{b_{22}} \Delta'(A_{\mathrm{i},t+1} - OE_{\mathrm{i},t+1})^{(4)} + c_{22} \Delta' \pi_{\mathrm{i},t+1} + \underline{d_{22}} \Delta' A_{\mathrm{M},t+1} \,, \tag{3.22}$$

$$\Delta' W_{\mathrm{s},t+1} = a_{23} W_{\mathrm{s},t} + \underline{b_{23}} \Delta'(A_{\mathrm{s},t+1} - OE_{\mathrm{s},t+1})^{(4)} + c_{23} \Delta' \pi_{\mathrm{s},t+1} + \underline{d_{23}} \Delta' A_{\mathrm{M},t+1} \,, \tag{3.23}$$

(3) The underlined coefficients are negative.

(4) Ratios amongst variables have been transformed into differences; this is possible since all variables are expressed in indices, and this maintains linearity.

$$\Delta' W_{a,t+1} = a_{24} W_{a,t} + \underline{b_{24}} \Delta'(A_{a,t+1} - OE_{a,t+1})^{(4)} + c_{24} \Delta' \pi_{a,t+1} + \underline{d_{24}} \Delta' A_{M,t+1} , \qquad (3.24)$$

$$\Delta' W_{c,t+1} = a_{25} W_{c,t} + \underline{b_{25}} \Delta'(A_{c,t+1} - OE_{c,t+1})^{(4)} + c_{25} \Delta' \pi_{c,t+1} + \underline{d_{25}} \Delta' A_{M,t+1} , \qquad (3.25)$$

$$\Delta' R_{t+1} \equiv \Delta' W_{i,t+1} + \Delta' W_{s,t+1} + \Delta' W_{a,t+1} + \Delta' W_{c,t+1} + \Delta' A_{i,t+1} + \Delta' A_{s,t+1} + \Delta' A_{a,t+1} + \Delta' A_{c,t+1} + 4\Delta' A_{R,t+1} - 4\Delta' P_{R,t+1} - 4\Delta' A_{t+1}{}^{(5)} , \qquad (3.26)$$

$$\Delta' B_{t+1} = a_{27} B_t + b_{27} \Delta' R_{t+1} , \qquad (3.27)$$

$$\Delta' P_{R,t+1} = a_{28} P_{R,t} + b_{28} \Delta' V_{t+1} , \qquad (3.28)$$

$$\Delta' AF_{t+1} = a_{29} AF_t + b_{29} \Delta' B_{t+1} , \qquad (3.29)$$

$$\Delta' Di_{t+1} = \underline{a_{30}} Di_t + \underline{b_{30}} \Delta' I_{d,t+1} , \qquad (3.30)$$

$$\Delta' I_{d,t+1} = a_{31} I_{d,t} + b_{31} \Delta' B_{t+1} + \underline{c_{31}} \Delta'(A_{R,t+1} - OE_{t+1})^{(4)} , \qquad (3.31)$$

$$\Delta' S_{t+1} = a_{32} \Delta' P_{R,t+1} + c_{32} \Delta' A_{t+1} , \qquad (3.32)$$

$$\Delta' DC_{t+1} = a_{33} DC_t + b_{33} \Delta' OE_{id,t+1} , \qquad (3.33)$$

$$\Delta' V_{t+1} = a_{34} V_t + b_{34} \Delta'(AF_{t+1} - P_{R,t+1})^{(4)} + c_{34} \Delta' OE_{s,t+1} + d_{34} \Delta' R_{t+1} + \underline{e_{34}} \Delta' S_{t+1} . \qquad (3.34)$$

The meaning of the symbols representing the 34 endogenous variables of the model is as follows:

PIV is the urban product,
A_i is the population occupied in industry,
A_s is the population occupied in services,
A_a is the population occupied in the public sector,
A_c is the population occupied in building activities,
A is the total employment,
A_R is the residential employment,
A_M is the commuting employment,
A_v is the commuting adjustment,
π_i is the productivity in industry,
π_s is the productivity in services,
π_a is the productivity in the public sector,
π_c is the productivity in the building sector,

(5) The identity expressing *per capita* income should be written:

$$\frac{\Delta' W_{i,t+1} A_{i,t} + W_{i,t} \Delta' A_{i,t+1} + \Delta' W_{s,t+1} A_{s,t+1} + \ldots}{\Delta' P^*_{R,t+1}} .$$

Since all variables are expressed in indices, the linear form of equation (3.26) is equivalent once more.

OE is the total supply of jobs,
OE_i is the supply of jobs in industry,
OE_{ie} is the supply of jobs in existing industry,
OE_{id} is the supply of jobs in induced industry,
OE_c is the supply of jobs in building industry,
OE_s is the supply of jobs in services industry,
OE_a is the supply of jobs in the public sector,
De is the demand for industrial products,
W_i are the wages in industry,
W_s are the wages in services,
W_a are the wages in the public sector,
W_c are the wages in the building sector,
R is the *per capita* income of resident population,
B is the public budget,
P_R is the resident population,
AF are the infrastructure expenditures,
Di is the distance between the city and its attraction zone measured in travelling time,
I_d are the investments in communications,
S is the population density,
DC is the interindustrial demand within the complex,
V is the attraction power of the city.

The graph shown in figure 1 illustrates the relations between groups of variables.

The model has the same structure as the theoretical one described in section 2. Its B-matrix is shown in figure 2, after quasi-triangulation.

For a triangular matrix, the eigenvalues are equal to the corresponding diagonal entries of the matrix. In fact, the relevant eigenvalues are those of $C = A^{-1}B$, which is even more complex than B, so that complex eigenvalues and cycling can be expected under certain conditions. The graph shown in figure 3 demonstrates that this has actually been the case.

The interesting point is that the cycling has been obtained by lowering the service–population ratio; this confirms what has been stated in section 2 as a proposition on urban dynamics.

Another interesting feature is the fact that a single parameter in the system is able to govern its behaviour. This is probably due to the fact that, in a sense, a city is a 'looser' system than a region which, in turn, is more 'disconnected' than a nation. The importance of good estimators for the parameters in *econometric* dynamic urban models becomes apparent; section 4 will be devoted to this topic.

It is evident that, before implementing the model, a certain number of improvements ought to be introduced. Time lags should become more realistic. Variables should become more operational in terms of urban policy. Land-use equations should be rewritten in terms of their defining factors.

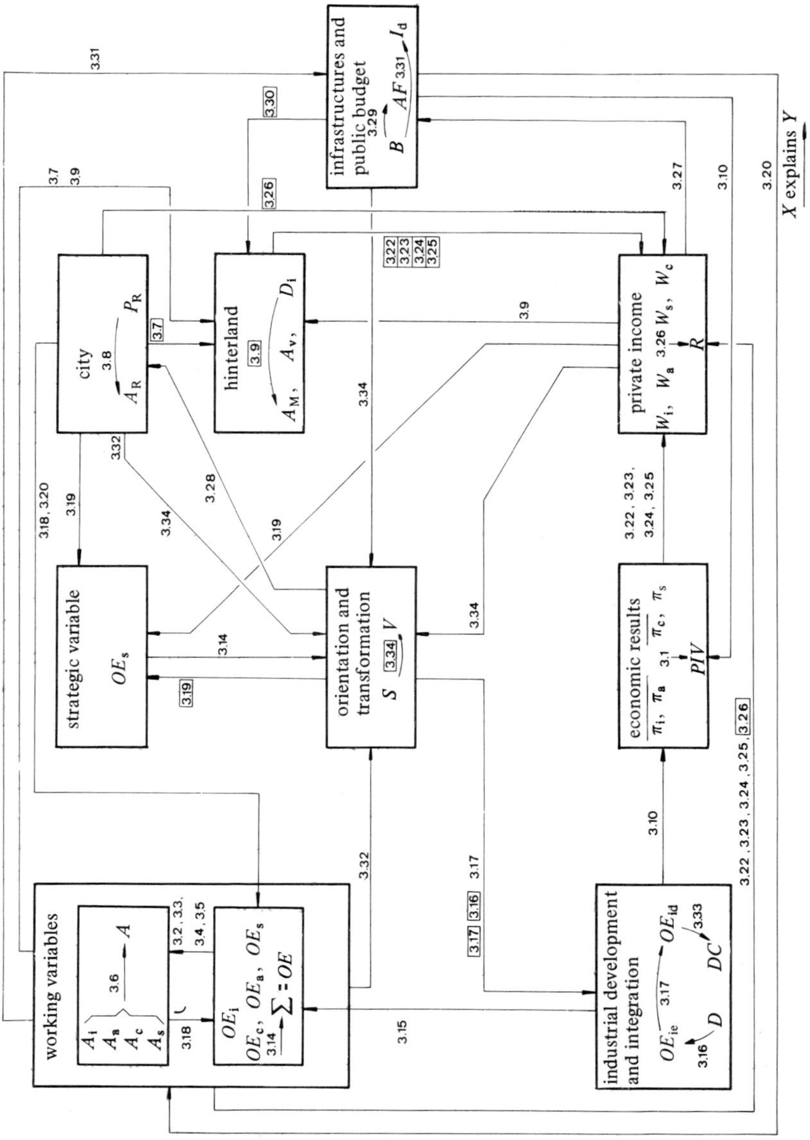
working variables
city
hinterland
strategic variable
orientation and transformation
infrastructures and public budget
private income
economic results
industrial development and integration
X explains Y

Figure 1.

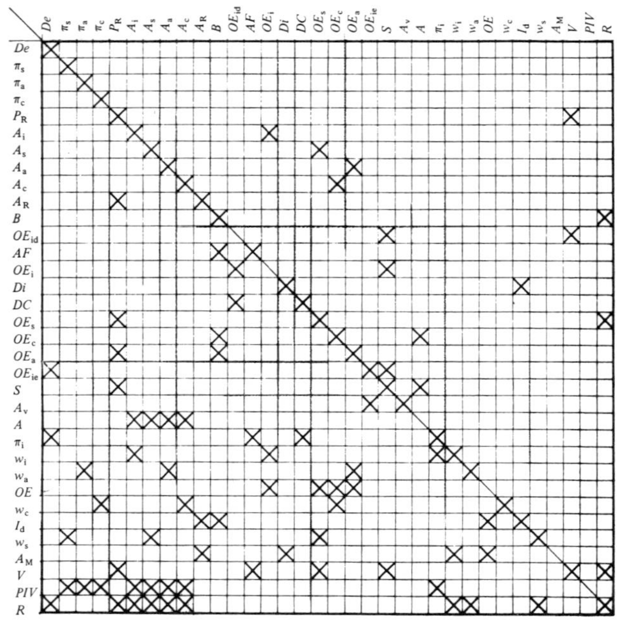

Figure 2.

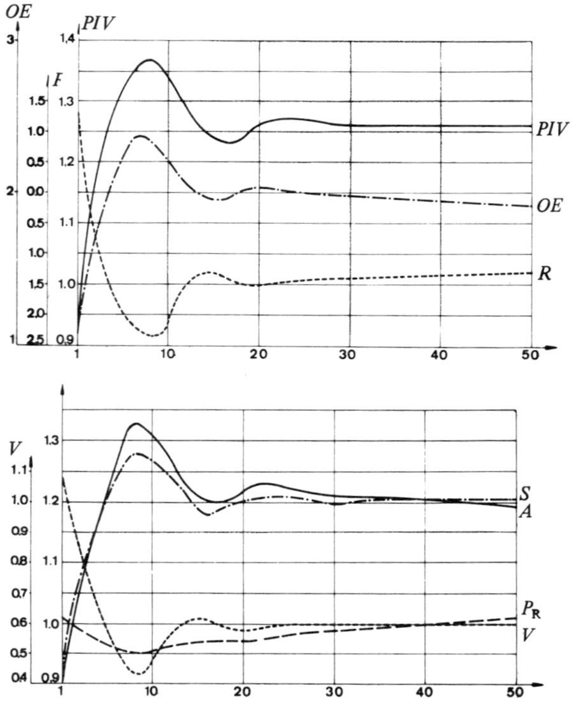

Figure 3.

The main difficulty will probably be that indispensable data will not become available at the desired rate.

4 Urban econometrics[6]

In future years, urban data will certainly become more readily available than at present. Moreover, they will probably allow the generation of time-series, and these will be stored in urban data-banks.

Implementation of the models described in sections 2 and 3 will then be possible, though the first trials will still have to be adapted to available figures; further pressure from urban policy will generate the missing ones.

The need for good estimators has already been stressed. The only experience as yet available stems from national models (de Biolley and Paelinck, 1970). The poor results obtained by classical methods, especially in non-linear systems, have led the author and one of his assistants, to look for alternative methods of estimation.

Historically a first set of estimation procedures has been derived, in a more or less sophisticated fashion, from the classical single-equation least-squares estimation methods: such methods are 'the ordinary least squares', the 'indirect least squares', and the 'multi-stage least squares'. The advantages of these methods are, on the one hand, their computational simplicity and, on the other, the absence of restrictive assumptions such as those concerning a particular distribution of the disturbances, and the availability of large sample data. Nevertheless they leave the statistician rather unhappy in the sense that they lack methodological rigour. Indeed, these methods fail to meet the real problem requirement, which is to estimate parameters of simultaneous equation systems. Instead they have been derived in one way or another, not with the idea of generalizing the single equation approach to simultaneous equation systems, but rather with that of reducing the simultaneous equation problem to a sort of single equation problem. The same idea applies to single dynamic equations (Markov processes, etc.).

A second set of simultaneous equation estimation methods is based on the principle of maximum likelihood. This is theoretically quite satisfactory as it takes full direct account of the interdependences of the complete model. In turn it is based on such assumptions, quite uncomfortable for the econometrician, as the multivariate normal distribution of the disturbances, and the availability of large sample data: the normality assumption may not be met at all closely in small samples, which is the rule in economics. Whatever the methods used, they largely break down when non-linearities are liberally introduced.

[6] For further details see Ancot and Paelinck (1970).

The purpose of this section is to describe some first results of an analysis based on the following leading principles.

(1) The approach aims to take full account of the generality of the non-linear model, whether static or dynamic.

(2) The parameter estimators must be such that they produce good values of the endogenous variables in small samples and regardless of any particular distribution of the disturbances. Another reason for the statement of this principle, apart from that given above, is that when one uses a model to simulate the economy, one usually neglects the stochastic part of the model; consequently there is the risk in dynamic models of the random disturbances being transmitted cumulatively from one time period to the other. These effects in such models should be minimized.

(3) Dynamic systems, when simulated, must be started somewhere. Initial values for the endogenous variables are usually taken to be the observed values of these variables for the initial time periods, if the model includes lagged variables up to time $t-s$. Now, these initial values are not necessarily the best possible starting point of the simulation model when considering the goodness of fit of the simulated values with the observed values of the endogenous variables. Therefore, why not regard these initial values as other parameters to be estimated?

(4) Not all endogenous variables fulfill an 'equally important' role in the model, either for reasons of economic status (there are 'strategic variables' and so on) or for reasons of statistical estimation (errors of observation and measurement affect differently the different variables of the model). Therefore the possibility of weighting these variables, in the course of the estimation procedure, according to their relative 'importance'.

(5) Finally, the estimations need not necessarily be simple to compute: modern high speed electronic computers provide us with calculation facilities which were unavailable in the past.

The principles enumerated in the preceding paragraphs lead quite naturally to the minimization of a function (the 'loss-function') of the weighted differences between observed and calculated, or estimated, values of all the endogenous variables. The most obvious of these is the function defined as the weighted sum of these differences squared. Thus, estimators of the parameters should be obtained through the minimization of the loss-function M so that

$$\mathrm{M} = \sum_{i=1}^{m} \left[w_i \sum_{t=0}^{T} (Y_{it} - Y_{it}^*)^2 \right] , \tag{4.1}$$

where Y_{it} represents the value of endogenous variable i observed at time t, Y_{it}^* represents the value of the same variable calculated from the model for the same time period, w_i is the weight associated with endogenous variable i and depends on the importance attached to that particular variable relative to the other endogenous variables

$$\left(0 < w_i < 1; \qquad \sum_{i=1}^{m} w_i = 1\right).$$

Of course, other loss functions could be preferred, but the advantages of this function are its simplicity and its close relationship to the classical least squares principle; some of the sophisticated versions of the latter will be derived as special cases.

We shall first consider the linear simultaneous dynamic model and its properties; the non-linear case will then appear as a simple generalization. First empirical results will be presented at the end of the study.

Model 1

On considering the most general linear simultaneous equations model—the static model appearing thus as a trivial case of the general model—and allowing for endogenous variables lagging up to time $t-s$, the following matrix notation is used:

$$\begin{bmatrix} B & B_{-1} & \dots & B_{-s} & 0 & \dots & 0 \\ 0 & B & \dots & B_{-s+1} & B_{-s} & \dots & 0 \\ & & & & & & \\ & & & & & & \\ 0 & 0 & \dots & 0 & 0 & \dots & B \end{bmatrix} \begin{bmatrix} \mathbf{y}_t \\ \mathbf{y}_{t-1} \\ \cdot \\ \cdot \\ \cdot \\ \mathbf{y}_0 \end{bmatrix} - \begin{bmatrix} C & 0 & \dots & 0 \\ 0 & C & \dots & 0 \\ & & & \\ & & & \\ 0 & 0 & \dots & C \end{bmatrix} \begin{bmatrix} \mathbf{x}_t \\ \mathbf{x}_{t-1} \\ \cdot \\ \cdot \\ \cdot \\ \mathbf{x}_0 \end{bmatrix} = \begin{bmatrix} \mathbf{u}_t \\ \mathbf{u}_{t-1} \\ \cdot \\ \cdot \\ \cdot \\ \mathbf{u}_0 \end{bmatrix} \qquad (4.2)$$

where $\mathbf{y}_t$ is a vector of m endogenous variables at time t,
$\mathbf{x}_t$ is a vector of n exogenous variables at time t,
$\mathbf{u}_t$ is a vector of m errors at time t,
B is a $(m \times m)$ matrix of coefficients of $\mathbf{y}_t$,
B_{-i} $(i = 1, ..., s)$ is a $(m \times m)$ matrix of coefficients of $\mathbf{y}_{t-1}$, and
C is a $(m \times n)$ matrix of coefficients of $\mathbf{x}_t$.

Equation (4.2) corresponds to a system of m simultaneous linear equations of m endogenous variables and n exogenous variables, including lagged variables up to s unit time lags, with $t+1$ observations of all variables being available. An important feature of this approach is the fact that the lagged variables are no longer considered as predetermined, but that they become really endogenous.

For the sake of convenience, the above equation can be written as

$$\mathsf{B}\mathbf{y} - \mathsf{C}\mathbf{x} = \mathbf{u}\,. \qquad (4.3)$$

Provided B is non-singular (which is not a very restrictive assumption), the latter can be written as

$$\mathbf{y} = \mathsf{B}^{-1}\mathsf{C}\mathbf{x} + \mathsf{B}^{-1}\mathbf{u} = \pi\mathbf{x} + \mathbf{v} \qquad (4.4)$$

which, although similar in notation, should not be confused with the usual reduced form equation (this is only so if $s = 0$, the static model).

Model 2

Model 1 is, of course, slightly incorrect in that it truncates matrix B by omitting for the s initial periods some or all of the lagged dynamic structure. In order to correct for this, and also to introduce the initial conditions in a more explicit fashion, a second model is proposed:

$$\mathsf{B}\mathbf{y} - \mathsf{C}\mathbf{x} - \begin{bmatrix} 0 & 0 & \dots & 0 \\ & & & \\ 0 & 0 & \dots & 0 \\ B_{-s} & 0 & \dots & 0 \\ B_{-s+1} & B_{-s} & \dots & 0 \\ & & & \\ B_{-1} & B_{-2} & \dots & B_{-s} \end{bmatrix} \begin{bmatrix} \mathbf{y}^{\mathrm{o}}_{-1} \\ \cdot \\ \cdot \\ \cdot \\ \mathbf{y}^{\mathrm{o}}_{-s} \end{bmatrix} = \mathbf{u}\,, \tag{4.5}$$

where $\mathbf{y}$, $\mathbf{x}$, $\mathbf{u}$, B, C, and the B_{-i} $(i = 1, ..., s)$ are defined as in model 1. $\mathbf{y}^{\mathrm{o}}_{-i}$ $(i = 1, ..., s)$ is a vector of m values corresponding to the initial conditions for the endogenous variables.

Let the above equation be written as

$$\mathsf{B}\mathbf{y} - \mathsf{C}\mathbf{x} - \mathsf{B}^{\mathrm{o}}\mathbf{y}^{\mathrm{o}} = \mathbf{u}\,, \tag{4.6}$$

or again, provided B is non-singular

$$\begin{aligned} y &= \mathsf{B}^{-1}\mathsf{C}\mathbf{x} + \mathsf{B}^{-1}\mathsf{B}^{\mathrm{o}}\mathbf{y}^{\mathrm{o}} + \mathsf{B}^{-1}\mathbf{u} \\ &= \pi\mathbf{x} + \mathsf{N}\mathbf{y}^{\mathrm{o}} + \mathbf{v}\,. \end{aligned} \tag{4.7}$$

The loss-function (4.1), corresponding to equation (4.4) of model 1, is:

$$\mathsf{M} = \mathbf{v}'\hat{w}\mathbf{v}\,, \tag{4.8}$$

where $\hat{w}$ is a diagonal matrix in which the diagonal consists of $(T+1)$ repetitions of the vector w $(w > 0$ and $i'w = 1)$, which is a vector of weights associated with the endogenous variables, as commended in principle (4) of our approach.

Equation (4.8) can be expanded

$$\mathsf{M} = \mathbf{y}'\hat{w}\mathbf{y} + \pi'x'\hat{w}\pi\mathbf{x} - 2\mathbf{y}'\hat{w}\pi\mathbf{x}\,, \tag{4.9}$$

and equation (4.9) can be expressed as a function of the unknown parameters π_i $(i = 0, ..., T)$:

$$\mathsf{M} = \sum_{t=0}^{T}\mathbf{y}_t'\hat{w}\mathbf{y}_t + \sum_{t=0}^{T}\left[\left(\sum_{i=0}^{T}\mathbf{x}'_{t-1}\pi_i'\right)\hat{w}\left(\sum_{i=0}^{T}\pi_i\mathbf{x}_{t-1}\right)\right] - 2\sum_{t=0}^{T}\mathbf{y}_t'\hat{w}\sum_{i=0}^{T}\pi_i\mathbf{x}_{t-1}\,. \tag{4.10}$$

Now, we want to find estimators of π_i such that they minimize the loss function M. This minimization process produces the normal equation:

$$\frac{\partial\mathsf{M}}{\partial\pi_i} \equiv 2\hat{w}\left[\sum_{t=i}^{T}\left(\sum_{j=0}^{T}\pi_j\mathbf{x}_{t-j}\right)\mathbf{x}'_{t-i}\right] - 2\hat{w}\sum_{t=i}^{T}\mathbf{y}_t\mathbf{x}'_{t-i} = 0\,; \qquad (i = 0, ..., T) \tag{4.11}$$

or

$$\sum_{t=i}^{T}\left(\sum_{j=0}^{T}\pi_j \mathbf{x}_{t-j}\right)\mathbf{x}'_{t-i} - \sum_{t=i}^{T}\mathbf{y}_t\mathbf{x}'_{t-i} = 0 \,. \tag{4.12}$$

Equation (4.12) does not give an estimator for the π_i's that is simple to compute. Nevertheless, provided some approximate value of the π_i's is known (for example, from ordinary least squares), an iterative procedure such as the Gaushaus algorithm (Marquardt, 1963) is feasible, at least in small models. The Gaushaus algorithm is essentially a compromise between the method of steepest descent and the Newton–Raphson method. The former converges faster when the process is relatively far from the solution, but becomes very slow as soon as the solution is approached; the latter converges faster in the neighbourhood of the solution and, apart from the risk of divergence elsewhere, the estimation is feasible, at least, in relatively small models.

Note finally that the weights vanish in equation (4.12).

Theorem: In the case of the static model, the estimators are indirect least squares estimators. Indeed, all the B_{-i}'s ($i = 1, ..., s$) are zero, so that all the π_i's become zero, except π_0 which is equal to $B^{-1}C$. Equation (4.12) then becomes

$$\sum_{t=0}^{T}\pi_0\mathbf{x}_t\mathbf{x}'_t - \sum_{t=0}^{T}\mathbf{y}_t\mathbf{x}'_t = 0 \,, \tag{4.13}$$

or

$$\pi_0 = \left(\sum_{t=0}^{T}\mathbf{y}_t\mathbf{x}'_t\right)\left(\sum_{t=0}^{T}\mathbf{x}_t\mathbf{x}'_t\right)^{-1} , \tag{4.14}$$

the indirect least squares estimators of the reduced form parameters.

On expanding (4.8) in the case of model 2,

$$\mathsf{M} = \mathbf{y}'\hat{w}\mathbf{y} + \mathbf{x}'\pi'\hat{w}\pi\mathbf{x} + \mathbf{y}^{\mathbf{o}\prime}\mathsf{N}'\hat{w}\mathsf{N}\mathbf{y}^{\mathbf{o}} - 2\mathbf{y}'\hat{w}\pi\mathbf{x} - 2\mathbf{y}'\hat{w}\mathsf{N}\mathbf{y}^{\mathbf{o}} + 2\mathbf{x}'\pi'\hat{w}\mathsf{N}\mathbf{y}^{\mathbf{o}} \,, \tag{4.15}$$

and writing z for $\mathsf{N}\mathbf{y}^{\mathrm{o}}$, where both N and $\mathbf{y}^{\mathrm{o}}$ are parameters of the system, and expressing the terms in N as a function of the π_i and z_i ($i = 0, ..., T$):

$$\mathsf{M} \equiv M_1 + M_2 + M_3 + M_4 + M_5 \,, \tag{4.16}$$

where:

$$M_1 \equiv \mathbf{y}'\hat{w}\mathbf{y} = \sum_{t=0}^{T}\mathbf{y}'_t\hat{w}\mathbf{y}_t \,,$$

$$M_2 \equiv \mathbf{x}'\pi'\hat{w}\pi\mathbf{x} = \sum_{t=0}^{T}\left[\left(\sum_{t=0}^{T}\mathbf{x}'_{t-1}\pi'_i\right)\hat{w}\left(\sum_{i=0}^{T}\pi_i\mathbf{x}_{t-i}\right)\right] ,$$

$$M_3 \equiv \mathbf{z}'\hat{w}\mathbf{z} = \sum_{t=0}^{T} \mathbf{z}_t'\hat{w}\mathbf{z}_t \,,$$

$$M_4 \equiv -2\mathbf{y}'\hat{w}\pi\mathbf{x} = -2\sum_{t=0}^{T}\left(\mathbf{y}_t'\hat{w}\sum_{i=0}^{T}\pi_i\mathbf{x}_{t-i}\right),$$

$$M_5 \equiv -2\mathbf{y}'\hat{w}\mathbf{z} = -2\sum_{t=0}^{T}(\mathbf{y}_t'\hat{w}\mathbf{z}_t)\,,$$

$$M_6 \equiv 2\mathbf{x}'\pi'\hat{w}\mathbf{z} = 2\sum_{t=0}^{T}\left[\left(\sum_{i=0}^{T}\mathbf{x}_{t-i}'\pi_i'\right)\hat{w}\mathbf{z}_t\right].$$

The following normal equations are then obtained from equation (4.16) by differentiating with respect to π_i and z_i, the latter being the corrective term for 'optimal initial conditions':

$$\frac{\partial M}{\partial \pi_i} = 2\hat{w}\sum_{t=i}^{T}\left[\left(\sum_{j=0}^{T}\pi_j\mathbf{x}_{t-j}\right)\mathbf{x}_{t-i}'\right] - 2\hat{w}\sum_{t=i}^{T}\mathbf{y}_t\mathbf{x}_{t-i}' + 2\hat{w}\sum_{t=i}^{T}\mathbf{z}_t\mathbf{x}_{t-i}' = 0\,,$$

or

$$\sum_{t=i}^{T}\left[\left(\sum_{j=0}^{T}\pi_j\mathbf{x}_{t-j}\right)\mathbf{x}_{t-i}\right] - \sum_{t=i}^{T}\mathbf{y}_t\mathbf{x}_{t-i}' + \sum_{t=i}^{T}\mathbf{z}_t\mathbf{x}_{t-i}' = 0\,, \qquad (4.17)$$

and

$$\frac{\partial M}{\partial \mathbf{z}_i} = 2\hat{w}\mathbf{z}_i - 2\hat{w}\mathbf{y}_i + 2\hat{w}\sum_{j=0}^{i}\pi_j\mathbf{x}_{i-j} = 0\,,$$

or

$$\mathbf{z}_i - \mathbf{y}_i + \sum_{j=0}^{i}\pi_j\mathbf{x}_{i-j} = 0\,. \qquad (4.18)$$

Now eliminating the vectors $\mathbf{z}_i$ between equations (4.17) and (4.18) produces the identity $0 = 0$, so that there are too few equations for too many unknowns.

This would be a difficulty if formulae for the estimators of the π_i's and the $\mathbf{z}_i$'s had to be derived. However, this is impossible here as has already been pointed out in model 1; some sort of 'tâtonnement' device must be used anyway. This suggests the following.

A synthesis of models 1 and 2

If we consider both models 1 and 2, that is essentially equations (4.12), (4.17), and (4.18), an iterative estimation process can be imagined. The estimates of π_i are corrected, for the initial conditions, by means of the following steps.

(a) Compute a first estimate of the π_i's from model 1, using equation (4.12).

(b) Compute the corrections for initial conditions from equation (4.18).

(c) Introduce these corrections into equation (4.17) and compute new estimates of the π_i's.
(d) Go back to (b) unless convergence is attained.

As to the non-linear case, two types of non-linear simultaneous equation systems can be distinguished.

The first type is not fundamentally non-linear in the sense that it can easily be converted into a linear system through simple transformations of variables. Single equation examples of this are the double logarithmic, the semi-logarithmic, and the log-inverse functions. In the case of a system of equations, however, it is much less likely that this process will transform the whole non-linear system of equations into a linear system. Indeed the variable will not appear in all the equations with the same 'type' of non-linearity, so to speak. Eventually this could happen, particularly in small models, as is exemplified in the empirical test below.

Nevertheless, the general case will be the one where the system is 'fundamentally' non-linear. Here again there is an escape. Such a system could be linearized using Taylor–MacLaurin expansions for all non-linear variables appearing in the model. This would also reduce the estimation problem to the one dealt with in the preceding sections.

The real problem, however, is to derive an estimation procedure in the case of the 'fundamentally' non-linear system along lines similar to those which have guided the analysis of the linear case. This has not yet been done in general and it will obviously be the purpose of subsequent research work. A non-linear version of the model used to produce an elementary test of the estimation procedure has, however, been considered; in this case the variable Jacobian could be easily estimated.

In the modest empirical test made to produce a first indication of the performances of the proposed estimators, five cases have been considered.

(1) linear static system: $\begin{cases} C_t = \alpha Y_t + \beta \\ Y_t \equiv C_t + I_t \end{cases}$

(2) an alternative of (1): $\begin{cases} \lg C_t = \alpha \lg Y_t + \beta \\ \lg Y_t \equiv \lg(C_t + I_t) \end{cases}$

(3) linear dynamic system: $\begin{cases} C_t = \alpha Y_{t-1} + \beta \\ Y_t \equiv C_t + I_t \end{cases}$

(4) an alternative of (3): $\begin{cases} \lg C_t = \alpha \lg Y_{t-1} + \beta \\ \lg Y_t \equiv \lg(C_t + I_t) \end{cases}$

(5) non-linear static system: $\begin{cases} C_t = \alpha Y_t^{\beta} \\ Y_t \equiv C_t + I_t \,. \end{cases}$

Moreover, the linear dynamic systems (3) and (4) have also been simulated with optimisation of the initial value Y_0. The optimal initial value for Y_0 has not been obtained in the way proposed in model 2, but only by the introduction of one other parameter in model 1, y_0, with respect to which the given loss function has been minimized as well.

For each of these systems, estimators of the structural parameters have been calculated following the method proposed in model 1 and using the Gaushaus algorithm as suggested in section 5. Data have been collected from Belgian National Statistics for the period 1953–1966.

Using the sum of the squares of residuals as a crude criterion for comparing the different results, one notices that for all five cases the method proposed in model 1 (Gaushaus) reduces this sum of squares when compared with a single equation least squares estimation. In the dynamic models, where an 'optimal' initial value y_0 has been computed, this reduction in the sum of squared residuals is even more important.

In table 1, these reductions are expressed as approximate percentages of the sum of squared residuals value obtained by the single equation least squares estimation.

These figures suggest two points. On the one hand, they suggest that it is really worthwhile to take full account of the dynamic structure existing between the endogenous variables in the dynamic model while estimating its parameters. On the other hand, they suggest that if the simulation of the same model is started from an initial value for Y_0 which is 'optimal' from the point of view of the goodness of fit rather than from the observed initial value of Y_0, this also reduces the sum of the squared residuals considerably.

The burden of the computations resulting from the proposed estimation procedure seems to be enormous, as it increases simultaneously with the number of observations, the number of endogenous variables in the model, and the number of time-lags. However, this judgement could tend to be exaggerated for the following reasons.

(1) The number of time-lags built into a dynamic linear model is currently very small. This reduces the number of submatrices B_{-i} and the number of time periods for which an 'optimal' starting point must be found.

(2) The number of variables traditionally called 'lagged variables' is also usually very small, and their influence on the mechanism of the model is normally small compared to that of the current variables. These facts imply that the submatrices B_{-i} will contain very few non-zero elements, and that those elements will be small in absolute value compared to those of B.

Therefore it is possible that in practice a certain number of submatrices B_{-i}, and hence also of π_{-i}, being algebraic sums of

Table 1.

	Method of Model 1 (Gaushaus)	Method of Model 1 + optimal Y_0 (Gaushaus)
Linear static model	2	-
idem in logs	2	-
Linear dynamic model	10	22
idem in logs	3	4
Non-linear static model	1	-

terms of the type

$$(B^{-1}B_{-i})(B^{-1}B_{-j}) \ldots (B^{-1}B_{-e})B^{-1} \qquad (i, j, \ldots, e = 1, \ldots, s)$$

can be approximated to zero. This would reduce the number of parameters to be estimated.

The results obtained are independent of the weights originally introduced. This is due both to the definition of the loss-function and to the linearity of the model. Consequently, at least in this linear hypothesis, another weighting system should be considered.

The important feature of the analysis is the generality of the approach and more specifically the integration of 'lagged variables' into the class of endogenous variables proper. Only two sets of variables remain, the exogenous and endogenous variables, and this dichotomy is preserved throughout.

5 Conclusions

These can be brief.

The history of urban dynamics will in fact be the same as that of national dynamics. So far, propositions have been generated by simple dynamic models (Schouten, 1967), more complex models have been simulated (Holland and Gillespie, 1963), and interdependent non-linear dynamic models have now been simulated and run under alternative policy conditions (de Biolley and Paelinck, 1970).

The general trend is clear and it now remains to be realized—and efforts are underway to prove the pudding by the act of eating. Optimistically our next paper on the subject will be a progress report.

References

Ancot, J. P., Paelinck, J. H. P., 1970, "A proposal for the estimation of parameters of simultaneous nonlinear equations systems", Faculty of Economics, Laboratory for Mathematical Economics, Econometrics and Operations Research, Namur, Working Papers No.3.

de Biolley, T., Paelinck, J. H. P., 1970, "Un modèle dynamique pour l'économie Belge: simulation et optimisation", *Optimisation et Simulation de Macro-Décisions: Recherches Théoriques et Appliquées*, Econometric Series, **3**, Laboratory for Mathematical Economics, Econometrics and Operations Research, Faculty of Economics, Namur.

Holland, E. P., Gillespie, R. W., 1963, *Experiments on a Simulated Underdeveloped Economy* (MIT Press, Cambridge, Mass.).

Jaumotte, C., Paelinck, J. H. P., avec la collaboration de Leheureux J. M., Pietquin, M., 1969, *Un Modèle de Simulation Dynamique pour une Région Urbaine,* Recherches Economiques de Louvain, **5**, 371-400.

Marquardt, D. L., 1963, *Journal of Industrial and Applied Mathematics,* **6**, 431-446.

Paelinck, J. H. P., 1970, "Some dynamic urban growth models", Papers of the Regional Science Association (Copenhagen Conference, 1969), **24**, Philadelphia.

Schouten, D. B. J., 1967, *Dynamische Macroeconomie*, 2 volumes (Stenfert-Kroese, Leiden).

Equilibrium versus Optimum: Spacing of Firms, and Patterns of Market Areas†

M.J.BECKMANN
Brown University, Providence, Rhode Island, USA

Introduction

Problems of optimum location are very much under discussion again (Mills and Lav, 1964; Bos, 1965; Beckmann, 1968; Schärlig, 1969; Serck-Hanssen, 1970). There has not been such interest in this topic since the pioneering work of Christaller (1966) and Lösch (1964). The purpose of this paper is to clarify, through direct calculations, what happens in a homogeneous market of one and two dimensions when markets are liberalized from a single firm monopoly to multiple firm monopoly to free entry; and to demonstrate how the market falls short of welfare maximization. At the same time we shall solve some of the mysteries that have surrounded the shapes of market areas under free entry in a two-dimensional economy. We shall limit ourselves to mill pricing for reasons that will become apparent in the course of the analysis. The reader is invited to extend the calculations to the cases of uniform, and perfectly discriminating, market prices.

1 One-dimensional model

Let firms be spaced at equal distances $D = 2R$. Following tradition assume that population density is uniform and that demand functions are linear and the same everywhere.

$$q = a - bp ,$$

where q is the quantity demanded, p is the price, and $a, b > 0$ are parameters of the demand function.

Also let each firm have the same fixed cost F and the same constant marginal cost c. Let transportation cost be proportional to amount and distance, and equal to k for sending one unit of the commodity over a unit distance.

† Research Papers in Theoretical and Mathematical Economics under NSF Grant #2325.

By a suitable linear transformation of price, and by suitable choices of the commodity unit and distance unit, the problem can then be standardized so that the demand function is given by

$$q = 1-p\,,$$

and such that marginal production cost is zero and transportation cost equals distance. In this section we assume that each firm sets a mill price p and that it is the same for all firms. If the firm sets a mill price p, the demand at distance r is $1-p-r$. The firms profit on a unit sale (before fixed cost) is p. The firms total profit is then

$$\int_{r\in S} p(1-p-r)\,\mathrm{d}r - F\,,$$

where S denotes the market area of the firm. In the following discussion we want to study and compare pricing for a single monopolist; pricing and spacing: (1) for a monopolistic industry (a cartel); (2) under free entry; (3) that maximizes social welfare as measured by the sum of consumers' and producers' surplus; and (4) pricing and/or spacing under price control and/or control of entry. It is useful to begin by expressing the following variables as functions of mill price p and market radius R both in absolute terms and per unit area (length): profit, consumers' surplus, quantity sold, and transportation required.

Definitions:

$$\text{profit } G = 2\int_0^R p(1-p-r)\,\mathrm{d}r - F$$

$$= 2Rp(1-p) - pR^2 - F\,,$$

$$\text{profit/area} = p(1-p) - \tfrac{1}{2}pR - \tfrac{1}{2}F/R\,,$$

$$\text{welfare} = G + H\,,$$

where H is the consumers surplus given by

$$2\int_0^R \tfrac{1}{2}(1-p-r)^2\,\mathrm{d}r = (1-p)^2R - R^2(1-p) + \tfrac{1}{3}R^3\,,$$

$$\text{consumers' surplus/area} = \tfrac{1}{2}(1-p)^2 - \tfrac{1}{2}(1-p)R + \tfrac{1}{6}R^2\,,$$

$$\text{welfare/area} = p(1-p) - \tfrac{1}{2}R + \tfrac{1}{2}(1-p)^2 + \tfrac{1}{6}R^2 - \tfrac{1}{2}F/R$$

$$= \tfrac{1}{2}(1-p^2) - \tfrac{1}{2}R + \tfrac{1}{6}R^2 - \tfrac{1}{2}F/R\,,$$

$$\text{quantity sold} = 2\int_0^R (1-p-r)\,\mathrm{d}r = 2(1-p)R - R^2\,,$$

$$\text{quantity sold/area} = 1 - p - \tfrac{1}{2}R\,,$$

$$\text{transportation required} = 2\int_0^R r(1-p-r)\,\mathrm{d}r = (1-p)R^2 - \tfrac{2}{3}R^3 ,$$

$$\text{transportation/area} = \tfrac{1}{2}(1-p)R - \tfrac{1}{3}R^2 .$$

Throughout we must have $0 \leqslant p \leqslant 1, \quad 0 \leqslant R \leqslant 1.$

1.1 *Single monopolist*

In this case firms are spaced so far apart that their actions do not affect one another. The market extends to a radius of $R = 1-p$. Thus,

$$\text{profit } G = 2\int_0^{1-p} p(1-p-r)\,\mathrm{d}r - F .$$

To determine the price giving maximum profit this term is differentiated with respect to p and set equal to zero,

$$0 = -2(1-p-1+p) + 2\int_0^{1-p} (1-2p-r)\,\mathrm{d}r ,$$

$$\hat{p} = \tfrac{1}{3} .$$

The market radius R is $\frac{2}{3}$, the quantity sold is $\frac{4}{9}$, and the profits are $\frac{4}{27} - F$. Total transportation is $\frac{8}{81}$.

A monopolist operating under price control $p = \overline{p}$ where $\overline{p} < \frac{1}{3}$ would maximize profits by selling in a market of radius $1-\overline{p}$. The quantity sold would be $(1-\overline{p})^2$, and his profit $\overline{p}(1-\overline{p})^2 - F$. There is, of course, no guarantee that profits are positive, even without price control. As long as profits are positive and the firm stays in business, the quantity sold, and presumably the consumers' welfare, increases as prices are lowered. (It will be shown later that the consumers' plus the producers' surplus can be raised by lowering prices as long as prices are positive.)

1.2 *Monopolistic industry*

The object of a monopolistic industry, or cartel, is to maximize total profit by choosing not only an optimal price, but also an optimal number of firms. In a linearly extended economy without bounds this means that the optimal spacing D of firms has to be chosen. The objective function is profit/area, that is, in a linear economy

$$g = \frac{2}{D}\int_0^{D/2} p(1-p-r)\,\mathrm{d}r - \frac{F}{D} ,$$

where $D = 2R$. On integrating we obtain the expression

$$g = p(1-p-\tfrac{1}{2}R) - \tfrac{1}{2}F/R .$$

The first term represents profit at the half-way point, which is the average of profits at all distances.

To determine optimum price and optimum spacing we set the derivatives of g with respect to p and R to zero:

$$0 = 1-2p-\tfrac{1}{2}R ,$$

from which we derive

$$\hat{p} = \tfrac{1}{2}-\tfrac{1}{4}R .$$

Thus mill prices never exceed $\tfrac{1}{2}$, which is the monopoly price in a spaceless economy.

$$0 = -\tfrac{1}{2}p+\tfrac{1}{2}F/R^2 ,$$

from which

$$\hat{R} = \left(\frac{F}{p}\right)^{1/2} .$$

This formula is reminiscent of the optimum lot size in inventory control, with the mathematical problems of the spacing of firms being equivalent to the spacing of orders to stock.

Combining the two equations we have

$$\phi(R) \equiv \tfrac{1}{2}R^2-\tfrac{1}{4}R^3 = F \quad \text{(see figure 1)} .$$

To determine which of the two roots is applicable we substitute $p = \tfrac{1}{2}-\tfrac{1}{4}R$ in g and differentiate twice with respect to R. The result is

$$g'' = \tfrac{1}{8}-\frac{F}{R^3} < 0$$

for the smaller root. It follows that spacing increases with rising fixed cost, for it is then optimal to substitute transportation for plants. The largest fixed cost with which the industry can live is equal to the monopoly profit $\tfrac{4}{27}$, and then $R = \tfrac{2}{3}$ as before. Hence, a monopolistic industry will—except in this limiting case—space its plants more densely than a single independent monopolist.

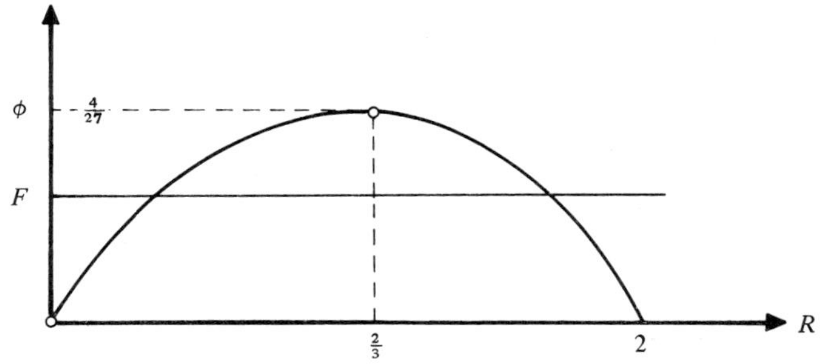

Figure 1.

If prices are controlled, $p = \overline{p}$, the industry will again space its plants according to the square root formula

$$R = \left(\frac{F}{\overline{p}}\right)^{1/2} .$$

Thus, the lower the price the fewer the plants. When entry is controlled, and hence R is predetermined at $\overline{R}$ say, then the optimal price is still

$$p = \tfrac{1}{2} - \tfrac{1}{4}\overline{R} ,$$

and hence smaller, the smaller the number of firms. However, once the spacing exceeds $D = \frac{4}{3}$, each firm is free to act as a monopolist, so that mill prices never fall below $p = \frac{1}{3}$ (nor do they rise above $\frac{1}{2}$). For a further treatment see Lovell (1969).

1.3 *Free entry*

The case that represents monopolistic competition in space is that of an industry composed of firms each maximizing profits on the assumption that others will set the same mill price, and such that spacing is determined by free entry. Then as long as profits are positive, additional firms will enter and spacing D will decrease until profits are eliminated. This is by far the most interesting situation and the one that has attracted the most attention (Lösch, 1954; Mills and Lav, 1964; Beckmann, 1968; Lovell, 1969). The possibility of noncollusive oligopoly (where firms assume that prices of others remain unchanged—Edgeworth type—or that quantities sold remain unchanged—Cournot type) are not considered in this paper (see Lovell, 1969).

At spacing $D = 2R$ the optimal price is, as before,

$$p = \tfrac{1}{2} - \tfrac{1}{4}R ,$$

and profits are given by

$$\begin{aligned} G &= 2Rp(1-p) - pR^2 - F \\ &= 2R(\tfrac{1}{2} - \tfrac{1}{4}R)(\tfrac{1}{2} + \tfrac{1}{4}R) - (\tfrac{1}{2} - \tfrac{1}{4}R)R^2 - F \\ &= \tfrac{1}{2}R - \tfrac{1}{2}R^2 + \tfrac{1}{8}R^3 - F . \end{aligned}$$

Thus, equilibrium under free entry is reached when profits vanish, that is, when

$$\tfrac{1}{8}R^3 - \tfrac{1}{2}R^2 + \tfrac{1}{2}R = F \qquad \text{or} \qquad \tfrac{1}{8}R(2-R)^2 = F .$$

Equilibrium is reached at the smallest positive root R_0 of this equation. One verifies that $F = \frac{4}{27}$ is the maximal fixed cost and that firms are then maximally spaced at $R = \frac{2}{3}$.

Since free entry drives spacing $D\ (= 2R)$ down to its minimum value consistent with the survival of firms at nonnegative profits, it also reduces mill prices to the minimum consistent value, each reduction of distance by one unit leading to a price decrease of one-quarter unit. Then, in agreement with Lösch, the number of independent existences is maximized. The average delivered price $p+\frac{1}{2}R$ $(=\frac{1}{2}+\frac{1}{4}R)$ is (apparently) minimized and average consumption (defined as consumption per linear area) is maximized. But does this mean that price control necessarily results in fewer firms and higher average prices to the consumer?

At a controlled mill price $p\ (=\bar{p})$ and spacing R profit is given by

$$\phi(R,\bar{p}) \equiv 2R(1-\bar{p})\bar{p}-\bar{p}R^2-F\ ,$$

and free entry results in this being zero.

To determine the effect of $\bar{p}$ on R we take the implicit derivative

$$\frac{\mathrm{d}R}{\mathrm{d}\bar{p}} = -\frac{\phi_{\bar{p}}}{\phi_R} = -\frac{2R(1-2\bar{p})-R^2}{2\bar{p}(1-\bar{p}-R)}\ .$$

Now the numerator is positive when $\bar{p} < \frac{1}{2}-\frac{1}{4}R$, that is, when the controlled price is below the free market price. The denominator is positive unless firms are spaced as independent monopolists (in which case it vanishes)—a case to be disregarded. Hence, spacing decreases as prices are raised, if prices are below the free market level $\frac{1}{2}-\frac{1}{4}R$. Conversely, when the controlled prices are above the free market price, spacing decreases as prices are lowered. Hence, price control will necessarily result in increased spacing and a decrease in the number of firms, confirming Lösch's theorem.

Average delivered price $\bar{p}+\frac{1}{2}R\ (=u)$ satisfies the equation

$$4\bar{p}u(u-\bar{p}) = F\ ,$$

(which is obtained by substituting u for R) and u is minimized when

$$0 = \frac{\mathrm{d}u}{\mathrm{d}p} = -\frac{\phi_p}{\phi_u} = -\frac{u(u-2\bar{p})}{\bar{p}(2u-\bar{p})}\ .$$

Now $\bar{p} = \frac{1}{2}u = \frac{1}{2}\bar{p}+\frac{1}{4}R$ implies that $\bar{p} = \frac{1}{2}R$ and upon substitution in the function ϕ,

$$\frac{R^2}{2}-\frac{R^3}{2} = F\ ,$$

which is different from the free market case.

Thus free entry does not minimize average delivered price and hence does not maximize average consumption. This is achieved by a controlled price $\bar{p}$ satisfying the equation

$$F = 2\bar{p}^2-4\bar{p}^3\ ,$$

and allowing free entry to reduce profits to zero.

It would be strange if price control could achieve a social optimum. We now, therefore, ask for that mill price and that spacing of firms which result in maximal consumers' plus producers' surplus, regardless of institutional constraints (such as firms needing to break even).

1.4 *Maximizing social welfare*
With demand functions and fixed cost as the only data in our problem the obvious measure of welfare is the consumers' plus producers' surplus, on a *per capita* basis taken per unit area. The expression for this is

$$w \equiv \tfrac{1}{2} - \tfrac{1}{2}p^2 + \tfrac{1}{6}R^2 - \tfrac{1}{2}R - \tfrac{1}{2}F/R \ .$$

Maximization of w with respect to p requires that $p = 0$. This is, in fact, only the principle of marginal cost pricing (cost of production having been transformed to zero). The optimal spacing requires that

$$\frac{\partial w}{\partial R} = \tfrac{1}{3}R - \tfrac{1}{2} + \tfrac{1}{2}F/R^2 = 0$$

or

$$F = R^2 - \tfrac{2}{3}R^3 \ .$$

Notice that maximal monopoly profit of $\frac{4}{27}$ is no longer the limit on fixed cost. Instead welfare will be positive as long as

$$R - R^2 + \tfrac{1}{3}R^3 \geqslant F \ ,$$

at the largest possible range $R = 1$. Thus fixed cost must not exceed the level

$$F \leqslant \tfrac{1}{3} \ .$$

Conversely for $F = \frac{1}{3}$ a market radius $R = 1$ is socially optimal. Due to the monopoly position of firms this spacing and pricing cannot be achieved through the market. Even price control by itself is insufficient. A comparison of formulae shows that optimal price control attracts fewer than the optimal number of firms to the market, since the smallest root of $\frac{1}{2}R^2 - \frac{1}{2}R^3 = F$ is always above that of $R^2 - \frac{2}{3}R^3 = F$. Thus optimal price control can achieve no more than second best, and even that is only achieved by having fewer firms in order to bring mill prices closer to zero than under free entry.

Let us now drop the restriction to mill pricing. Assume that a price $p \ [= p(r)]$ is to be charged, $0 \leqslant r \leqslant R$. Profit is then given by

$$2\int_0^R [p(r) - r][1 - p(r)]\,\mathrm{d}r - F \ ,$$

and profit/area

$$\frac{1}{R}\int_0^R [p(r) - r][1 - p(r)]\,\mathrm{d}r - \tfrac{1}{2}F/R \ .$$

The consumer surplus per area is

$$\frac{1}{R}\int_0^R \tfrac{1}{2}[1-p(r)]^2 \mathrm{d}r \,.$$

Then we seek,

$$\max_{p(r),R} \frac{1}{2R}\int_0^R [1-p(r)]^2 + 2[1-p(r)][p(r)-r]\,\mathrm{d}r - \tfrac{1}{2}F/R$$

$$= \frac{1}{2R}\int_0^R [1-r]^2 - [p(r)-r]^2 \mathrm{d}r - \tfrac{1}{2}F/R \,.$$

It follows at once that setting $p(r) = r$ is the welfare maximizing price policy, and hence mill pricing is no restriction. Consider now the 'second best'. What spatial pricing system and what market size maximizes social welfare under the constraint that firms break even? We require

$$\max_{p(r),R} \frac{1}{R}\int_0^R \tfrac{1}{2}[1-p(r)]^2 + [p(r)-r][1-p(r)]\,\mathrm{d}r - \tfrac{1}{2}F/R \,,$$

subject to

$$\int [p(r)-r][1-p(r)]\,\mathrm{d}r - \tfrac{1}{2}F \geqslant 0 \,.$$

If a Lagrangian multiplier λ/R, $\lambda \geqslant 0$, is introduced, the optimal p can then be obtained by differentiating under the integral with respect to p, and setting the result equal to zero, viz.

$$-(1-p)+(1+\lambda)[1-p]-(1+\lambda)[p-r] = 0$$

which gives

$$p(r) = \frac{\lambda+(1+\lambda)r}{1+2\lambda} \,.$$

The optimal pricing system imposes a tax $\lambda/(1+2\lambda)$ $(<\frac{1}{2})$ on the consumer per unit of the commodity; and a tax rate $(1+\lambda)/(1+2\lambda)$ $(>\frac{1}{2})$ for transportation. In the absence of the constraint that the fixed cost F must be recouped from consumers, $\lambda = 0$, and the price system reduces to marginal cost pricing and $p = r$. If the constraint is at its tightest then $\lambda = \infty$, $p = \frac{1}{2}$, and $k = \frac{1}{2}$. This is the pricing system of a perfectly discriminating monopolist (Singer, 1937; Beckmann, 1968). But how does optimal spacing under the break-even constraint compare with that under unrestricted welfare maximization?

If we write $p(r) = 1-\beta+\beta r$, where

$$\beta = \frac{1+\lambda}{1+2\lambda} \quad \text{and} \quad \tfrac{1}{2} \leqslant \beta \leqslant 1 \quad \text{since} \quad 0 \leqslant \lambda \,,$$

then we obtain

$$\lambda = \frac{1-\beta}{2\beta-1} \,.$$

On substituting in the welfare integral we obtain

$$\frac{1}{R}\int_0^R \tfrac{1}{2}[1-(1-\beta)-\beta r]^2 + \frac{1-\beta}{2\beta-1}\frac{1}{R}[1-\beta+(\beta-1)r][1-(1-\beta)-\beta r]\,\mathrm{d}r$$
$$-\frac{1-\beta}{2\beta-1}\frac{F}{2R}$$
$$=\left[\frac{\beta^2}{2}+\frac{\beta^2(1-\beta)}{(1-\beta)}\right]\frac{1}{R}\int_0^R (1-r)^2\,\mathrm{d}r - \frac{1-\beta}{2(2\beta-1)}\frac{F}{R}$$
$$=\frac{1-\beta}{2(2\beta-1)}\left[\beta(2-\beta)\left(1-R+\frac{R^2}{3}\right)-\frac{F}{R}\right].$$

To determine the maximum of the welfare function with respect to market size R, this is now differentiated and set to zero,

$$R^2-\tfrac{2}{3}R^3 = \frac{F}{\beta(2-\beta)} \, .$$

But

$$0 \leqslant \beta(2-\beta) = \frac{1+4\lambda+3\lambda^2}{1+4\lambda+4\lambda^2} \leqslant 1 \, ,$$

for $\lambda \geqslant 0$ but equals 1 only for $\lambda = 0$. Hence, the effect of the break-even constraint is to raise the right-hand term of the equation for the welfare optimal R, thereby increasing the solution R (which is the smaller root, as seen from the second-order conditions). Thus, firms are made larger than under unrestricted welfare maximization.

2 Two-dimensional region

It is well known—and we shall not repeat the argument here—that a hexagonal lattice maximizes the distance between nearest neighbors for a given number of lattice points per area (Lösch, 1954). Assume that firms are located in a hexagonal lattice of mesh width D, and that they will all set the same price, thus behaving like firms in a competitive economy. Then the market area of each firm is limited by the hexagon marked out by the normal bisectors between any pair of adjacent lattice points. What is the optimal sales area of a firm selling in this admissible region at a given mill price?

Clearly the firm cannot sell in those points of the admissible region where demand is nil, since mill price plus transport cost exceeds the maximum demand price of one. Thus, the admissible region is further limited to that part of the admissible hexagon which is inside the radius of $1-p$. This will be called A. Now, since the firm realizes a positive marginal revenue p on all sales, it will sell throughout A. The general shape of the optimal sales region is thus a hexagon with its corners possibly rounded off by a circle of radius $1-p$. As limiting cases, we have a complete circle and at the other extreme, the complete hexagon. Let each flat portion of the market boundary (which is on the contour of the hexagon) have an angular width of 2α. The distance from each neighbor is D and the radius of the limiting circle $R = D/2\cos\alpha$ (see figure 2). The profit function, in terms of polar coordinates r, φ, is now

$$G = 12\int_0^{\alpha}\int_0^{D/2\cos\alpha} p(1-p-r)r\,\mathrm{d}r\,\mathrm{d}\varphi + \int_0^{2\pi-12\alpha}\int_0^{D/2\cos\alpha} p(1-p-r)r\,\mathrm{d}r\,\mathrm{d}p - F\,,$$

$$= b_1(\alpha)D^2p(1-p) - b_2(\alpha)pD^3 - F\,,$$

where, for instance,

$$b_1(\alpha) = \tfrac{3}{2}\tan\alpha + \left(\frac{\pi}{4}-\frac{3\alpha}{2}\right)\frac{1}{\cos^2\alpha}\,,$$

and

$$b_2(\alpha) = \tfrac{1}{4}\left[\frac{\sin\alpha}{\cos^2\alpha} + \ln\left(\frac{1}{\cos\alpha}+\tan\alpha\right)\right] + \left(\frac{\pi}{12}-\frac{\alpha}{2}\right)\frac{1}{\cos^3\alpha}\,.$$

Now at the circular boundary

$$1 = p+R = p+\frac{D}{2\cos\alpha}\,.$$

Thus

$$p = 1-\frac{D}{2\cos\alpha} \qquad 0 \leqslant \alpha \leqslant \tfrac{1}{6}\pi\,.$$

Thus in setting a price the firm will also choose an angle α, and profit maximization requires that α be optimized. The profit function is therefore differentiated with respect to α and set equal to 0.

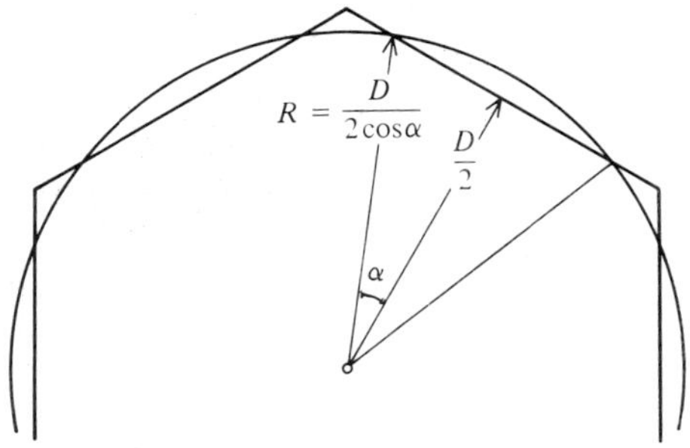

Figure 2.

$$0=\frac{\mathrm{d}G}{\mathrm{d}\alpha}=\frac{\partial G}{\partial\alpha}+\frac{\partial G}{\partial p}\frac{\mathrm{d}p}{\mathrm{d}\alpha}$$
$$=\frac{\partial G}{\partial\alpha}+\frac{\partial G}{\partial p}\left(-\frac{D\sin\alpha}{\cos^2\alpha}\right).$$

On substituting for G we obtain

$$0=b_1'(\alpha)D^2p(1-p)-b_2'(\alpha)pD^3+[b_1(\alpha)D^2(1-2p)-b_2(\alpha)D^3]\left(-\frac{D\sin\alpha}{\cos^2\alpha}\right)$$
$$=\frac{\sin\alpha}{\cos^2\alpha}\left(\frac{\pi}{2}-3\alpha\right)D^2\left(1-\frac{D}{2\cos\alpha}\right)\frac{D}{2\cos\alpha}+\left(\tfrac{3}{2}\alpha-\frac{\pi}{4}\right)\frac{\sin\alpha}{\cos^4\alpha}\left(1-\frac{D}{2\cos\alpha}\right)D^3$$
$$-\frac{\sin\alpha}{\cos^2\alpha}\left[\tfrac{3}{2}\tan\alpha+\left(\frac{\pi}{4}-\tfrac{3}{2}\alpha\right)\frac{1}{\cos^2\alpha}\right]\left(\frac{D}{\cos\alpha}-1\right)D^3$$
$$+\frac{\sin\alpha}{4\cos^2\alpha}\left[\frac{\sin\alpha}{\cos^2\alpha}+\ln\left(\frac{1}{\cos\alpha}+\tan\alpha\right)+\left(\frac{\pi}{3}-\tfrac{3}{2}\alpha\right)\frac{1}{\cos^3\alpha}\right]D^4.$$

By cancelling

$$\frac{D^3\sin\alpha}{2\cos^2\alpha},$$

we obtain

$$0=(\pi-6\alpha)\left(1-\frac{D}{2\cos\alpha}\right)\frac{1}{2\cos\alpha}+\left(3\alpha-\frac{\pi}{2}\right)\frac{1}{\cos^2\alpha}\left(1-\frac{D}{2\cos\alpha}\right)$$
$$-\left[3\tan\alpha+\left(\frac{\pi}{2}-3\alpha\right)\frac{1}{\cos^2\alpha}\right]\left(\frac{D}{\cos\alpha}-1\right)$$
$$+\tfrac{1}{2}\left[\frac{\sin\alpha}{\cos^2\alpha}+\ln\left(\frac{1}{\cos\alpha}+\tan\alpha\right)+\left(\frac{\pi}{3}-\frac{3\alpha}{2}\right)\frac{1}{\cos^3\alpha}\right]D.$$

For a given value of D, the optimal α in the range $0<\alpha<\frac{1}{6}\pi$ is thus determined. In order to find the limits on the range of D for which α is in the interval $0<\alpha<\frac{1}{6}\pi$ we set, respectively $\alpha=0$, and $\alpha=\frac{1}{6}\pi$ and solve for D. The results are

$$D(0)=\tfrac{3}{2}, \qquad D(\tfrac{1}{6}\pi)\approx\tfrac{5}{4}.$$

For distances of D exceeding $\frac{3}{2}$, each firm sets a monopoly price of $p=\frac{1}{4}$ and sells in a circular market of radius $R=\frac{3}{4}$. For distances of D below $\frac{5}{4}$ the firm sells in a hexagonal market area bordered on all sides by the market areas of its neighbors. When $\frac{5}{4}<D<\frac{3}{2}$, then the market area is a rounded hexagon. Customers in the corners are excluded by the fact that mill price plus transport cost exceeds the maximum demand price 1 for these locations.

In the case of a uniform delivered price (not presented here) firms will refuse to sell to points for which price no longer covers production plus transport cost (see Beckmann, 1968, p.46). The distance D of firms from each other is determined either by profit maximization in joint monopoly, or by the condition that profits are wiped out under free entry. The relationship between fixed cost F and the resulting distance D in each case is not presented here.

To repeat, under free entry, circular market areas emerge only in the hairline case that fixed cost equals monopoly profit, and then $D = \frac{3}{2}$. For the case when fixed cost is small enough, so that $D < \frac{5}{4}$, market areas are hexagonal. The equilibrium distances for this latter case can be calculated. Profit per area is given by,

$$G = 12\int_0^{\pi/6}\int_0^{D/2\cos\varphi} p(1-p-r)r\,\mathrm{d}r\,\mathrm{d}\varphi - F$$

$$= \frac{\sqrt{3}}{2}\tan\tfrac{1}{6}\pi D^2 p(1-p) + \tfrac{1}{4}pD^3\left[\frac{\sin\frac{1}{6}\pi}{\cos^2\frac{1}{6}\pi} + \ln\left(\frac{1}{\cos\frac{1}{6}\pi} + \tan\tfrac{1}{6}\pi\right)\right] - F$$

$$= \frac{\sqrt{3}}{2}D^2 p(1-p) - pD^3(\tfrac{1}{6} + \tfrac{1}{8}\ln 3) - F\,.$$

The profit maximizing price is

$$p = \tfrac{1}{2} - \left(\frac{1}{6\sqrt{3}} + \frac{1}{8\sqrt{3}}\ln 3\right)D$$

$$= \tfrac{1}{2} - \frac{b_2}{2b_1}D\,,$$

where

$$b_1 = \frac{\sqrt{3}}{2} = 0\cdot866 \quad \text{and} \quad b_2 = \tfrac{1}{6} + \tfrac{1}{8}\ln 3 = 0\cdot303\,.$$

On substituting this price we obtain

$$\frac{D^2}{2\sqrt{3}}\left[(\tfrac{1}{6} + \tfrac{1}{8}\ln 3)D - \frac{\sqrt{3}}{2}\right]^2 = F$$

$$0\cdot288D^2(0\cdot303D - 0\cdot866)^2 = F\,.$$

Of the two positive roots the smaller is taken since free entry pushes firms to the minimum distance consistent with non-negative profits. This can be compared with formula 8H of Mills and Lav (1964, p.280).

An analysis of welfare maximization follows along similar lines. The computations are straightforward but cumbersome and are not presented here.

The main conclusion is that welfare maximization requires hexagonal market areas so that all customers are supplied at marginal cost.

References

Beckmann, M. J., 1968, *Location Theory* (Random House, New York).

Bos, H. C., 1965, *Spatial Dispersion of Economic Activity* (Rotterdam University Press, Rotterdam).

Christaller, W., 1966, *Central Places in Southern Germany*, translated by C. W. Baskin (Prentice-Hall, Englewood Cliffs, N.J.).

Lösch, A., 1954, *The Economics of Location*, translated by Yale University Press, New Haven, Connecticut (C. B. Mohr, Tübingen).

Lovell, M., 1969, "Product differentiation and market structure", *Western Economic Journal.*

Mills, E. S., Lav, M. R., 1964, "A model of market areas with free entry", *Journal of Political Economy,* **72**, 278-288.

Schärlig; A., 1969, *Localisation Optimale et Theorie des Graphes* (Librairie Droz, Geneva).

Serck-Hanssen, J., 1970, *Optimal Patterns of Location* (North Holland, Amsterdam).

Singer, H. W., 1937, "A note on spatial price discrimination", *Review of Economic Studies,* **5**, 75-77.

A Model of Household Locational Preferences

B.HARRIS
University of Pennsylvania

1 Exploring the basic market assumptions

This paper deals with the assumptions used in a research project to investigate certain aspects of metropolitan location in a policy-making context. The results of a pilot project are summarized in an extensive Interim Report (see Harris *et al.,* 1966).

The project rests on three very simple concepts which are a theory of the land market, a method for simulating market competition, and a method for analyzing consumer preferences in housing and location. These concepts can be very briefly explained and related to one another. However, in the application of these concepts, a fundamental decision has been taken to attempt to simulate a very large system and to make it possible to vary a great many aspects of that system's state, history, and environment. This amounts to abandoning in many respects the classical assumption of *ceteris paribus.* As a result, the models developed are rich in implications and complex in their interactions, despite their simplicity of concept.

In the original design of these experiments it was necessary to make a choice (conscious or unconscious) between two fundamental approaches. One of these would be in the first instance largely empirical, drawing on detailed observation of some aspects of behavior in housing choice and attempting to proceed one step at a time in the direction of more general statements. The second approach would be to base oneself on general knowledge crystallized in well formulated theories and to define certain deductive consequences of these theories. These deductions would then be applied to the real world and, hopefully, tested.

One of the implications of the second view is that any working hypothesis to be used in a deductive experiment must be testable. By their very nature, the counsels of despair with regard to the diversity and unclassifiability of human behavior rest on untested and untestable hypotheses. An investigator who is concerned to advance scientific understanding is virtually compelled to expose himself to failure by testing hypotheses which may be untrue. This risk is increased, first, by the difficulties of the experimental method in the social sciences and, second, in proportion to the investigator's ambition to deal with scientific theories which are both parsimonious and general.

There is an aspect of our approach towards theory and scientific research which requires mention. It seems that frequently theories are successfully constructed out of concepts which are not in common currency, and such theories may not naturally occur or even be readily comprehensible to either scientists or laymen familiar with the general subject matter. This belief does not imply a desire in any sense to insulate science from practice by mystification. It means rather that often the true form of relationship which science attempts to uncover may not correspond with widely held ideas. In this case, there is a further difficulty in that the description of the theory will make use in part of ordinary language in special senses, and this may compound the confusion. In this note an effort is made to define the terms used as they are introduced.

The general theory on which this research effort is based is the Alonso (1964) theory of the land market, which in turn is based on classical agricultural rent theory and locational theory.

In brief, it is maintained that residential locators in the urban land market seek to achieve an equilibrium between their expenditures for space for residential accommodations, their ease of access to other opportunities, especially employment, and their expenditures on all other commodities. It is especially emphasized that the utilities from space and accessibility are a *joint* outcome of the locational decision. The possession of land in central locations confers a transportation advantage, and consequently this land enjoys higher rents in direct relation to the savings on transportation cost and inconvenience.

The individual locator cannot indefinitely expand his expenditures on land or on transportation or both, because to do so under budget constraints would reduce his capacity to purchase other goods. Similarly he cannot indefinitely reduce his locational expenditures, since the needs for shelter and for interaction are basic necessities. In a given market situation, each consumer has a certain level of expectation as to his achievable level of utility, and on the basis of this expectation, can establish a number of bid rents for land parcels in various locations. If all of the conditions of market equilibrium can be met, one or more of these bid rents will be just sufficient to secure the use of a parcel of land. Since different groups of consumers have different budgetary constraints, and possibly different preferences for space and convenience, there are a number of distinct patterns of bid rent offers. The prices of land at market equilibrium are determined simultaneously by the interaction of these bid rent curves and depend in a complicated way on their shapes, on the total level of demand, etc. Alonso examines the conditions under which equilibrium is achieved and the general shape of the urban rent surface which results from his theory.

There are a number of restrictive assumptions in the Alonso theory and other similar efforts (see also Wingo, 1961). Some of these are necessary for the theory whilst others are imposed in order to simplify drawing immediate conclusions. Of the second class of restrictions, we have tried to relax as many as possible in the development of our work.

There are three equilibrium conditions necessary for the general development of the theory. First, it must be assumed that in equivalent locations land rents for the same price, as modified, however, by zoning and land use controls.

The second essential assumption is that at equilibrium all members of the same locator group, wherever located, enjoy the same levels of utility—that is, are on the same indifference surface. In theory, this assumption probably offers very minor difficulties. In application to the real world, however, it is quite plainly contrary to fact. The attainment of maximum utility is probably achieved only by households which have recently relocated after careful review of the market. In practice, therefore, owing to changes in family status, changes in neighborhoods, changes in transportation, and changes on the location of employment, most locational situations are less than optimal. Adjustments are impeded by the cost of moving.

A third essential assumption of the Alonso model is embodied in the budget equilibrium conditions mentioned above, which in classical economic terms state that at equilibrium, equal marginal expenditures on all components of the consumer's budget should yield equal marginal returns in utility. For reasons which will become more clear in the discussion of utilities which follows, this equilibrium condition is not actively applied in the elaboration of our model except in a somewhat weakened form with regard to trade-offs between locational expenditures and all other expenditures. In his development, Alonso was able to assume uniform land qualities and infinitely divisible land quantities, thus satisfying certain conditions necessary for defining this equilibrium. In actual fact, however, many of the variables entering into locational decisions are discrete or discontinuous and not infinitely divisible. In this case, the principle of marginal substitution is not directly applicable.

Let us now examine some of the simplifying assumptions made by Alonso, Wingo, and others.

The assumption that various segments of the population have well-defined utility functions, and the assumed shapes of these functions, are discussed in a separate section. The simulation of a mechanism whereby market equilibrium can be studied in detail is also separately discussed.

Alonso's theoretical discussion is cast entirely in terms of the market for land. His discussion therefore chooses to overlook the obvious and important fact that at any point in time the residential land market is in fact constrained by the existence of structures which have hitherto been put in place and which are not in general rented or purchased for purposes of demolition. In brief, the actual market to which Alonso's theory applies is a market in housing, and only at the margin of urban expansion, a market for land. Both in theory and in practice it is very difficult to separate the value of land from the value of the house in situations where the structures are already in place. By focusing on rents for housing units and reproduction costs for new units, Alonso's land model may be converted to a housing model. The models become identical at the development margins of the metropolitan area where the market mechanism deals with land itself.

Alonso and Wingo assume that all employment in their hypothetical cities is concentrated at the center. This assumption greatly simplifies the exploration of the properties of their models with respect to preferences for space. Other investigators have taken a diametrically opposite view. Lowry's (1964) model of residential and retail location takes the location of basic employment, and a rigidly defined willingness to travel, as almost the sole determinants of residential choice. Density, housing quality, and neighborhood characteristics do not enter into his calculations.

We assume that locational utilities can be measured by accessibility constructs. This assumption is weak theoretically in that it fails to take into account the actual location of place of work in defining residential choice. The great advantage of the use of accessibility measures is that it may be expected to improve the realism of the model in the event of changes in the distribution of activities or in the performance of the transportation network.

There would be no difficulty in introducing both the location of employment and the qualities of housing into an analysis of housing preferences. Such an investigation might indeed be highly desirable. In a simulation model, however, this solution of the problem becomes extremely cumbersome.

If the utility functions (preference structures) of all locators are known, if the locational attributes of sub-areas of a region are well defined, and if the attributes of housing either in existence or permitted to be constructed in any particular location are also well defined, then it is possible to estimate the rents which any particular locator group would offer for any particular type of housing in any particular area. This set of bid rents implies a situation of competitive offers for the available or constructable housing stock.

Given this set of bid rents, the actual process of determining such a market equilibrium using the methods of linear programming was developed in some detail by Herbert and Stevens (1960). This development embodied many other features, but essentially it solved the problem of determining market equilibrium for the land and housing market, given the assumptions outlined in the preceding sections and given a stratification of the locator population into groups with homogeneous and defined preferences.

The application of the Herbert–Stevens model to present purposes was extensively revised in PJ Paper #20 (see Harris, undated). Most of these revisions are not relevant to the present discussion, but those that are, are newly summarized in the following paragraphs, along with a discussion of some additional points. Above we have already dealt with the general meaning of changes that make it possible to deal with the existing housing stock and vacant land simultaneously.

The most serious ambiguity inherent in the Herbert–Stevens model is the fact that, with a fixed set of bid rents, solutions to the model yield dual household variables which imply the existence of consumer subsidies or surpluses. These dual variables are unrealistic, indicating as they do that the 'bid' rents actually offered were not adjusted to market conditions, and consequently could not reflect the real expectation of renters and buyers in this market. An appropriate adjustment of expectations leads, however, to a change in consumers' utility levels, and in the operation of the Herbert–Stevens model with adjustments to the utility levels, the household subsidies may be made as close to zero as we desire.

The Herbert–Stevens model, like any linear programming model, will in general locate only one household type in one area, and will work properly only if each model area is defined as having a single housing type. If it were computationally possible to extend the application of the model to individual dwelling units and locators, this difficulty would disappear. This matter is discussed in more detail in Harris (1966b).

A problem exists in the application of any equilibrium model to a large and polynucleated metropolitan region, which arises as a direct consequence of the relaxation of Alonso's assumption of a central concentration of employment. In a polynucleated region, the various labor markets focused on different centers are in part disjoint. If this difficulty becomes of practical importance, it will be possible to avoid it by using an iterative scheme with a choice of variables which permits the model to enforce a carefully defined equilibrium between population and employment for subsections of the labor market. Harris (1966a) provides a more detailed discussion of this subject.

The original definition of the problem in the Herbert–Stevens model, as redefined to permit the inclusion of the existing housing stock, prescribes the form of the linear programming problem. If only an existing or planned housing stock is offered to locators, the problem reduces to transportation problem, in which all coefficients in the constraints are unity. If, however, locators are permitted to choose between various types of housing at different densities in the development of vacant land or in the redevelopment of existing urban areas, then the problem becomes in part a version of the 'machine loading problem' in which nonuniform density coefficients enter into one set of the constraints. This machine loading problem can be converted into an iterated application of the transportation problem, with very substantial savings in computer time. This conversion requires that the choice of housing types for each household in each area where choice exists be determined before the problem is submitted to a solution by linear programming. The housing type usually chosen for vacant areas is that which results in the highest bid rent per area, it being the most competitive.

The actions of the market which are simulated in our adaptation of the Herbert–Stevens model function entirely on the demand side. With respect to supply through redevelopment under market conditions, it seems likely that an iterated use of the model will be necessary, in order to establish the relevant alternate use prices. A somewhat deeper consideration of supply conditions suggests, however, that the model as it now stands is somewhat less than adequate. Even existing housing may be changed in character by rehabilitation and by varying levels of maintenance. These investment decisions are sensitive to government policy, to market influences, and to investment alternatives. Much more intensive work along the lines initiated in the Arthur D. Little study for the San Francisco Community Renewal Program (Robinson *et al.,* 1965) will be necessary before such market simulation from the supply side can be incorporated into the present model.

2 Household utility functions

As indicated, the theory of Alonso and its embodiment in the Herbert–Stevens model requires a predefinition of a household preference structure which is capable of generating bid rents for housing of all types in all areas throughout the region. These bid rents are assumed to depend on the socioeconomic status of the household, the characteristics of housing and neighborhoods, and the accessibility of the location to urban activities. The systematic development of such preference functions in the past has been undertaken only on a limited basis, and the present effort may be regarded as very preliminary. Nevertheless in this project we have attempted for the first time to bring all of these locational factors together and to undertake massive statistical testing. We outline here the conceptual basis of this testing and the assumptions which are involved.

While it is not appropriate in these notes to engage in an extended theoretical discussion of preference structures, some statement as to the sense in which we refer to various concepts in this section is in order. We adopt the general concept of a utility function as defining a level of well-being or self-gratification of the spending unit through the command which its pattern of expenditures gives it over a variety of commodities.

Thus,

$$U = f(Q_1, Q_2, Q_3 \ldots) .$$

In general, over some range of each Q, U is an increasing function of Q. Utilities derived from various commodities may in general be independent or interacting. In principle, utility functions are internal to the spending unit, and utilities may not be aggregated across individuals. This assumption is relaxed in ways which are specified below.

If the level of utility of a spending unit is held fixed in the preceding definition, then all possible sets of the Qs which will satisfy this equation are an indifference surface. This surface will in general be convex toward the origin, by virtue of the fact that the marginal utility of each commodity will decrease as the quantity of that commodity commanded increases. The collection of indifference surfaces, which exists for all different levels of utility for a given spending unit, constitutes a definition of the preference structure of that spending unit. This use of the term 'preference structure' is not to be confused, for example, with the preference ordering of choices which a spending unit might make in a real-life situation or a social survey experiment. Rather, it is our contention that a knowledge of the preference function at a given level of U enables us to simulate an experiment which consists in the determination of a large number of indifferent choices defined by one indifference surface drawn from a preference function.

The confusing feature of this indifference concept in ordinary parlance arises from the fact that the preference structure generates 'equally preferred choices'. This in turn rests on the fact that the category of 'all other goods' or non-locational expenditures is included in the structures, from which is implied indifference to specified combinations at a particular price, namely the bid rent. Ordinarily the bid rent will be below the actual rent, and the magnitude of these differences establishes a preference ordering in the ordinary sense. Those dwelling units with the smallest differences are the most preferred, and *the preference ordering is related to market conditions.*

Thus in a broad sense we follow conventional practice with regard to preferences and utilities, defining with Alonso a budget plane and a utility function. The utility function defines not one preference surface, but a family of preference surfaces. At any fixed level of utility, the utility function becomes a preference function which implicitly defines the trade-offs between the goods embodied in it. These two equations may be written as

$$Y = M + R + T , \tag{1}$$

$$U = f_1(M) + f_2(Q) + f_3(A) . \tag{2}$$

Equation (1) states that total income Y viewed as expenditures must be divided between expenditures on all other goods M (including savings), expenditures on house rent R, and expenditures on transportation T. Equation (2) states that separate and independent utilities are derived from expenditures on other goods, from expenditures on a particular quantity Q of housing (including land or space), and from the accessibility consequences A of a locational decision. It is important to note that Alonso and we both view the choice of housing and location as a joint decision, so that R and T are jointly determined, as are the second and third terms in equation (2). Essentially, therefore, the decision framework which is sketched in these two equations represents the choice between locations, considering their cost and utility implications as to housing and transportation on the one hand, and as to other expenditures on the other hand.

This difficulty in applying standard methods to a preference analysis of housing choices leads naturally into some exploration of the manner in which these concepts are treated in theory and practice in the development of our models.

In the first place, it is appropriate to point out that the definition of utilities, as stated in equation (2), is so far largely formal in nature, and that it is indeed inadequate not only for operational purposes, but also from the viewpoint of theory. The theoretical difficulty arises principally from the fact that each of the sources of utility—other goods, quantity of housing, and accessibility—is a composite commodity containing many different attributes and objects of expenditure, each of which provides some utility. In reality, each consumer probably has a set of basic needs for such general purposes as food, clothing, shelter, housekeeping, social interaction, recreation, etc., which are satisfied severally or jointly through the acquisition of bundles of commodities. Within these bundles there may be considerably more substitutability and freedom of consumer choice than there is between bundles. This circumstance introduces severe difficulties in the analysis of consumer choice, and it is claimed that only a very small beginning has been made in dealing with these difficulties in this project.

We assume, first of all, that each of the purposes served by the three terms on the right of equation (2) is a fundamental necessity of life in the metropolitan area. This means that a considerable disutility should attach to a situation in which M, Q, or A becomes very small or zero. For this reason, we give somewhat more specific content to equation (2) by writing

$$U = \lg M + k_1 \lg Q + k_2 \lg A \ . \tag{3}$$

This form of the equation has been chosen mainly for statistical convenience, and does not exhaust the large variety of possible forms for which U would approach $-\infty$ as M, Q, or A approaches zero[1]. The choice of the appropriate function in fact deserves substantially more investigation.

The effect of using an equation of the form of (3) or (3a) on consumer choice is to introduce very strong consumer resistance to the expansion of housing expenditures to high proportions of income, and this results, as housing prices increase, in ever more severe reductions in the quantities demanded. Similar observations apply with regard to accessibility.

For practical reasons we choose to treat M as a single commodity and two factors regarding the interaction of Q and M are omitted, in spite of their possible serious consequences. First, changes in the relative prices of individual components of the market basket of other goods (M) may change directions of consumer expenditure in such a way as to affect the whole structure defined by equation (4). Second, technological and social changes may result in the satisfaction of needs through expenditures on other goods rather than through joint expenditures on Q and A.

We must now also recognize that even though M is to be treated as a single commodity, Q and A cannot be so defined. In line with our recognition that bundles of various commodities can satisfy basic needs in a variety of ways, we must now plan to disaggregate Q and A, and to deal with a number of dimensions of housing quantity and quality, and of accessibility. What we have in fact done is to measure housing qualities along a number of dimensions such as land area per dwelling unit, number of rooms, age, condition, and structure type, and to construct a number of orthogonal descriptions of accessibility. In this connection, it is important to note that in principle only one measure of housing and one measure of accessibility must enter into this equation in logarithmic form. This measure in each case should be of such a type that if the available amount of this quantity goes to zero, the consumer essentially has command over no housing or no interaction. Thus, for example, a logarithmic measure of number of rooms and acres per dwelling unit is more logically compelling than a logarithmic measure of age or condition.

We now rewrite equation (1) in the following form:

$$M = Y - R - T\,, \tag{4}$$

(1) An equivalent and more familiar definition for utility would be

$$U = MQ^{k_1}A^{k_2}\,. \tag{3a}$$

In this case, as M, Q, or A approaches zero, utility also approaches zero. A consistent treatment of either form of this equation leads to identical results in the analysis, except in curve fitting. A nonlinear regression on equation (3a) would emphasize high-income families unduly. Even equation (3) suffers in this respect, and is modified below.

and substitute this value for M in equation (3).

$$U = \lg(Y - R - T) + k_1 \lg Q + k_2 \lg A \ . \tag{5}$$

We now have an expression in which the level of utility enjoyed by a locator is a function of his income, his command over housing and accessibility, and his costs for housing rent and transportation. If we now apply the equilibrium assumption of the Alonso theory (discussed above), that all members of a particular socioeconomic group are at the same level of utility wherever located, U becomes a constant, and we have an equation in Y, R, T, Q, and A, all of which may be observed and measured. Thus we may estimate the values of the k's which apply to the various measurements of housing and accessibility.

By assuming a fixed utility level for defined population groups, we have converted a more general utility function into a preference function which defines a single set of indifference points in the market for housing and location. In the ordinary case, for a household not experienced in the local housing market, this indifference 'surface' might be too high or too low. That is, housing opportunities might first be ordered in a subjective preference ranking and given tentative bid rents. Either several of these bid rents might be higher than market prices, or all might be lower. In either case, the family will adjust its preference structure so that just one bid rent is equal to the market price, while others are below the market.

The significant question now arises as to whether bids for other houses in other locations may in general be expected to be well below the market prices, or not. If these other bids are very close to a number of other market prices, it is apparent that this family could equally well locate in a variety of situations, and thus *uniform preferences* could give rise to *heterogeneous behavior.* If, on the other hand, only a single location is eminently satisfactory to this household, then all other bid prices will be well below the market prices, and families of this type would uniformly make a unique locational decision. This point is of vital importance for statistical reasons and in the interpretation of the meaning of the model and of the term 'preferences'.

There are strong reasons for believing that between these two situations a locational group would tend to find itself with a number of alternative bids at or near the market prices, thus exhibiting a diverse pattern of behavior while maintaining a constant preference structure. The rents or values of existing housing are determined by market forces and not usually by considerations of replacement cost, depreciation, and so on. In the case of new housing, the cost of the house itself is a function of construction prices, but the rental or purchase value of the land is also determined by market forces. If we now imagine that one particular location and house type is of salient importance to a particular type of household, we must consider what the course of events regarding the price of this house type is apt to be. If this population group is growing, the demand for the salient locational package will rise and, unless it is in copious supply, the price will also rise. This will force this population group to accept a lower level of utility, and its offers for alternative locational packages will also rise. These will go closer to the market values, and the situation will approach one in which this particular group has in fact a number of indifferent choices. The combination of constraints on the housing market, and competition within and between household groups, thus tends to lead in real life to diverse behavior patterns, especially in a growing metropolis.

We may reiterate at this point, therefore, that the possibility of this diverse behaviour rests on three assertions about the nature of preference functions and the market:

First: That basic needs for shelter and interaction can be met by a variety of combinations of locational quantities;

Second: That the cost of location may legitimately enter into a preference structure so defined, so that every location will *at some price* be on one indifference surface; and

Third: That the mechanism of competition tends to create (but does not guarantee) a situation in which more than one type of location yields bid rents close to market levels—that is, more than one of these locational choices is, for a given family, achievable.

We may now turn our attention to some of the problems of a statistical application of the foregoing discussion to data concerning the real world. In this discussion we shall omit some of the detailed aspects which are treated in the Interim Report (Harris *et al.,* 1966), and confine ourselves to some outstanding questions of principle.

It is most difficult to secure a data source consisting of suitable observations over a wide range of behavior, and containing information regarding income, expenditures, socioeconomic status, housing, and location. For this reason our initial efforts have focused on the use of census tract median and average information, assuming that each tract represents a typical family. Later efforts will hopefully make use of survey data on a household basis.

There is a basic issue as to whether in certain cases different behaviors are due to genuinely different preference structures or not. This is a classical example of missing variables, which would be needed to subdivide the population or explain differing preferences. It seems likely that this whole issue will be greatly clarified in the future when it becomes possible to work with data on recent movers, and thereby to split the locational decision into two parts—the decision to move away from a given place and the decision to locate in a different place.

This problem is of course related to considerations of the diversity of behavior which may or may not be expected among locators with the same or similar preferences. The more finely the population is divided into locator groups for purposes of analysis, the more improbable it becomes that these groups will display diverse behavior. In this case, it then follows that estimates of a general preference structure for housing types, neighborhood conditions, and accessibilities outside of the range of observation become increasingly unreliable. In this sense, therefore, market conditions which result in the location of populations in diverse settlement patterns and without a complete matching of population to housing type are statistically useful rather than the reverse, provided only that this does not conceal diverse preferences.

We now introduce one more set of modifications to the mathematical formulation of utility functions so far discussed. In order to account statistically for the disparities introduced into an analysis, by possible differences between utility levels within a population group due to measurable within-group variables, we introduce the assumption that in any given situation utility levels in the abstract are a function of the socioeconomic position of each particular family. Thus even if a defined group is not uniform on all dimensions, some of this non-uniformity can be admitted to the model by permitting utility levels to vary in relation to a defined function of its socioeconomic status variables. For reasons which will become apparent, we separate a part of that variation in utility which is due to income from this definition of utility levels and write

$$U = \mathrm{f}_4(S) + \lg Y\,, \tag{6}$$

where S refers to socioeconomic variables. If we now substitute equation (6) in equation (5) and rearrange terms, we have a final estimating equation which was considered for our work:

$$\lg\left(\frac{Y-R-T}{Y}\right) = \mathrm{f}_4(S) - k_1 \lg Q - k_2 \lg A\,. \tag{7}$$

In this form, the dependent variable is taken to be the logarithm of the ratio of nonlocational expenditures to total income. This form of the dependent variable was chosen because it is well known that locational expenditures, and consequently nonlocational expenditures, vary in close relation to income. In social analysis of many popular types, reference is made to the 'rent-income ratio'. We could also refer to a 'location-income ratio' $r = (R+T)/Y$. If r is small, a good approximation to the left side of equation (7) is the first term in its series expansion: $-M$. Since we are primarily concerned not with the influence of income, but with the influence of Q and A on the level of expenditures, the form developed in equation (7) has seemed more appropriate for estimating purposes[(2)]. In most metropolitan areas, income will explain 90% to 98% of the variance in rents. Equation (7) in turn explains from 50% to 90% of the residual variance.

[(2)] Also, see the last two sentences of footnote (1).

There are a number of statistical problems of a relatively less important nature than those so far discussed which are nonetheless troublesome and will be subject to further investigation and reports.

In working with census tract data, it was almost, but not entirely, mandatory to combine information regarding owner-occupied and renter-occupied dwelling units. The considerations which would permit a proper conversion of owner-occupied housing values to an annualized rental cost are extremely intricate. They require data and analysis which are not readily feasible in conjunction with the whole remainder of this analysis. For this reason we have currently adopted a standard conversion factor.

Depending on historical and dynamic conditions, the use of a large number of variables regarding subareas of a metropolis introduces severe dangers of collinearity. To a very considerable extent, these difficulties are unavoidable, since it is precisely the difference, for example, between accessibility and density which motivates people to offer higher rents in particular locations. If we component-analyze the correlation matrix of the independent variables, this fact is reflected when components with low eigenvalues have a high correlation with the dependent variables. This has frequently occurred in our analysis. Since our accessibility variables are an artificial concept of a type which may be expected to show strong collinearity, we have entered them into the analysis only in the form of the first five principal component scores, which are of course mutually independent. Other evidences of collinearity, however, reflect the historical and self-equilibrating nature of the metropolitan structure. Since historical accident and residential disequilibrium may be expected to influence the market behavior of locators, this collinearity must be retained in order to retain the divergences from it.

3 Projective uses of the models

We have now described the somewhat cumbersome apparatus by which we define a set of preference structures, and the solution method for market equilibrium which we hope will permit us to conduct projective experiments regarding the structure and performance of the metropolitan housing market and of arrangements affecting it. We intend to explore not only those changes in the housing market which may be expected to eventuate as a result of foreseeable changes in population size and composition, income, age and condition of the housing stock, and so on, but also those changes which might be anticipated to result from drastic changes in policy regarding zoning, redevelopment, industrial location, transportation, and other factors. Using these models, it may be simpler in some respects to explore equilibrium conditions than to explore a path of development. In this sense, therefore, the models explore ultimate consequences and their extreme implications, and not actualities.

The simplest and most appropriate tests of these models in any case would be to see if they can reconstruct *de novo* the distribution of households found in the period of observation on which the preference functions were fitted. Owing to the equilibrium assumptions, this test is impossible, but application to the original city at the date of fitting would produce an equilibrium pattern which can be compared and contrasted with the existing pattern. A more interesting and useful test is to calculate bid-rents in all locations for a variety of household types. In any location where a household type is poorly represented, its bids should be lower than the going rent in that area. In preliminary work on this test, we have already observed that, while the rule is generally applicable, the non-white population frequently has high bid rents in areas occupied by whites. This is *prima facie* powerful evidence of discrimination in the housing market.

Once adequate tests of the validity of the model have been carried out for a particular metropolitan area as of the date of analysis, it will be possible to extend the tests of the model in a more interesting and powerful way. We intend to test the implications of the model with respect to other cities at the same time, or with respect to the same city at different times. This amounts to changing the conditions surrounding the use of the model and thus constitutes a true test of its generality and validity.

Even if the model were to pass a number of tests on the foregoing hypothesis successfully, there would still be certain grounds for doubting its applicability to greatly changed situations. The most cogent of these grounds is that preference structures will have been defined in the absence of important data applicable to future behavior and future arrangements. Until experimental measurements can be made, a projective evaluation of proposed new arrangements is probably not possible.

In any projective use of these models, therefore, there are many dubious (or at least daring) assumptions above and beyond those which are necessary to define the relationship in the model as an analytical tool. Despite the possible imperfection of the model in these respects, we believe that it has important uses in evaluating future plans. These uses fall into three main categories, which may be listed in order of increasing importance.

First, the models can offer an effective and rapid method of sketch planning, in that they deal with the extensive and troublesome problem of locating population and housing types in a rational pattern at a future date. This step in sketch planning is a necessary precedent to planning the location of transportation facilities, open space, schools, sewers, etc.

Second, the models produce, as an output rather than as an input, measurements of land value which should be extremely useful in planning redevelopment, industrial location, fiscal policy, and the like. While the importance of land values in urban projections and planning has long been recognized, it becomes very difficult to project these magnitudes far beyond the immediate present. In principle, at least, the models described herein provide the possibility of detaching this calculation from present circumstances and developing a projective inspection of the far distant future under very drastically changed circumstances.

Finally, substantial information can be derived from the changes in locators' utilities which are necessary, as described above, to adjust their bid rents so as to clear the market. Under varying market restraints, this adjustment affects different groups differently, and these effects depend in part on the planned arrangements. It is furthermore possible to set monetary values to the utility adjustments, and as between two plans to determine the amount of compensation (positive or negative) which would be necessary to equalize the circumstances of each locator group under one plan by comparison with its circumstances under another plan. Dependent on assumptions regarding the aggregation of utilities, this equivalent monetary difference is a measure of the superiority of the second plan over the first. By experimenting with the effects on utilities of different plan changes, including densities, transportation arrangements, the location of employment, etc., we may thus derive measures of benefit which can be weighed against the costs. These measures of benefit are far more general and far more closely related to the purposes of plans than most previously suggested measurements. On the other hand, they apply to the residential population only, and either omit the effects on businesses or omit the effects which businesses would transmit to consumers by virtue of increased or decreased costs. They also measure, in most applications so far proposed, the benefits which would be derived at equilibrium. This is unrealistic in that equilibrium will never be attained, but this unrealism is mitigated by the fact that the figures are comparative and relate equilibrium under one plan to equilibrium under another. The comparisons are also subject to all the qualifications outlined above about the validity of this model system as a whole. It may be noted, however, that some criticisms of the model as such may not have very serious implications for comparisons between plans which are made by using the models.

As has been made clear at numerous points in the preceding discussion, several advantages might accrue from adapting these models to a growth model context. This adaptation is under study, and it may be expected that it will entail some sacrifice in capacity to explore the ultimate consequences of a plan, but it will sharpen the accuracy of the estimating procedures and will permit projections that are more realistic and more useful for certain purposes. At the same time, it is of interest to note that the development of a growth model will introduce the opportunity to pinpoint the sources of change in metropolitan residential arrangements. This will be the decision to move, which we believe can be made to depend in a realistic way on the comparative disutility of remaining in a particular area and a particular house. This part of the model would provide an immediate and perfectly general test if an effort were made to describe the changes which take place and which are observed in aggregate between two dates in the metropolis. These changes themselves would not be the source of the parameters in the model.

4 Preliminary statistical results

After the preceding sections of this report were first drafted substantial statistical investigations were undertaken, but the model has still not been completely tested as of July 1970. This section provides a very brief summary of the statistical procedures and results.

The approximately 4000 census tracts in the New York region provide a large number of observations which have been rather homogeneously 'sorted' by locational differentiation. For each of these tracts for 1960, we estimated the distribution of households by 70 categories of race (2), size (5), and income (7)—using tract marginal distributions and metropolitan area joint distributions. We also calculated and component-analysed the accessibilities of approximately 170 zones in which these tracts are grouped by the New York Regional Plan Association (RPA), using RPA data on travel times, employment, and open space. We calculated measures of local displacement of tracts within zones, and we prepared estimates of tract elevation and average slope. From the census data we computed densities using RPA estimates of residential land, and we assimilated measurements of median number of rooms, condition, age, structure type, etc. A dummy variable for rent control within New York City was constructed on the basis of age and type of dwelling units.

We computed for each tract an average weighted sum of values and rents, based on tract median figures. For each of 70 household types within each tract we estimated transport costs on the basis of census data regarding automobile ownership, journey to work, and mode of travel data. These estimates are probably the most crude and inaccurate in the entire study.

We experimented with a number of methods of manipulating these data. We decided that as a result of the stratification of the households, the use of $f_4(S)$—see equation (7)—to take care of the effects of within-stratum variation was unnecessary. Using tract means on the household stratifier variables, we combined tracts into a large number of strata, and computed product-moment matrices for each stratum. We then conducted 70 regression analyses, one for each class of the population, using sums of these product-moment matrices weighted by the representation of each population class. For each analysis a different dependent variable was used. The analysis was conducted by way of principal components analysis, correlating the dependent variable with the component scores, and adding them successively in a stepwise fashion.

The results of these efforts in ordinary statistical terms have still not been completely studied. In general the values of R^2 range from 0·70 to 0·95. For all variables, the 't' values are high. The pattern of approximately

70 by 20 correlation coefficients is generally consistent and reasonable, except in the case of small and very low-income households. Here some distinctions as to age must probably be made to separate out retired families with their unique preferences.

A striking finding from the study of residuals and of bid-rents calculated from equation (7), was that, as described above, the model with largely economic variables failed to define properly the behavior of the upper income groups. Their projected bid rents for inferior housing were universally too high. This indicated that a model based on these preferences would not predict properly the location of the 'well-to-do' outside of the central urban core. Since density and age of housing enter into the model in a major way, it seems unlikely that missing variables concerned with housing proper could explain this difficulty. We experimented with a few major approaches, and found that the best results in remedying this situation were produced by adding variables regarding the accessibility of low- and high-income groups, and of non-whites.

This result conforms, of course, with popular conceptions of locational preferences. It deals a heavy blow to Alonso's belief that market behavior can be explained without reference to externalities. It also introduces possible difficulties in a projection model, since household location becomes both an input and an output. In this case an equilibrium must be sought by iteration, and it may not be unique. Because of the extreme implications of the result, it is advanced here very tentatively, and will be further studied in detail.

References

Alonso, W., 1964, *Location and Land Use—Toward a General Theory of Land Rent* (Harvard University Press, Cambridge, Mass.).

Harris, B., undated, *Linear Programming and the Projection of Land Uses,* PJ Paper No.20, Penn-Jersey Transportation Study, Pennsylvania State Department of Highways, Harrisburg, Pa.

Harris, B., 1966a, *Note on Residential Location in a Subnucleated Region,* Institute for Environmental Studies, University of Pennsylvania, Philadelphia.

Harris, B., 1966b, *Note on Residential Mixture in the Herbert-Stevens Model,* Institute for Environmental Studies, University of Pennsylvania, Philadelphia.

Harris, B., Nathanson, J., Rosenburg, L., 1966, *Research on an Equilibrium Model of Metropolitan Housing and Locational Choice—Interim Report,* Institute for Environmental Studies, University of Pennsylvania, Philadelphia.

Herbert, J., Stevens, B. H., 1960, *A Model for the Distribution of Residential Activity in Urban Areas,* PJ Paper No. 2, Penn-Jersey Transportation Study, Pennsylvania State Department of Highways, Harrisburg, Pa. Abridged in: *Journal of Regional Science,* **2**, 21-36.

Lowry, I. S., 1964, *A Model of Metropolis,* Memorandum RM-4035-RC, The Rand Corporation, Santa Monica, California.

Robinson, I. M., Wolfe, H. B., Barringer, R. L., 1965, "A simulation model for renewal programming", *Journal of the American Institute of Planners,* **31**, 126-134.

Wingo, L., 1961, *Transportation and Urban Land* (Resources for the Future Inc., Washington, D.C.).

Utility Systems as Determinants of Settlement Patterns: A Typology

D.BÖKEMANN
Universität Karlsruhe

1 Introduction

1.1 Hypotheses

This topic comprises the following hypotheses:

1 that infrastructure includes a defined set of different utility systems, each producing and/or delivering a certain supply good;
2 that these systems are locally interconnected by the user's demands for combining different supply goods in production or consumption processes;
3 that the systems' characteristics are the cause or result of changes in settlement patterns.

Confirmation of these hypotheses requires the demonstration that a significant contribution to the region's character occurs in this way.

To begin with, features of utility systems will be defined which, from the aspect of serving an area, are characteristically common or distinctive. By weighing the different determinants we shall be able to derive specific trends in the individual system's development. Through the confirmation that compound individual demand for various supply goods connects different utility systems locally, the term 'location-quality' will be given a new interpretation.

1.2 Definitions of infrastructure

The term 'infrastructure' first came into use in army language after the Second World War, meaning 'the sum of facilities which enables the flow of a supply from the hinterland to the combat force at the front'. This definition is rather vague insofar as the connection to the troops is relative: today they may need this, tomorrow something quite different, here this, there quite a different set of facilities may be of use.

Social scientists use the term 'infrastructure' in a similarly unpragmatic way, but they also use it in a wider sense to mean the sum of all local prerequisites for entrepreneurial activities to develop. Most authors in this field favour this rather vague definition in preference to specific enumeration of supply sectors and systems. Hirschman (1958) for example, states:

1 infrastructure is the prerequisite for any economic activity;
2 infrastructural goods are produced or controlled by public enterprises;

3 infrastructural goods cannot be imported;
4 infrastructural investments are characterized by technical units which cannot be divided, and by a high capital coefficient.

An extended interpretation is given by Tinbergen's (1962) hypothesis on the division of the real capital stock of an economy into the two sectors, infrastructure and superstructure, whereby investments into infrastructure indirectly increase the productive capacity of the enterprises (superstructure). In a similar way Jochimsen (1966) associates the external economies of enterprises with the term infrastructure. See also Stohler (1965).

Thus the common meaning of the term 'infrastructure' is public local investment. Such an interpretation has probably hindered appreciation of intersectoral, qualitative, and interlocational aspects of infrastructure.

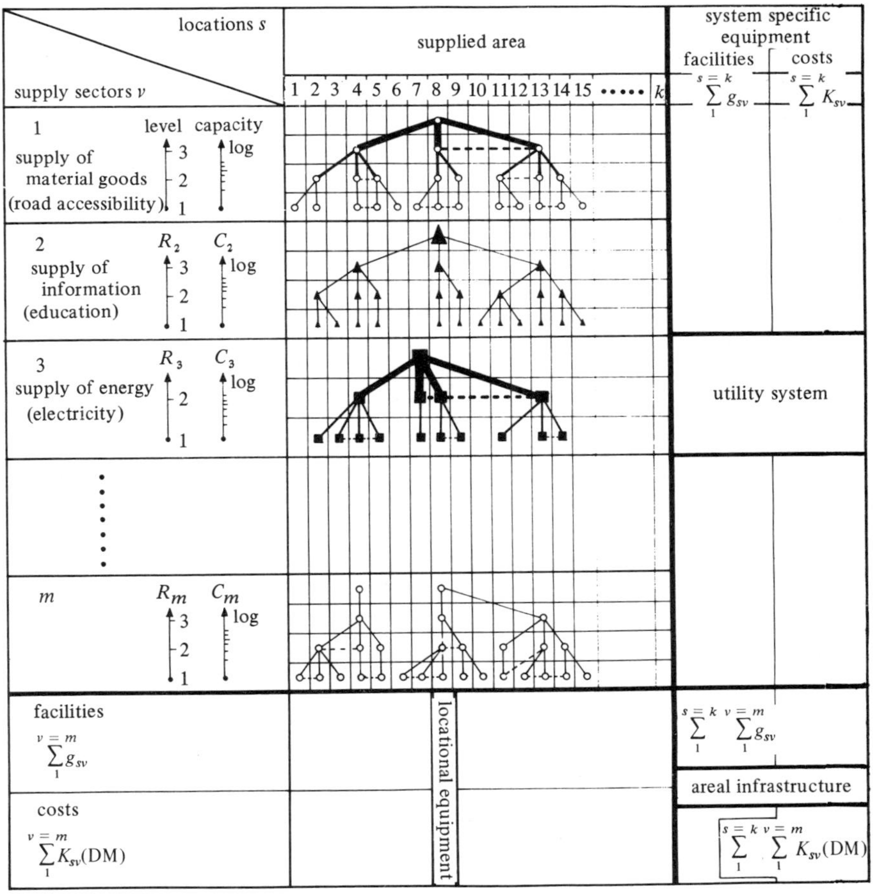

Figure 1. Infrastructure as a defined set of utility systems.

These aspects, however, have to be included in any effective policy dealing with the improvement of locational quality, because of the limits these interdependencies set up (see figure 1).

2 Description of individual utility systems

2.1 General features

A water supply system for a delimited area is used as an example of a utility system in terms of this study. A water supply system contains as its main elements the waterworks, in which the 'supply good, water' is produced, and the pipe network, as the necessarily complementary transportation facility, which connects the producing plant with the consumers.

The utility systems to be dealt with are characterized by the following general criteria.

1 Each household and enterprise connected with the system has the chance to share the advantages of an economical production of the supply good.
The utilization of economies of scale leads to centralized production.

2 The supply goods which are produced on a large scale at central places have to be transported to the consumers over paths (roads, railways, channels, and pipelines). Both production and transportation facilities constitute utility systems in a complementary way.

3 The spatial extension of a utility system is limited to adjacent areal elements, which are connected through paths (roads, railways, channels, and pipelines) to the production place of the supply good.

The following questions help to characterize our problem.

(1) What specific purpose does a utility system serve? (See section 2.2, differentiation by functions.)

(2) What relations exist between the quantity and quality of supply goods produced by utility systems? (See section 2.3, differentiation by qualities.)

(3) How are the supply goods distributed to the consumers by the utility system? (See section 2.4, network structure.)

(4) What are the utility systems' characteristic trends in development? (See section 2.5, dynamic considerations.)

2.2 Differentiation by functions

There is a complex set of certain technical standards which define the function of each utility system as well as the purpose of the associated supply good. The question of the extent of the general applicability of the technical standards reflects the limitations in range and consistency for each utility system. The more technical standards that exist to constitute a certain utility system, the more specialized is the purpose of the associated supply good.

Utility systems adapt only with a certain time lag to changes in the social and economic needs of a region. Usually a certain threshold of demand has to be exceeded before fresh investments are undertaken. This threshold is determined by the degression of average production cost and the increase of average delivery cost.

Therefore new utility systems tend to develop in a process of division of functions on the base of the locally existing systems. We can assume that this process of functional specialization (for each utility system determined by the number of applied technical standards) will continue, and our growing supply problems will have to be solved by more and more specialized supply systems.

2.3 Differentiation by qualities

Supply goods of the same kind may vary considerably in quality, if we define the comparatives 'faster, cleaner, more exact, more reliable' or, express generally, 'more adapted to special needs'. The corresponding degree of adaptation is determined by the strictness of applied technical standards like guaranteed stressability, speed permitted, required purification effects, etc. From this aspect the technically complicated expressways represent a 'supply good' (i.e. accessibility) of the same kind but of higher quality than a country road.

Usually different qualities of the same good are produced and distributed in one and the same system, since low quality goods are in general, the input for aggregates producing a high quality output. Thus, for instance, in a water supply system, aggregates for the mechanical

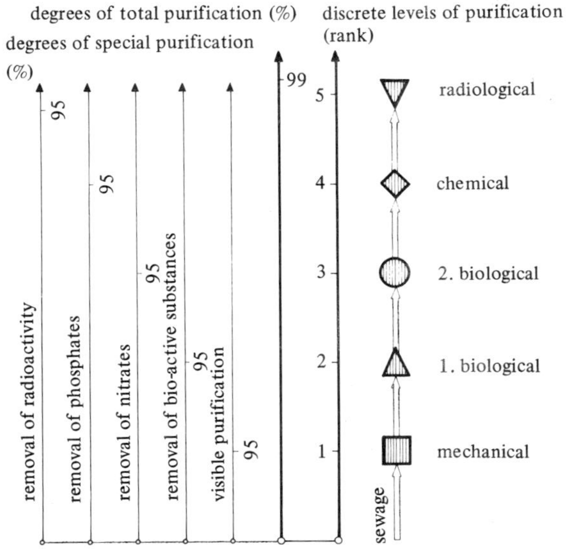

Figure 2. Differentiation of supply goods by quality: concentrated production (for example, sewerage).

purification of sewage (low quality output) are prerequisite to purification from biologically active substances (higher quality output). Therefore, production plants for high quality goods are frequently linked at one location with those for lower quality goods of the same kind. If the total of a demanded supply good has to be of one quality the production capacity may be nearly constant at all levels. In this case the spatial concentration of all production levels is significant. However, in the case of demand for a supply on different quality levels, only partial output of the lower production level becomes input to the next higher level (figure 2). For an optimal combination of minimal transportation costs with maximum scale economies it may, in cases of spatial dispersion, be necessary to associate with each production aggregate a certain number of lower ordered ones, in the manner of satellites (figure 3). The number of lower ordered production aggregates associated with a higher ordered one is determined by the amount of output being used as input for the higher level. This explanation of the spatial organization of public administration, education, and social services confirms a distribution according to central place theory.

In this sense the quality of supply goods can be identified with the level of production by specialization. The level of specialization is derived from the process of functional division. The analogy to evaluation of labour quality is obvious: the higher the guaranteed educational standards, the higher the specific investments needed for educational institutions. Or, to express it more generally, for high qualities of supply goods the production of one unit of output needs more investment than for low qualities.

It can be assumed that technological developments and increasing demographic and economic concentration will cause further differentiation of the utility systems by qualities. This tendency will be accompanied by an increasing areal extension of the systems.

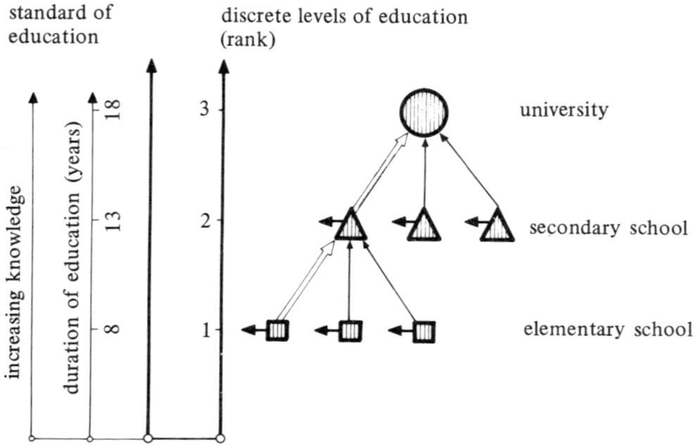

Figure 3. Differentiation of supply goods by quality: dispersion of production (in this example, as applied to education).

2.4 Network structures

Utility systems are topographically realized by paths for transportation of material, energetic, and informational supply goods between the places of production and the places of consumption. The aggregate of interconnected transportation paths of the same type is called a transportation network (road network, railway network, canal network, pipeline network).

Networks have been constructed in a great variety of patterns, marked by the extreme types of 'minimally ramified' like a tree (in terms of graph theory) and 'completely meshed by cycles' (see Garrison and Marble, 1962; Kansky, 1963).

Minimally ramified networks contain the feature that transportation flows can be collected or distributed only in the same flow direction, and cannot intersect. In comparing the extreme types of network patterns we state that a minimally ramified transportation network will provide only one supply route between the location of production and each place of demand. On the other hand a meshed network, in which the adjacent nodes or vertices are interconnected, provides a certain number of alternative routes between the location of production and demand (redundancy). Through minimal ramification, all points of access (locations of demand) are connected with the root (location of production) by minimal path length. That is the reason why a minimally ramified transportation network is considered as the one with the lowest investment costs (for instance, a sewer network).

Minimally ramified networks can only operate either in a market system like von Thünen's (1826) isolated state, where only one city is allowed to distribute all the supply goods for a limited area, or by specialization in one single supply good. A completely meshed network must develop if the total supply is carried by the same transportation network and if each location is specialized in the production of one single good and consumes all kinds of goods. This relation may partially explain the patterns of historically evolved road networks which, in most cases, connect all adjacent communities directly.

These almost completely meshed road networks are the most flexible transportation facility with respect to their adaptability to a great variety of needs. On the other hand, a minimally ramified network for a single good transportation system has optimum adaptability to extremely specialised standards.

The connectivity of transportation networks, however, cannot only be explained through the constraint of interlacing transportation flows but also by the individual need for reliability of a supply (or for minimization of potential disturbances in the supply routes) provided by the network.

If only one path (or one edge) in a minimally ramified transportation network is interrupted all the inhabitants and enterprises connected by a branch beyond the interruption are cut off from supply. In a meshed network however, supply goods may be diverted through an alternative route to the consumers.

The transportation network's reliability is defined by the probability of breakdown which happens when the supply route at any point between production and consumer is interrupted. We can therefore assume that the breakdown of supply is complementary to a continuous flow of supply goods on the supply route between the locations of production and consumption. We define the probability of disturbance p for a certain edge (that is part of the supply route) as

$$p = \frac{\text{disturbance frequency} \times \text{disturbance period}}{\text{period of observation}} \ .$$

This edge-specific probability of disturbance is mainly determined by:
1 the length of the edge,
2 its constructional quality, and
3 the proportion of its capacity that is utilized.
If the supply route is composed of a certain number of edges we can calculate the probability of disturbance for the whole supply route p_{tot} relative to the connectivity of the network, *ceteris paribus,* as follows:

(1) In a minimally ramified network the supply to the consumers is endangered more, the greater the number of edges n used. In this case the edges j are combined in series connection, which yields

$$p_{\text{tot}} = 1 - [(1-p_1) \times (1-p_2) \times \ldots \times (1-p_n)] = 1 - \prod_{j=1}^{n} (i-p_j) \ .$$

(2) When there are m parallel independent routes in a meshed network (parallel connection), the probability of disturbance is decreased. The single probabilities multiply, giving

$$p_{\text{tot}} = p_1 \times p_2 \times \ldots \times p_m = \prod_{j=1}^{m} p_j \ .$$

In these simple cases it was not considered that the interruption of a certain edge in a meshed network can affect the disturbance probabilities of adjacent edges.

Of course, these assumptions must be revised if the ratio of load to capacity becomes part of the calculation. At least in the case of the overloading of a certain edge's capacity, negative feedback effects develop for the probabilities of disturbance for adjacent edges (conditional probabilities).

Disregarding these limitations we may consider a network's degree of connectivity as a measure of its reliability in serving an area with supply goods.

The necessity to mesh a mainly ramified transportation network by higher investment costs must be considered with reference to

1 the number of people being supplied by a single branch only, and
2 whether the supply good is of vital importance to the population and enterprises affected.

As soon as the activities of great industrial plants or the health of a large population depend heavily on supply systems, the reliability has to be maintained at a very high level. In this sense the utility systems—the traffic system, electricity, water supply, and sewerage and solid waste management (that is, the public systems especially)—have become depended upon more and more. We cannot manage without them even for short periods.

For the following considerations the conduits' flow capacity is introduced as a characteristic feature of utility systems' networks. Using the compound advantages we will show that a network's total length of conduits can be substituted by the conduits' flow capacity.

By installing transportation networks for its distribution of goods two kinds of compound advantages may be obtained:

(1) if several larger flows are combined in one conduit of higher capacity, construction costs may be saved;
(2) running costs may be reduced as the resistance against motion decreases with increasing capacity.

Compound flows effect discontinuities of capacity within the network's conduits which we define as discrete ranks r of conduits. Each rank of conduits is characterized by a collecting function for conduits of the next lower rank. The greater the number of lower rank conduits that are compound to a higher rank conduit, the greater is the value of β_r which characterizes the amount of the discontinuity between the rank-specific capacity C_r and $C_{(r-1)}$

$$\beta_r = \frac{C_r}{C_{(r-1)}} , \qquad \beta_r \geqslant 1 . \tag{1}$$

If we assume the capacity multiplier β is constant over all the ranks of a network then

$$\begin{aligned} C_2 &= C_1\beta \\ &\vdots \\ C_r &= C_{(r-1)}\beta \\ &= C_1\beta^{(r-1)} , \end{aligned} \tag{2}$$

where C_1 means the capacity of the terminal branches by which the consumers are connected to the supply system.

To supply a certain area F_r by an artificial utility system it is necessary that:

(1) one conduit exists for access l_r which connects the area served with the higher rank network;

(2) lower rank conduits $l_{(r-1)}$ distribute supply goods to the lower rank areas $F_{(r-1)}$ which are elements of F_r. This principle of distribution by conduits of different ranks is continued down to the parcels F_1 where the consumers are served by the terminal conduits l_1.

α_r gives the ratio of conduit lengths between two sequential ranks in related areas served.

$$\alpha_r = \frac{l_r}{\sum^{F_r} l_{(r-1)}} , \qquad \alpha_r \leqslant 1 . \tag{3}$$

α_r varies with the shape of the area served and the type of compound. We can use a constant α as length multiplier in our calculations, if the shape and organisational principle of the area served do not change across the ranks as in central place theory.

We then have

$$l_2 = \sum^{F_2} l_1 \alpha$$

$$l_3 = \sum^{F_3} l_2 \alpha$$

$$l_r = \sum^{F_r} l_1 \alpha^{(r-1)} = {}_r L_1 \alpha^{(r-1)} . \tag{4}$$

There is a close relation between the length multiplier α and the capacity multiplier β because

$$\sum^{F_r} l_{(r-1)} = \beta l_{(r-1)} . \tag{5}$$

From equations (3) and (5) it follows that

$$\alpha = \frac{l_r}{\beta l_{(r-1)}} . \tag{5a}$$

By associating the served areas F_r with the capacities of the conduits K_r in a rank-specific way, we find

$$\beta = \frac{C_r}{C_{(r-1)}} = \frac{F_r}{F_{(r-1)}} . \tag{1a}$$

The assumed uniformity of the areas served over all ranks, includes also the assumption that enough symmetry exists for setting a constant geometrical shape factor a:

$$F_r = a l_r^2 , \qquad F_{(r-1)} = a l_{(r-1)}^2 ,$$

and

$$\beta = \frac{l_r^2}{l_{(r-1)}^2} . \tag{1b}$$

From equations (1b) and (5a) we obtain

$$\alpha \cong \frac{l_{(r-1)}}{l_r} , \qquad (6)$$

which results in the expression

$$\alpha \cong \beta^{-\frac{1}{2}} . \qquad (7)$$

Contrary to our assumptions so far, in reality flow capacity of the compounded conduits is reduced on each level of the networks' hierarchies. These frictions can be considered as capacity used at central places for local activities. Assuming that there is a relation between central place activities and city size, we can now define two different but completing capacity multipliers, ${}^{c}\beta$ for the conduits, and ${}^{p}\beta$ for the central place size. Then

$$\beta = \frac{{}^{c}\beta}{{}^{p}\beta} . \qquad (8)$$

The relations between α and β are valid if the discontinuities in capacity are generated by the fact that all associated lower rank conduits join the higher rank conduit exclusively at its root (central place type). This can be caused by the necessity to adapt the state of transported goods, for instance by speed, tension, pressure, and degree of coding, to the standards of the higher rank conduits in special transformation aggregates. Thus the central place type compound is, for instance, enforced in electricity networks by function and location of the transformer stations, in telephone networks by the different ranks of telephone exchanges. The capacity multiplier satisfying the conditions of the central place type compound is defined by $\beta_r \geqslant 2$ [compare this to Lösch's (1940) *k*-values].

If the state of the moved goods does not change over the various ranks of a supply system (for instance in sewer systems operating without excess pressures) it is not necessary to compound the lower rank conduits in the root of the higher rank conduit. It is, however, possible to compound the lower rank conduits by distributing the access over the whole alignment of the higher rank conduit (series type compound).

The use of a capacity multiplier $\beta \geqslant 2$ in adaptation to the central place type compound, would give a very unfavourable load capacity ratio. For the series type compound the capacity multiplier may become smaller than 2. By introducing intermediate ranks, which adapt the capacity at every point of flow to the real load, we can define the capacity multiplier β_s satisfying the conditions of the series type compound between 1 and 2. Then we can define a scale of β-values characterizing various ways to combine conduits of different rank. This scale is limited on one side by the central place type compound where β can increase *ad infinitum* ($\beta \to \infty$). This occurs when an infinite number of consumption places is connected to one production place with each connection established by a distinct conduit. Radio and television information may be considered as examples for this kind of direct serving with supply goods. On the other hand, there is the extreme series type compound when β converges to 1. $\beta = 1$ when the distribution function of a higher rank conduit is operating by a continuous flow in such a way that there is a steadily growing load along the alignment. We can regard a rain gutter as an example of an extreme series type compound flow (see figure 4).

Only under the condition of single supply routes between the locations of production and consumption, does the capacity multiplier β characterize

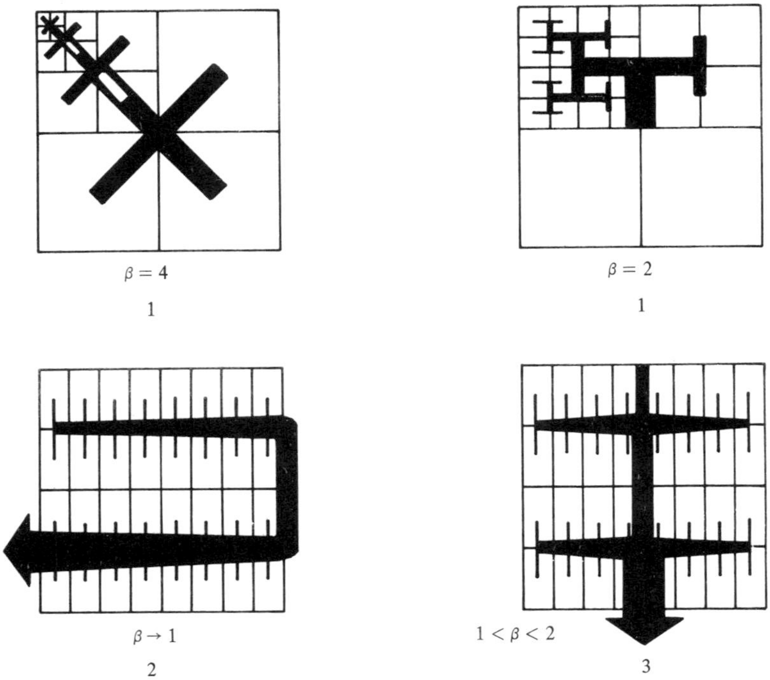

$$C_r = C_1\beta_r^{(r-1)}, \qquad \beta_r = \frac{C_r}{C_{(r-1)}} \qquad \beta_r > 1$$

$$L_r = {}_rL_1 \text{ are } \alpha_r^{(r-1)}, \qquad \alpha_r = \frac{L_r}{{}_rL_{(r-1)}} \qquad \alpha < 1$$

L_r is the total length of the conduits of rank r in the considered supply area F_r;
L_r is the rank-specific conduit length;
α_r is the rank-specific length multiplier;
C_r is the rank-specific conduit capacity;
β_r is the rank-specific capacity multiplier.

Figure 4. Network patterns and conduit capacity. 1. Patterns of the central place compound type. 2. Pattern of series compound type. 3. A mixed pattern.

a supply network's pattern as well as its hierarchical structure (although this includes many idealizing assumptions). Considering the network hierarchies from the viewpoint of connectivity, we can deduce that the process of meshing a mainly ramified network will affect the reliability, so that the greater the reliability of supply to the average consumers served, the higher will be the rank of the meshed conduits.

The highest reliability of supply relating to the whole network is obtained by minimization of the summed probabilities of disturbance p_{tot} for all supply routes m, which connect the served individuals with the production centre.

$$\sum_{j=1}^{m} p_{tot} \overset{!}{=} \min .$$

In the case of ramified networks the formula shows that a greater number of individuals are affected by interrupting a higher rank conduit than by interrupting a lower rank one. This is because the higher rank conduit compounds a greater number of individual supply routes. Under these circumstances the cyclic compound, formed by connecting a certain number of different plants producing the same supply good (for instance electric power stations) makes a maximum contribution to the reliability of a supply network; however, meshing the same number of terminal conduits does not affect the total reliability very much.

From the relations derived between the capacity and length multipliers on the one hand, and the degree of connectivity on the other, it should be possible to define different types of supply networks by shape and hierarchical structure. These types may be associated with various utility sectors.

However, all these types cannot fit exactly the real utility systems such as those for the distribution of water, electricity, gas, information by telephone etc. because:

1 land use is heterogenous with respect to the kind as well as to the intensity. Therefore neither the demand for goods nor the accessibility of the systems can accord with the assumed homogenous spatial distribution;
2 immobility of infrastructural investments effects that each local improvement must adapt to the already existing systems. In this sense technical standards, which were initially set on an almost arbitrary basis, have become tradition. As examples of such arbitrarily fixed technical standards we may consider the voltage levels in electric networks (220 V, 10 kV, 30 kV, 110 kV, 380 kV) or the width and critical load of roads and railways. Thus, technical standards are very important as shaping constraints in the functional limitations of network patterns, and of their hierarchical structures.

It may be useful to analyze for different utility systems the defined characteristics C_1, L_1, α_r, β_r (or β_s), μ_r, and p_{tot}, for discussing the various determinants and economic criteria because the real networks may deviate from predetermined ideal types.

If we intend to estimate an existing or planned system's quality by design, it would be necessary to include in our calculation topographical characteristics, data for land use, indices of spatial concentration, social behaviour etc.

At first, after having integrated this knowledge into the concept, we can expect some results for planning assistance. There might be a chance to set up a linear programme whose objective function would be minimization of a spatial network's construction costs by using the relation between rank and length. The constraints may be defined by a certain demand for reliability of supply including a function of rank-specific degrees of connectivity. Besides this the constraints must of course include the individualities of the planned region. Neglecting the length and capacity multipliers, α and β, which may be considered as parameters describing the individual systems' pattern and hierarchical structure, we can simplify from the formulae (2), (5), and (7) to get

$$L_r = L_1 \left(\frac{C_1}{C_r}\right)^{1/2} , \tag{9}$$

$$C_r = C_1 \left(\frac{L_1}{L_r}\right)^{2} . \tag{9a}$$

(1)

2.5 Dynamic considerations: modifications of utility systems under '*ceteris paribus*' conditions (an example)

Growing specific demand for supply goods by inhabitants as well as enterprises usually effects increasing capacities in the utility systems. In the following, the hierarchical structure of urban road networks is analyzed and discussed under conditions of '*ceteris paribus*'. This example may also help to evaluate the weight of different determinants for other utility systems (see figure 5) (Bökemann and Herz, 1967).

Two simplifying assumptions are made.

1 Households are dispersed homogeneously throughout the urban area. This should effect the same spatial distribution of traffic generation. The city is the mainpoint of destination for the whole traffic.

2 The network pattern is characterized by the right angle (square served areas) and by partial connectivity which allows two alternative traffic routes to the centre for each rank of the network hierarchy.

These assumptions produce a rank-specific multiplier equal to four ($\beta = 4$), for the total of areas F_r, served by one conduit

$$F_r = F_1 \times 4^{(r-1)} .$$

(1) This derivation is analogous to Beckmann's mathematical formulation of central place theory. (See Beckmann, 1958; Christaller, 1933; and Lösch; 1940.)

At the same time the total length per rank is reduced for each rank added ($\alpha = 0 \cdot 5$)

$$L_r = {}_rL_1 \times 0 \cdot 5^{(r-1)} .$$

Because of the proportionality between the population density d and the traffic generation v, we can assume that the city streets and rank-specific traffic load V_r also increase in proportion to the size of the associated areas served F_r.

$$V_r = vdF_1\beta^{(r-1)} . \qquad (10)$$

Substituting this expression into our theoretical calculations (formula 9), we can conclude

$$\log L_r = \log_r L_1 + \tfrac{1}{2}\log(vdF_1) - \tfrac{1}{2}\log V_r , \qquad (11)$$

and substituting formula (10) we obtain

$$\log L_r = \log_r L_1 - \frac{(r-1)}{2}\log\left(\frac{V_r}{V_{(r-1)}}\right). \qquad (12)$$

After logarithmic transformation the relation between the total length per rank L_r and the rank-specific capacities C_r necessary to facilitate traffic is a straight line graph.

Because of the deduced proportionalities in the model, we are able to draw in the above graph an axis of the city's population parallel to the L_r abscissa. Under the assumed constraints, the graph shows the population thresholds beyond which supply services must be organized on a new level: new higher ranked centres may use the facilities given by higher ranked streets with greater capacity.

At this point the following three determinants, being involved implicitly in the model, are discussed under '*ceteris paribus*' conditions: (1) city size, (2) degree of motorization, and (3) population density.

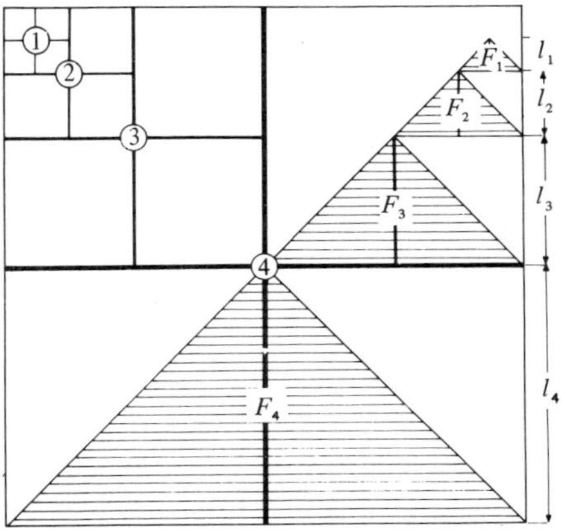

F_r is the served area of one street of the rank r;
l_r is the length of one street of the rank r.

Figure 5. Street lengths and served areas ($\alpha = 0 \cdot 5$).

(1) *City size*

With increasing population in a city, not only do the city streets grow proportionally (parallel shift of the function's straight line) in each rank, but after exceeding certain threshold's of population or traffic load respectively, new ranks of streets become necessary. Thus the necessity may arise of constructing major arterial streets or expressways in addition to the existing residential streets and collectors with or without access to the land parcels. As the construction of streets of the next higher rank becomes necessary after the threshold associated with a certain existing rank has been reached, the neglect of this fact may have a negative influence on the city's growth (see figure 6).

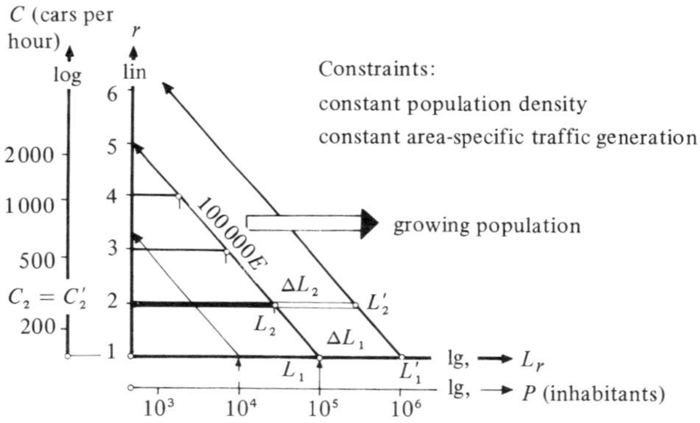

Figure 6. Network structure for urban streets by rank and length depending on the city's population.

(2) *Degree of motorization*

With increasing traffic generation per unit area (produced, for instance, by a higher degree of motorization) the length of the lowest ranked streets L_1 remains constant, although the city's population does not grow. Even the width of these residential streets need not usually be changed because the

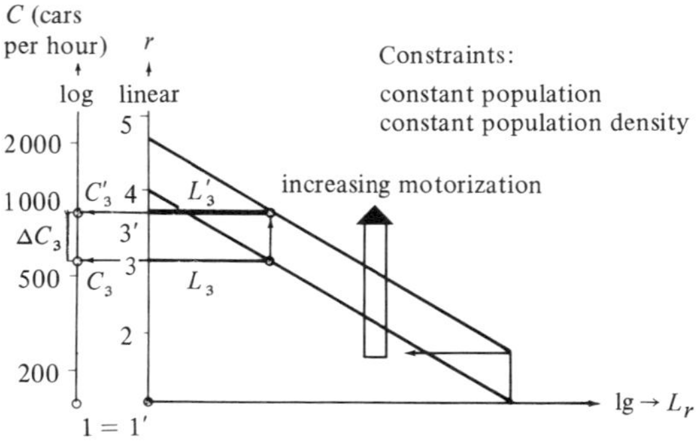

Figure 7. Network structure for urban streets by rank and length depending on area-specific traffic generation.

basis for capacity calculation is not the traffic load but the function of access to parcels. Because of the urban streets' hierarchical structure, the increased traffic generation places additional traffic loads (enforcing a greater street capacity) the higher the rank of the streets. A growing basic traffic load V_1 requires, according to formula (11), that the rank-specific discontinuities in capacity must increase the higher the rank. For an existing urban street system the increase of motorization means that the higher the rank of the streets under consideration, the greater the urgency to adapt them to load increases by constructional means, as spare capacity is less available the higher the rank and the area-specific traffic generation (figure 7).

(3) *Population density*
If, *ceteris paribus* the population density decreases, the total number of streets of length L_r, necessary to provide access to areas F_r, grows in inverse proportion to the rank of the street. Because the parcels of land become larger as a consequence of decreased density, the necessary length increase is highest for the lowest rank streets. None of the existing street capacities, however, will suffer from an additional load of traffic (see figure 8).

In the following, the basic intention of regional planning—serving for land use potentials—is introduced as a determinant of developing utility systems' networks.

Public utility systems are generally planned for increasing future strains, as the data deduced from the planned land use are multiplied with a factor σ

$$\sigma = \frac{\text{planned capacity}}{\text{planned load}} \; .$$

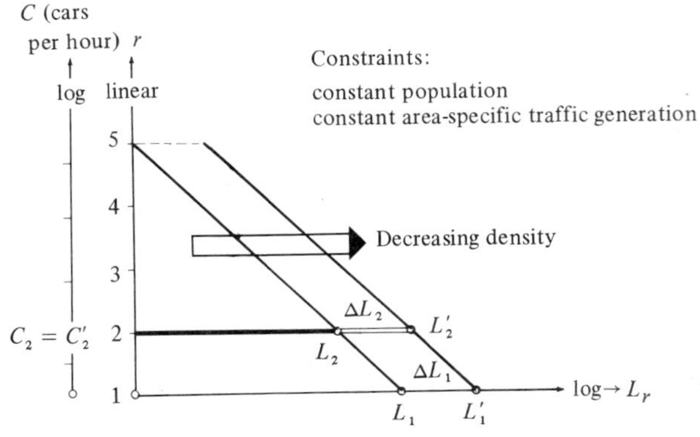

Figure 8. Network structure for urban streets by rank and length depending on population density.

This procedure of calculating the capacity includes a local free capacity ΔC_r which does exist under normal conditions. This may be considered as depending on the conduit's rank

$$\begin{aligned}\Delta C_r &= (\sigma - 1)C_r \\ &= (\sigma - 1)C_1\beta^{(r-1)} \; . \end{aligned} \tag{13}$$

Thus, the capacity calculation procedure favours the infrastructural equipment at single locations insofar that, in the case of usage, there is a greater potential of supply goods available than at other locations. This differentiation also arises if the considered utility system has been constructed for the purpose of providing a certain level of supply service in the total of the served area.

Locally existing free capacities of artificial utility systems may be defined as local potential for utilization, which is qualified by ranks like the associated conduits. This system's utilization potential becomes effective in connected (respectively accessible) parcels at the micro-level and accordingly also in communities at the macro-level. Under the condition that the number of access facilities on the supply conduit's path is limited by a critical distance $\Delta l_{r\,\mathrm{min}}$, which varies with technical specification across the ranks, we can derive a maximum number of possible locations $A_{r\,\mathrm{max}}$ as ranked discretely by the local potential of utilization,

$$A_{r\,\mathrm{max}} = \frac{L_r}{\Delta l_{r\,\mathrm{min}}} \; . \tag{14}$$

In the case of the central place type compound representing an extreme network pattern, access is given only to the root of each rank-specific conduit because the mode of transportation (for instance levels of tension or pressure) does not allow any further junction on the conduit's route. We can derive therefore the minimum possible number of locations accessible to a utility system of the central place type compound as depending on the area-specific number of lowest ranked locations and the capacity multiplier β,

$$A_{r\,\mathrm{min}} = \frac{A_1}{\beta^{(r-1)}} \; . \tag{15}$$

These results correspond with the respective studies by Christaller (1933), Lösch (1940), and Beckmann (1957) in the framework of central place theory.

Also in the case of the series type compound networks (systems without rank-specific varying transportation modes) the critical distances between the points of access increase exponentially with the rank (for instance the critical access distances for the street hierarchy which are usually fixed by technical standards). In this respect the rank-sized proportion of the locations in a certain region is not significantly changed by the type of compound appropriate to the conduit.

Free capacities provided by supply systems cannot be evaluated as potential for utilization without reference to the specific case and to the particular time, because in the case of utilization the locally raised real load limits the capacity of all the other locations connected with the same branch.

For the case of a minimally ramified supply network, if there are no free capacities, no additional load at any one of the locations connected with the system's branch behind the considered point is possible.

Looking at it the other way round we see that the same case illustrates a decreasing influence for the utilization potential the higher the conduit's rank. Generalizing, we can state that a location utilization potential of utility systems increases not only by the rank but also by the distance from the location of production, because it becomes more probable that capacities are already blocked by other users the greater the distance between the considered location and the place of production.

Thus, at this stage, besides the availability of utility systems' capacities, there appears to be another factor of importance for calculating location quality: that is the opportunity to use certain free capacities at a location over a longer time period.

Enterprises generally settle only at such places where the entrepreneurs can expect extension. For the realization of such expectations future utilization of free infrastructural capacities must be guaranteed.

Naturally these ideas modify the assumption about the homogeneous distribution of supply goods over the area served. A close interrelation does exist, however, between the potential of utilization distributed over the system's alignment, on the one hand, and the real land use on the other. The higher the utilization potential offered by the utility systems the greater the inducement to settle; the greater the opportunity to have the use of free capacities in the future the stronger becomes the intention to intensify existing local land use.

3 Location quality defined by the access to infrastructural systems

Up to now we have analyzed the factors determining spatial patterns of single utility systems and the constraints under which these systems expand. In the following we shall deal with the rules under which the different systems superpose in space.

Utility systems offer utilization potentials at access points along their network's lines. Thus any part of the system's capacity already required at a certain point of the alignment can no longer be used at another point. Therefore, along their alignment, utility systems possess one degree of freedom in respect of the users' choice of location, as long as free capacities in the branch under consideration (and not in the conduit's cross section) are not exhausted. If conduits of various systems intersect, at the intersection a particular location quality arises, because this point is unique from all adjacent ones in being the only one offering two opportunities for usage.

If we consider the accessibility to a certain utility system as a single opportunity for usage, we can define location quality as the local cumulation of various facilities. Thus for any user external economies may arise from the linkage if his establishments are connected with a plurality of different supply systems. In this sense linkage advantages are going to be maximum at the places where infrastructural opportunities are highly concentrated and conversely, there will be a lack of external linkage advantages at places with only one available supply good.

It can be derived from the single system's characteristics in different compounds that facilities cumulated locally cannot be distributed homogeneously over an area. Not even all the main sectors of the supply services used can be available at all places because of the single system's own distinct ranges, their own degrees of connectivity, features of hierarchy, etc.

If we combine the concept of the facilities' local linkage with the contents of formula (15), we can derive the facilities' positions for the settlement patterns (in analogy to central place theory) that there are in a certain area. There will be a large number of places, each with a small population and few facilities (in other words, only a small utilization potential). However, very few places will exist containing a large population combined with a wide variety of facilities. It is characteristic of regional structure that only those cities with a large population can offer the higher ranked facilities (for example, in the traffic sector there is direct access to expressways, rapid transit railways, pipelines, etc.). However, at smaller settlements only the lowest ranked facilities are usually available (for instance, direct access to a small county road only).

Following these considerations, we shall now define a parameter reflecting the local availability of infrastructural facilities. This is the number of locally linked opportunities provided by the different utility systems.

The definition includes the assumption that the use of utility systems develops over time in a fixed sequence matched to the utility. This is because the existing variety of locally linked facilities is always the prerequisite and reason for their utilization and for the economic success of investments in new systems. The determination of the rank sequence of local facilities is affected by the structural similarity of residents' and enterprises' demand in each location of a region.

As all units of consumption and production (households and industrial plants) use different supply goods in specific combinations at the same places, the terminals of the coordinated utility systems have to be linked at these positions. On aggregating over whole settlements the maximum number of different types of user—each with a demand for a specific locational combination of supply goods—we can assume the demand structures of these single units yield an average structure which is similar for most settlements of the same size. According to central place theory settlements of the same size therefore use, within certain limits, the same combination of infrastructural facilities. The number of these facilities and their individual capacities increase with the settlements' size. Due to this reason different utility systems expand over space by similar network patterns, very often with similar alignments and compound types.

As an alternative to the infrastructural facilities offered locally we have also to consider the different demands of individual households and enterprises. Industrial establishments in particular, which are wanting to settle, decide on their location by comparing the opportunities offered locally by the communities with their own location conditions.

We can assume that in order for each industrial plant to settle, there must be a certain guaranteed minimum of infrastructural equipment (or utilization potential). The majority of the 24000 municipalities in Western Germany, however, cannot even offer this essential requirement in the case of mechanical production processes specialized at a low level. Only one in forty municipalities is suitable for the settlement of industrial plants; if we assume that their minimum requirement is correlated with the size of the population, the place must have 10000 inhabitants.

The potential likelihood for industrial plant to settle can be clarified by the following model (figure 9).

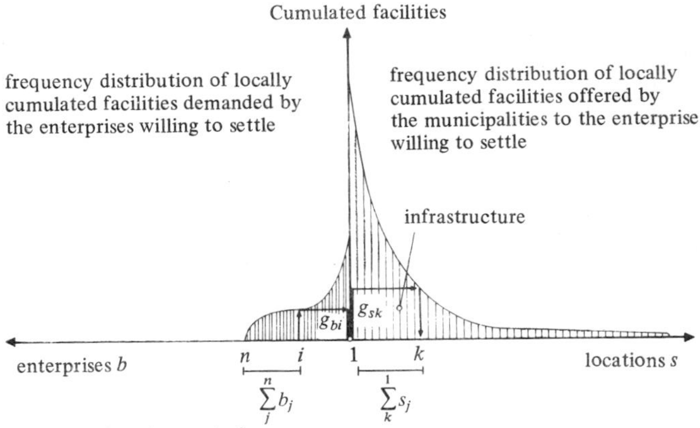

potential of settlement in k:

$$p_k = \sum_j^n b_j \Big/ \sum_k^1 s_j \qquad \text{where } g_{sk} = X g_{bi}$$

g_{sk} = facilities of location k
g_{bi} = facilities demanded by enterprises i
X = coefficient guaranteeing a certain combination of facilities within a local cumulation with a certain probability

Figure 9. Potential of settlement by enterprises.

Let us consider as equivalent decision alternatives all locations which satisfy the specific minimum requirement of containing associated types, or branches, or sizes of enterprise. On this assumption the location potential for settling by an enterprise is the ratio of the number of enterprises able and willing to settle $\sum_j^n b_j$, and $\sum_k^1 s_j$, the number of locations able and willing to satisfy the enterprises' conditions. We may assume that each municipality which we identify as one location is willing to attract new enterprises because of the stimulation to its growth which this will cause.

Thus, the location potential for settlement by enterprises p increases with the number of locally linked opportunities for utilization g_{sk}, and decreases with the number of locations competing $\sum_k^1 s_j$ (figure 9)

$$p = \sum_j^n b_j \Big/ \sum_k^1 s_j \tag{15}$$

where

$$b_j = \mathrm{f}(g_s) , \qquad \text{for } g_s < g_{sk} \tag{16}$$

$$s_j = x\mathrm{f}(g_b) , \qquad \text{for } g_b > g_{bi} . \tag{17}$$

Multiplication of the existing number of local facilities g_{si} by the coefficient x ($x > 1$) gives us a ficticious number of local facilities g_{sk} in which a certain combination of facilities demanded by a specific enterprise will most probably be available.

The exact allocation of individual facilities to ranks *ex genere* is, by analogy to central place theory, largely governed by division of function (a proportion of locally available facilities being a match of identified types).

Enterprises, on the contrary, need more random combinations of facilities; that is, supply facilities of certain ranks throughout the rank-series may not be demanded. For this reason the relation between supply and demand is more balanced in larger municipalities, where the different combinations of enterprises adjust the demand structure to the regular pattern of the rank-series, in correspondence to central place theory.

In this context the classification of local facilities into discrete ranks can be expressed formally by the help of division and specialization of functions. We assume the process of specialization to be synchronised for all supply sectors. However, this means the number of individual systems offering the discrete utilization opportunities g increases exponentially to the base 2 with the number of ranks.

$$g_r = s \times 2^{(r-1)} ,$$

$$g_{\mathrm{tot}} = \sum_{r=1}^{n} g_r = g_1 + g_2 + g_3 + \dots g_n = s(2^n - 1) ,$$

where s are the (basic) supply sectors; r is the level of specialization; g_r are the rank-specific facilities; g_{tot} is the total number of local facilities.

In a very similar way location factors, differentiated by ranks, have been allocated to branches of industry, depending on the degree of specialization of their production.

If local facilities and location factors of production are connected by the same criteria of the functional division process, then we can deduce the probability of an enterprise settling, p, as follows:

1 The local availability of an additional supply sector s will open up additional possibilities of settlement for such new enterprises and size of plant, as are associated in their demand with these new facilities. Dependant on the importance of the available supply sectors, the number of branches of industry willing to settle therefore, will rise at a certain rate.

2 If, however, we compare cities of different ranks (according to central place theory), we find an exponential increase in the branches willing to settle per rank-step, each one representing a higher level of the infrastructure's specialization. This provides an explanation of the fact that large agglomerations, with more differentiated and specialized infrastructural equipment, are much more attractive in relation to their population size to enterprises willing to settle, than are smaller municipalities; and it is also the reason for the much higher growth-rates of their populations.

From this relation between local equipment and location potential of settlement for growth inducing enterprises, we now can deduce a general law governing the stimulation effect of infrastructural equipment. Without any planning for adjustment, investment decisions in the infrastructural sector of any favourable place, which were originally made at random, will produce discrepancies which will be multiplied in future times.

References

Beckmann, M. J., 1958, "City hierarchies and the distribution of city size", *Journal of Economic Development and Cultural Change,* **6**, 243–248.

Bökemann, D., Herz, R., 1967, "Funktionsgerechte Gestaltung von Stadtstrassen", *Strassenverkehrstechnik,* **10**, (3/4).

Christaller, W., 1933, *Die Zentralen Orte in Süddeutschland* (G. Fischer, Jena).

Garrison, W. L., Marble, D. F., 1962, "The structure of transportation networks", US Army Transportation Command Technical Report, Evanston, pp.62–11.

Hirschman, A. O., 1958, *The Strategy of Economic Development* (Yale University Press, New Haven, Conn.).

Jochimsen, R., 1966, *Theorie der Infrastruktur* (Mohr, Tübingen).

Kansky, K. J., 1963, "Structure of transport networks: relationships between network geometry and regional characteristics", Dept. of Geography, Research Paper 84, University of Chicago.

Lösch, A., 1940, *Die Räumliche Ordnung der Wirtschaft* (G. Fischer, Jena).

Stohler, J., 1965, "Zur rationalen Planung der Infrastruktur", *Konjunkturpolitik,* **11**, (5).

Tinbergen, J., 1962, *Shaping the World Economy* (Twentieth Century Fund, New York).

von Thünen, J. H., 1826, *Der isolierte Staat in Beziehung auf Landwirtschaft und Nationalökonomie, Hamburg* (4th edition, 1966, G. Fischer, Stuttgart).

Toward a Reformulation of the Modal Choice Problem of Urban Transportation Planning

D.E.BOYCE
University of Pennsylvania

Introduction

The term, modal split model, refers to a class of procedures for estimating the proportion of trips or trip ends that will use one mode over another. Such models are an integral part of a sequence of models that comprise a well-defined travel demand forecasting methodology applied in urban transportation planning. The other models in this sequence—trip generation, trip distribution and traffic assignment—estimate other specific aspects of travel behavior. Different formulations of these models have resulted in two major sequences of model application, pre-distribution modal split and post-distribution modal split. In both cases, however, the modal split problem is a specifically defined procedure in the overall urban travel demand forecasting process. A review of nine such models and their relation to the other travel models is given in Fertal *et al.* (1966). The application of such models in the transportation planning process is reviewed by Boyce *et al.* (1970).

Shortcomings

It is well known that modal split models have a number of shortcomings that are becoming increasingly severe as the urban transportation planning process becomes oriented towards the specific problems of urban transit and the broad problem of a wider choice of urban transportation technology. These shortcomings are basically of two types. The first has to do with the difficulties imposed on the modal split model by the manner in which the overall sequence of models is structured. The second type has to do with the modal split model itself.

As an example of the first type, consider the problem of obtaining equilibrium forecasts of travel volumes on congested transportation networks. An equilibrium solution is one in which the properties of transportation networks predicted by the models are in agreement with the assumptions made about these properties as inputs to the model. Perhaps the most important example of such a property is link speed.

Equilibrium solutions at the traffic assignment model stage are obtained through capacity restraint procedures. However, it is typically the case that the final speeds predicted by the capacity restraint assignment model do not correspond with the speeds assumed in the modal split and trip distribution models. Therefore, the modal split and trip distribution forecasts are not consistent with the final solution obtained by the traffic assignment. In order to correct this inconsistency, it is necessary to reiterate through the modal split, trip distribution, and traffic assignment models until a convergence is obtained.

The error introduced in the modal split by the failure to obtain equilibrium solutions is no doubt quite large, perhaps as large as the differences in modal split between major alternative transportation plans. If equilibrium solutions over the entire sequence of trip forecasting models cannot be obtained, then it may not be technically feasible to test alternative levels of investment in highways versus transit. This problem is made even more difficult by (a) the need to estimate peak-hour volumes as well as 24-hour volumes, and (b) the different operating characteristics of the highway system and the transit system during peak-hour conditions.

An example of the second type of shortcoming internal to the modal split model itself is the importance of auto ownership or auto availability as a predictor of modal split (for example see Bock, 1968). Automobile ownership is clearly a very important variable in determining modal split. Moreover, auto ownership is highly correlated with household income, and very good estimating equations for car ownership can be obtained based on income, given that the transportation system remains *constant*. However, the transportation system is precisely the system that planners need to vary, particularly if the allocation of investment between highway and transit facilities is the primary question to be resolved. In other words, if the auto ownership behavior of households is a function of the total transportation system and household income, as well as price and taste, then one would prefer to estimate automobile ownership in response to these variables rather than as an independently determined input to the modal split prediction. This is particularly true for predicting whether households own more than one car, or for predicting the group of households that prefer to own no car at all. Therefore, if transportation planning procedures are to be able to predict the use of new transportation facilities, including major improvements in urban transit in a satisfactory way, automobile ownership should not be estimated on the basis of the past and existing transportation systems.

Behavioral concepts

Modal split models have been criticized by some researchers on the grounds that they are not behavioral. However, many models constructed to date, including the ones reviewed in Fertal *et al.* (1966), Mercadal (1968), and Warner (1962), include in their formulation many behavioral concepts.

Behavioral concepts are defined here to mean that households or trip makers with similar socio-economic status, age, sex, and other household characteristics tend to respond in a uniform way when confronted with a given environmental system, in this case the transportation system. That is, the internalized preference function of a homogeneous group of trip makers tends to be sufficiently similar that they respond to the perceived system characteristics, such as cost, time risk, convenience, status, etc., by choosing the same mode and path through the transportation network. However, as Mercadal (1968) has pointed out in detailed behavioral studies of modal choice, trip makers with similar characteristics do not always agree on their choice of mode; this may indicate that the number of group characteristics to be considered is large and that trip makers may have difficulty in perceiving and comparing modal options.

In fact, existing modal split models do categorize trip makers into homogeneous groups, for example by income, auto ownership, and family size. The dependent modal split variable is then predicted as a function of transportation systems characteristics, usually the relative time and cost characteristics of the two modes. What these models do not make explicit is the preference function by which trip makers reach a modal decision. Moreover, no distinction is made between actual system characteristics and those perceived by the trip maker.

These behavioral inadequacies of modal split models may be remedied by considering a more explicit behavioral approach. However, the literature potentially applicable to this problem is not sufficiently advanced to provide critical sensors of the relevant behavioral parameters. The problem is then to locate critical areas where strong economic assumptions of behavior appear inconsistent with observed behavior, in order that they can be replaced with measurable surrogates of observed characteristics.

Given the existing behavioral aspects of modal split models, and given the shortcomings of these models as discussed above, any extension of the existing approach to modal split will only lead to refinements of this approach and not to major improvements in transportation planning procedures. In particular, extensions of the existing approach will not help to solve the equilibrium problem discussed above, nor will it make the existing procedure more susceptible to iterative solutions. Furthermore, it will not solve the inconsistency caused by the need for an independent auto ownership forecast.

Therefore, in order to take a major step forward in making travel forecasting methods more responsive to a wider variation in transportation system modal characteristics, and at the same time to make these methods more behavioral in approach than at present, a substantial reformulation of the existing framework is required. Some desirable requirements for such a new approach are now discussed.

Model requirements

Before stating any specific requirements for a reformulated transportation planning procedure it is necessary to delineate the problem to be solved more precisely. In general, highway planning procedures have been applied in an attempt to solve a very wide range of problems, much wider than is probably effective or efficient for one such set. Instead, at least two levels of procedures seem to be indicated for two broad types of problems. This paper is concerned only with the second level as described below.

Level 1 transportation planning procedures

(a) Purpose—estimates of person-miles of travel by mode and facility type for large districts including estimates of total cost and time of travel by the above categories. An example of an attempt to develop such an approach is Balkus (1969).

(b) Application—evaluation of consequences of urban activity distributions (land use alternatives); evaluation of major investment alternatives, for example, highway versus transit, freeways versus arterials; determination of total cost of alternative transportation systems.

Level 2 transportation planning procedures:

(a) Problem—estimates of volumes of vehicles and passengers by transportation facility (link detail) for all modes, facility types and link locations and for peak-hour and 24-hour travel.

(b) Application—evaluation of detailed network layout; identification of design criteria for preliminary and detailed design of facilities; evaluation of terminal and modal interchange facilities.

Under Level 2 procedures, the objective is to produce estimates of link volumes for peak-hour and 24-hour travel for the total transportation system. Clearly, if link volumes are known for all facilities then the modal split is also known. Stated another way, once link volumes are known, the existing definition of the modal split problem is not relevant.

To understand more fully the implications of the above point, consider the early methods of assigning trips to freeways using trip diversion curves. When the all-or-nothing procedures were implemented, the number of trips diverted to freeways from arterials became a largely irrelevant problem. The information needed, that is the volume of vehicles on each link, was produced by the new method. In a similar manner, the modal split problem and its many difficulties may be largely a result of the way the problem had been defined historically. Therefore, through a reformulation of the problem it may be possible essentially to replace the modal split problem with a new one that can be solved in a more straightforward way.

What, then, are the desired characteristics of the new problem? They are:
(a) to enhance the feasibility of obtaining equilibrium solutions with well-behaved properties of stability and convergence over the entire set of transportation planning procedures;
(b) to incorporate input variables describing the socio-economic status of households and the characteristics of the total (multi-modal) transportation system; furthermore, that an independent prediction of auto ownership not be an exogenous input to these models;
(c) to utilize the existing expertise in highway and transit planning procedures outside the modal split problem (trip generation, distribution and assignment) to the maximum possible extent in any reformulated approach.

Statement of the approach

In this section the overall approach to a reformulation of a sequence of transportation planning procedures is first stated concisely, and then discussed with regard to method of solution, data requirements and estimate procedures, and the problems and uncertainties with the approach.

The problem

Assume that the following information is given:
(a) a single network description of the total (multi-modal) urban transportation system in conventional node-link terms, but with each link described by a set of characteristics (for example, travel time, travel cost, accident risk, delay risk, convenience, privacy, variance of travel time) instead of a single characteristic; this network description includes all modes integrated to the extent observed or proposed for a given metropolitan area;
(b) trip origins and destinations by zone, classified by trip purpose, and by the socio-economic status and other characteristics of the trip maker or the household.

Given the above information, if a preference function can be identified for each combination of trip purpose and class of households, and this function combines the set of link characteristics into a single composite characteristic such that the minimum path formed with the composite link characteristics corresponds to the trip makers' preferred path, then a behavioral solution to modal choice will be achieved. The preference function sought may consist of a linear equation of weighted link characteristics, or it may be more complex in form. If such a preference function can be identified, then minimum path trees over the total network can be computed for each origin zone for each combination of trip purpose and socio-economic status, and trip origins can be distributed to trip destinations using conventional trip distribution models.

Furthermore, these trips can then be assigned to the integrated (multi-modal) transportation network using conventional assignment methods. This assignment will provide the information usually provided by two separate traffice assignments—one for the highway network, and the other for the transit network. The network speeds and other link characteristics predicted for each class of link can be used to revise the input assumptions regarding each link's characteristics and the entire sequence of models can be reiterated until an equilibrium is achieved.

Method of solution

Two major departures from existing procedures are involved in solving the above problems, namely the transportation network description and the estimation of the form of the preference function and its parameters.

The use of two (or more) separate networks in urban transportation planning appears to be mainly a historical accident, in that the highway network was first considered as a separate system, and then transit was added as a second system. There now appear to be sound reasons for building a single network, that is, a network that corresponds more precisely to the single network faced by trip makers in the real world. Such an approach and its difficulties are discussed by Bock (1968). Because of the much wider range of link characteristics found in such a single network, several characteristics (comprising a vector) must be formed to replace the existing single characteristic—usually travel time. This vector offers an opportunity to introduce many behavioral variables; the manner in which they should be introduced is described below. In selecting a path to a given destination, including the selection of the type of link on which to travel (mode and facility types), a trip maker constructs internally a preference function on link and path characteristics. One simple way of defining this preference function is to identify a set of weights, one for each link characteristic, for inclusion in a linear equation resulting in a composite characteristic. Given these weights, the trip maker can then identify the preferred minimum path, that is the sequence of links that he prefers to all other sequences.

Given a network description, the socio-economic status of trip makers for a given trip purpose, and information on which path is chosen by these trip makers, the problem of determining the weights for a linear preference function is well defined in the algebra of linear inequalities. Consider the following *very* simple example:

A trip maker can choose between two links with characteristics (x_1, y_1) for a link one and (x_2, y_2) for link two. If he chooses link one, then there must exist weights, α and β, such that:

$$\alpha x_1 + \beta y_1 > \alpha x_2 + \beta y_2,$$

or

$$\alpha(x_1 - x_2) + \beta(y_1 - y_2) > 0.$$

Then suppose we have data on n such trip makers distributed over p types; then we might seek estimates for each of the p groups of trip makers for:

$$\alpha' = \alpha + e_1 \qquad \beta' = \beta + e_2$$

such that the sum of the squared error terms is minimized. Given such estimates for each group, a preference ordering on the two links can be defined, and the link preferred by each group identified. The problem may also be thought of as one of classification in which trip makers are classified according to their preferences for alternate paths. Procedures for solving systems of linear inequalities and estimating the required weights for linear preference functions have been developed to solve pattern recognition problems and appear to be applicable to the type of preference function problems defined here. The perceptron algorithm for solving such problems is discussed in Kanal (1968) and Watanabe (1969).

In order to extend this very simple case to a large multi-modal network, we have to identify the preferred and the alternative paths for each trip maker in a given group. The preferred path is the path (including its mode) actually taken by a trip maker for a given trip purpose. The alternative path could be obtained by questionnaire, or it could be defined as the next best path that incorporates an alternative mode. Similar approaches to this problem are discussed by Bock (1968) and Moses and Williamson (1963); the similarity to Schneider's formulation (1969) is also noted.

Data requirements and estimation procedures

The data required to implement such a method may not be substantially greater than for current models, but a much different use of the data is suggested. Two types of data are necessary. First, interview data on preferred and alternate paths for each group and trip purpose are highly desirable. This data might be constructed from typical home interview files; but an iterative process would be required to estimate the weights, since initial trial weights would be required to identify the preferred and alternate paths, given the origin, mode and destination of each trip.

The second set of data concerns the transportation network description. Several link characteristics are required; most of the information needed is presently simultaneously inventoried, but not necessarily used for this purpose. For example, risk of delay is largely a function of access limitation that permits or prevents a change of path *en route*. This information is usually available. Similarly, accident risks by facility types are usually known. Operating costs can be readily estimated from link length and speed.

The number and types of link characteristics required should be determined on a trial and error basis. Initially, the preference function should be estimated with only a few characteristics, for example, time and cost. Then others should be added one at a time in order to reduce the errors in the estimation of the function. In this manner the most satisfactory set of characteristics can be identified.

Problems and uncertainties with the approach

The problem reformulation outlined above is well founded on existing transportation planning methods and experience. It incorporates fully the proven concepts of network description, trip distribution and traffic assignment, and seeks to extend and attain the full potential of these approaches. At the same time the proposed approach contemplates major new directions—namely, multi-modal network description and preference function estimation for alternate paths. The risk associated with such innovations is clearly larger than the risk of refining existing approaches, in the short run at least. In order to clarify some of the problems associated with the approach, three difficulties are now discussed.

Existing modal split models are criticized here for their dependence on independent estimates of auto ownership. Any attempt to eliminate the need for such an important variable requires a significant advance in the understanding of modal choice phenomena. It is not clear if the approach proposed here has sufficient power to attain this goal. The preference function estimation procedure may in fact only place weak conditions on path choice. The degree of success that can be attained depends not only on the regularity of the phenomena, but also on the quality of the data available.

For these reasons, it is somewhat questionable whether the need for an independent auto ownership prediction can be removed straightaway. However, the use of such an independent prediction is compatible with the proposed approach. One way to implement this more limited approach is to code an 'auto availability' link into the highway network at every entry point. By this device, only the class of trips having an auto available would be able to pass through this link. Therefore, the need to develop an operational model can still be met, even if the overall objective of eliminating the dependence on an auto ownership prediction has to be abandoned.

A second question about the approach is whether the path preference functions for a multi-modal network are independent of trip destination. In the above discussion, it is implicitly assumed that modal path preference functions can be estimated for homogeneous groups of trip makers and trip purpose which apply to all destinations. Such an approach seems reasonable, and if attained would eliminate the pre-distribution versus post-distribution problem. However, the special character of CBD trips and past experience with the difficulty of this group of trip-ends requires that caution be exercised at this point. Therefore, the preference functions estimated should be tested for their sensitivity to location of trip destination. If it is found that different preference functions exist for some groups of destination than for others, a post-distribution modal choice process is implied, with additional iterations probably required. This approach, while feasible and operational, is not as desirable as the main approach described.

A final problem concerns the size of the network and the number of trees to be built. The multi-modal network description proposed will result in a much larger regional network. Not only are the highway and transit networks combined into a single network in this approach, but also much more detail in the connection between the two modal networks is proposed. Accordingly, networks with two or three times as many nodes and links as existing highway networks may be required. Furthermore, several link characteristics will be measured for each link.

Networks of this size can probably be efficiently employed in building minimum path trees through the application of network partitioning methods. Conceptually, the regional network can be partitioned into several sub-regional networks. Minimum path trees can be efficiently computed for these partitioned networks using conventional tree-tracing programs. These partitioned paths can then be efficiently combined to form regional paths through the use of matrix algorithms; see Land and Stairs (1967) for a description of such an algorithm.

In conclusion, the above problems represent several uncertainties associated with the proposed reformulation of the modal split problem. While difficult, they do not appear insurmountable, and they appear to offer the possibility of overcoming some of the problems that are inherent in existing approaches.

References

Balkus, K., 1969, "Metropolitan highway system in the framework of social welfare decisions", *Papers Regional Science Association,* **22**, 39 - 64.

Bock, F. C., 1968, "Factors influencing modal trip assignement", NCHRP Report 57, Highway Research Board, Washington, DC.

Boyce, D. E., Day, N. D., McDonald, C., 1970, *Metropolitan Plan Making, Monograph Series: No.4* (Regional Science Research Institute, Philadelphia).

Fertal, M. J., Weiner, E., Balek, A. J., Sevin, A. F., 1966, *Modal Split* (Bureau of Public Roads, US Department of Commerce, Washington, DC).

Kanal, L. (Ed.), 1968, *Pattern Recognition* (Thompson Book Co., Wayne, Penna.).

Land, A. H., Stairs, S. W., 1967, "The extension of the cascade algorithm to large graphs", *Management Science,* **14**,(1), 29-33.

Mercadal, M., 1968, *Choice of Mode of Transport, Psychological Motivation and the Econometric Approach* (European Conference of Ministers of Transport, Paris).

Moses, L., Williamson, H., 1963, "Value of time, choice of mode, and the subsidy issue in urban transportation", *Journal of Political Economy,* **76**, No.3, 257-264.

Schneider, M., 1969, *Transportation and Land Development* (Creighton, Hamburg Inc., for the Bureau of Public Roads, US Department of Transportation, Washington, DC).

Warner, S., 1962, *Stochastic Choice of Mode in Urban Travel: A Study in Binary Choice* (Northwestern University Press, Evanston, Illinois).

Watanabe, S. (Ed.), 1969, *Methodologies of Pattern Recognition* (Academic Press, New York).

The Question of City Size and National Policy

W.ALONSO*
University of California, Berkeley

Are big cities too big?

A great many countries, both developed and developing, believe that their biggest cities are too big, but there is no solid base for this conclusion either in fact or theory. While, as is frequently thought, the largest American urban areas may be too large, we do not know that this is the case and much of the evidence runs counter.

Most American studies and a scatter of foreign ones have addressed this question by studying how *per capita* public costs vary with urban size. The most common finding is that these reach their lowest point in the range of 50000 to 250000 population. However, these findings are not firm: more sophisticated multi-variate analyses show no correlation of these costs to population size. Further, these studies have not been able to measure the levels of public services produced, and it is of relatively little use to know how expenditures vary if we do not know what they buy. A more fundamental difficulty is that, for the purposes of public policy, we should be interested in economic costs rather than money costs. Not only do we lack figures in economic costs, we also lack a good theoretical basis for approaching them. For instance, in many cases it is unclear whether land costs should be counted as a cost or as a benefit, or whether differences in salary levels for schoolteachers or policemen are true costs or transfer payments.

In any case, it would seem that the minimizing of costs is a poor objective for public policy, even within a narrow focus of economic efficiency. There is strong evidence that, at least in cross section, output *per capita* increases strongly with urban size, so that economic efficiency would be better served by maximizing the difference between input and output. In this country we lack figures for the gross regional product of metropolitan areas, but German and Japanese figures show it to be rising much more rapidly than public costs. In this country, using *per capita* income as an index, we find the same pattern: income rises sharply with urban size. An objective of economic efficiency would thus be best served not by minimizing costs but by maximizing the difference between income and costs. However, since these figures are in money terms, one

* Supported by a grant from the Economic Development Administration.

might question whether interurban differences in costs and prices to private consumers and producers eliminate the effect of rising money incomes. No US figures are available for producers costs, but the Bureau of Labor Statistics data on comparative costs of living in metropolitan areas bear only a weak and slight association with urban size, so that the rise in incomes is real. Interestingly a recent Gallup Poll indicates that people feel they need more money in bigger cities, suggesting that it is risen expectations rather than objective facts that make large urban areas seem more expensive.

Examining the data on *per capita* income of metropolitan areas in certain ways (but not in others) suggests that there may be some decline in *per capita* income above a population of about three million. One cannot conclude from this, however, that diminishing returns set in after this size. In the first place, the definition of the Standard Metropolitan Statistical Area of the Census misses considerable exurban high-income population in the largest urban areas, so that the decline may be more apparent than real. Secondly, these few very large urban areas perform certain functions for the national system of cities which may lower their own *per capita* income while serving the national interest as a whole. They function as principal ports of entry and acculturators of immigrants from rural areas and from abroad, and they are seedbeds of new economic activities which, not being capital intensive in their early stages, pay relatively low wages. Considerable evidence shows that when the activities mature (and become more capital intensive) they move to smaller urban areas.

Why should productivity increase with urban size? In brief, because urban size is a measure of the opportunities to which an inhabitant or enterprise has access. Interestingly *per capita* income is also strongly correlated to population potential, which is a mathematical measure of the accessibility available to residents of the city to the population of the rest of the country. Thus, a small metropolis in an area of high population potential will usually have as high a *per capita* income as a larger but more remote metropolis. This phenomenon may account for the emerging megalopolitan pattern, which consists of constellations of metropoles. The nineteenth century city, which had a single dominant center of activity, has given way to the much larger metropolis, whose structure is a complex counterpoint of multiple nuclei which permit the advantages of concentration and specialization while keeping functional distances relatively small. The megalopolis, for all the negative associations this term has gathered in journalistic usage, seems to be a further adaptation permitting specialization and high connectivity among urban areas, while avoiding some of the penalties of excessive size.

This discussion has concentrated on urban areas as engines of production, but other things must be considered for the purposes of public policy and human welfare. Recent studies by Ornati (1968) and by Burns (1968) find that, in general, incomes are more evenly distributed in larger metropoles than smaller ones. The contrary popular impression may be attributable to the sheer mass of the concentration of poverty in the larger areas. In general, all indicators of status, such as education, skill levels, and the proportion of the population living above the poverty level, rise with urban size. Indicators of pathological conditions point in different ways. Levels of air pollution rise; some forms of morbidity and mortality rise, but others decline. Most indices of crime are too unreliable for comparison, and there are no systematic studies of mental health variations. In brief, there is very little information on these issues, although there is a great deal of opinion and anecdote. It would seem that research into these topics would be of great value.

Current approaches to policy

The emergence of public concern on a national policy with respect to city size is quite recent, becoming explicit with President Nixon's State of the Union Message in 1969, in which he called for a national growth policy. At this early stage most of the debate seems to focus on three approaches, which will be discussed briefly below, but as might be expected of first efforts in a complex area, these approaches are gross over-simplifications.

The three approaches most commonly cited may be summarized as follows:

1 a reversal of migratory flows back to the countryside and the development of economic opportunities there;
2 the development of hundreds of new towns as containers for further urban growth; and
3 the encouragement of growth in alternative urban centers.

1 Development of the countryside

This policy has received considerable publicity and has been advocated by some of the US Departments, most notably that of Agriculture, usually under the name of 'Urban–Rural Balance'. But it appears highly questionable on the grounds of its feasibility, its impact, and its consequences.

First, can the migration from the country to the cities be halted, let alone reversed? It seems extremely doubtful. It is a world-wide phenomenon that arises as much from the continued development of agriculture and other primary industries, as from industrial development. It is a response to fundamental economic and social processes and any effort to stop orreverse it must be enormous and radical. To illustrate the point, only two countries appear to have adopted such a policy with any effectiveness in recent years: Communist China, in some of its communes and 'Great Leap' experiments; and North Vietnam, under the pressure of

American air bombardment. In other words, a commitment to such a policy bespeaks the utmost degree of national reorientation, which is likely only under extreme crisis.

Second, should the countryside retain its population, would the impact be significant? Not very, from the point of view of the metropolitan areas. Their growth currently consists of 80% natural increase, 15% migration across national borders, and only 5% net migration from non-metropolitan areas. Even the reversal of migratory flows would not have a large numerical impact. These considerations would apply similarly to the black population, which is already far more urbanized than the white. The consequences of the success of such a policy would not then be very large for metropolitan America. The main impact would be felt in the rural areas and small towns, where, because the population base is smaller, these flows have a much larger relative magnitude.

Steering manufacturing to the countryside would improve local economic health, but there would be some mixture of blessings. Most of the plants would probably be branch plants, and thus the small local economies would be in a position of colonial dependence to some distant corporate headquarters. Moreover, since manufacturing plants are larger in smaller places (mainly because they must internalize many functions not otherwise available), there would be a great many one-industry towns, with their well-known vulnerability to cyclical downturns and to technological or demand obsolescence. From the point of view of workers in the towns or dispersed agro-industrial communities, there would be the limitations of career choices and of opportunities advancement and the dangers of unemployment which characterize such small economies. From the social point of view one must suppose that in many cases there would be the rigid social hierarchy that has characterized such places. From the point of view of the nation, for the reason suggested earlier in this paper, there would be some loss in the rate of economic growth.

Some further questions are posed by recent findings of Lowry (1966), Lansing and Mueller (1967), and others. It is well known that the out-migrants are the young, and that the more educated they are, the more likely they are to leave. The surprise is that their rate of departure seems to have little to do with local prosperity, and that the young leave big and prosperous places at about the same rate as small and depressed ones, but they tend to go to big and prosperous places. Thus, a population maintenance policy might, in fact, result in bringing new people to these depressed areas rather than retaining the young of the original population. A further irony is that improvement of local conditions, by improving the education and marketable skills of the young, may, in fact, accelerate their out-migration.

2 Development of new towns

Insofar as new towns are thought of as small independent places, much of the proceeding argument applies to them. The small places are less productive, less adaptable, and thus more vulnerable than larger ones, and they offer residents fewer choices and opportunities. One important difference is that, because the free market cannot produce housing for the poor or even for most of the working class, a national emphasis on new town development would be regressive and accentuate the separation and polarization of our society. The poor could only be accommodated in new towns through massive housing subsidies, which would then not be available to existing urban centers where most of them live. Nor is there much hope that new towns would be cheaper to build than comparable extensions of cities: the tremendous cost of carrying a very large initial investment appears to wipe out possible savings from pre-planning and control. Moreover, even if such savings were realizable, they would be insignificant compared to the lower productivity of smaller urban places. The *per capita* income in 1960 of urban areas of a population of 100000 to 200000 was $427.00 or 20% lower than in urban areas of more than one million.

It appears that a 'new town's' approach would have a rather modest impact on America's urban pattern. The most ambitious responsible proposal, that of the Advisory Commission for Intergovernmental Relations, would have us build 100 new towns of 100000 population and 10 completely new cities of one million by the year 2000. Even by this staggering undertaking 80% of the urban population increase, and 93% of urban construction, would occur in existing urban areas until the end of the century; and by the year 2000 only 7% of the population would be living in these new towns and cities. Thus a major new towns program, while clearly of importance to those who would live in them and to their neighboring districts, would have only a marginal impact on overall patterns of population distribution.

One great difficulty in speaking of new towns is that the idea is a fashionable one and the term is freely applied to almost any development of more than two houses. Not only are suburban developments called new towns, but also central city redevelopment becomes a 'new town in town'. In this sense rather conventional extension or rebuilding of existing urban areas comes under the umbrella of new towns. A national policy of new towns that included these would be basically indistinguishable from current modes of urbanization.

3 Alternative urban centers

A more plausible alternative to a strategy of directing population growth to new towns or back to the countryside is to promote growth in suitable middle-sized urban areas. In other words, rather than a policy of putting new towns where they do not exist, the policy would put them where they show signs of wanting to be, other than in the largest cities. Granting, for the sake of argument, the desirability of steering growth away from the larger urban areas, a policy of concentrating on smaller existing centers makes excellent sense. In 1965, there were nearly 200 Standard Metropolitan Statistical Areas (SMSA) below one million population. Clearly, in an arithmetical sense, if each grew by half a million, they could absorb the projected 100 million (probably an overestimate) population increase by the year 2000 with none of them ending larger than one and a half million, and with an eventual average size well below one million. America's population has urbanized largely in this way, but without such spreading. Of 26 SMSAs of more than one million population in 1965, nine had less than a quarter of a million population in 1900, and these nine absorbed one sixth of the population growth of all 212 metropolitan areas during those 65 years. In recent years the smallest metropolitan areas (below 200000) have as a group grown more slowly than larger areas, but one third of them have attracted migrants at twice the rate per inhabitant of all metropolitan areas, while only one fifth of those above one million have grown as rapidly. In fact the proportion of these small metropolitan areas which is growing fast (by attracting twice their share of migrants) is two and a half times higher today than it was in 1900. However, the largest proportion of fast growing metropoles is found among those between 750000 and one million, and the fastest growing class is that between one million and two million. The difference between the average growth rates for the group of metropoles of a given size and the number of high performers in that group derives from the large number of smaller metropolitan areas which are growing slowly.

The strategy based on encouraging the growth of smaller urban areas runs into the difficulty of smallness of impact. Thus ten metropolitan areas of 200000, each of which attracted ten times its share of migrants, would absorb together less than 3% of the national population growth. In fact all 101 SMSAs of less than 250000 in 1960 together account for only one tenth of metropolitan growth. Because of the limits and dangers of dispersion of efforts if too many centers are selected from growth, it would appear that such a strategy would have only marginal impact upon national urbanization patterns, although it would obviously have strong regional consequences. Based on the evidence of current rates of growth and consideration of the marginal contribution to population absorption, a policy of alternative centers would have to make use of larger centers, of the order of one million population, as well as of smaller centers. Whether such a policy would be desirable or enforceable is another matter.

In the current discussions of an alternative growth center policy, it is often assumed that these will be free-standing, isolated metropoles. But this is unlikely. While many of the 60 SMSAs which attracted migrants at twice the overall metropolitan rate in 1960–65 were independent, primarily in the South and West, ten were in the Atlantic megalopolis and substantial numbers in the other megalopoles. This may be understood in terms of the earlier discussion of the relation of income or productivity not only to urban size, but also to population potential as a measure of access to the national population. Smaller metropolitan areas within megalopolis draw many of the benefits of the agglomeration without many of the penalties of large size. In this respect it might be noted that in 1960 development covered only 12·2% of the land area in the core 104 counties of the Atlantic megalopolis, so that popular images of megalopolis as a teeming anthill are in error. It would appear that a policy of alternative centers would have to find a great many of these among the smaller metropoles of the megalopolitan constellation. From the point of view of the advantages and disadvantages of urban size, these may, in a way, have their cake and eat it too.

Some general comments on national urban growth policy

It is often commented that we have a great many urban growth policies hidden in the operational consequences of government programs such as highways and welfare, and in our laws relating to such matters as the treatment of depreciation and capital gains. Indeed it would appear that there is a great deal of explicit if piecemeal *regional* planning done by the legislative branch, whose members are territorial representatives and usually quite aware of the local consequences of the legislation and appropriations before them. But the early attempts we are now witnessing to formulate an explicit and coordinated *national* policy are doomed to triviality if they remain geometric statements searching for some vaguely intuited balance. Rather, the goals of a national urban policy must be the same as those of other national policies: economic growth, economic efficiency, distributional equity of consumption and democratic participation, private and public safety, ecological integrity, avoidance of cyclical instability, and so forth. It is likely that, in this field as in others, no simple unified policy can be formulated. Before one can propose useful and effective programs and operational guidelines, considerations of territorial policy as to city size, location of economic activity, interrelations among cities, urban and rural relations, and migratory movements must be placed in the context of the general national objectives. There is a range of topics with which these programs may deal: subsidies or taxes to alleviate local distress; the equation of private with public costs; subsidies to labor or capital to affect their movement or location; direct subsidies to mobility; locational licensing of industry; help in providing infrastructure; easing the cash-flow fiscal problems of growth and decline; helping to integrate the economy by improving information or transportation, and so forth. But specific programs can be developed and evaluated only in the broader framework of national purposes. A national growth policy cannot be a picture on a map. The map is only a two-dimensional projection of the many dimensions of the society that lives within the territory.

I would like to conclude with a plea that in the formulation of policy and programs there be not only realism as to how society actually works, but also realism as to how government works. Two instances will serve as illustrations. First, current suggestions that all government actions within a region be coordinated, and that all regional consequences of every action be taken into account, are naive and unworkable. They recognize neither the complex operational dynamics of the polity of agencies, nor the cost in time and resources of additional coordination and planning, nor the difficulty of prediction and the uncertainty that is involved. Of course, more planning and coordination would result in better and more effective public actions, but overly ambitious and unrealistic approaches will not achieve this and may discredit and impede potential advances. Second, there is a particular problem in territorial programs which is seldom recognized explicitly and which has led to the erosion of many programs in this country and in others. Much territorial policy is based on a principle of concentrating efforts and resources in some few areas, and consequently excluding most other areas. Political pressures, even in totalitarian countries, almost invariably oppose and undermine the resulting exclusion. In this country, recent experience with programs, such as Model Cities and growth centers, are witness to the power of this effect. It would be a pity if the emergent government leadership in a national growth policy ran aground for lack of understanding of the working of that government itself.

References

Burns, L. S., 1968, "The intra-urban income distribution", paper presented at the Annual Conference, British Section of the Regional Science Association, London, 1968.

Lansing, J. B., Mueller, Eva, 1967, *The Geographic Mobility of Labor* (Survey Research Center, Institute for Social Research, Ann Arbor, Michigan), pp.292-294.

Lowry, I. S., 1966, *Migration and Metropolitan Growth: Two Analytical Models* (Chandler Publishing Co., San Francisco).

Ornati, O. A., 1968, "Poverty in cities", in *Issues in Urban Economics,* Eds. H. Perloff, L. Wingo (Johns Hopkins Press, Baltimore).

A Policy-oriented Model of Regional Economic Growth

R.FUNCK
Universität Karlsruhe

1 Introduction

The post-Keynesian as well as the neoclassical theories of economic growth basically consist of macroeconomic dynamic models which, under partly differing assumptions, provide sets of conditions for an equilibrium growth of a national economy as a whole. Attempts toward sectoral disaggregation have been made by several authors, in different directions. Uzawa (1962, 1963), and others have introduced different production functions for the capital goods and the consumer goods industries in a two-sector model. Von Neumann (1937) and those following his ideas (e.g. Morishima, 1969) have developed multi-sector systems with explicit linear production functions, which may be regarded as microeconomic linear expansion models. Dynamic input–output models are formally related to von Neumann models. However, whereas these, and Uzawa-type models are equilibrium growth models, dynamic input–output systems may be regarded as projection models, that is as systems describing the structure of the economy for a sequence of periods during the process of economic growth.

In the theoretical literature on economic growth, very little attention has been devoted to the policy requirements guiding the actual economic development in industrialized countries. Growth theory, as it has been developed thus far, must be interpreted as a section of pure economic theory, and almost no bridging exists from here to economic growth policies.

Whereas sectoral disaggregation has been a major concern of economic growth theorists, few attempts have been made to construct regionally disaggregated growth models. The main body of regional economic theory, on the other hand, consists of static equilibrium statements, sets of tools for analyzing the regional relevance of economic activities, and spatial applications of linear or non-linear decision models. Little attention has been paid to the theoretical questions of economic growth, except with respect to dynamic versions of regional or interregional input–output systems. This statement outlines a rather curious situation, since regional economic policy in almost all practical cases is concerned with the achievement of a regional economic growth objective based on, or related to, a political value judgment.

It therefore seems appropriate that attempts be made to provide answers to the following questions.

(a) What are the possibilities to describe in model form the process of economic growth in a system of regions in an industrialized economy?

(b) What types of policy objectives or judgments are most significant in regional economic growth policy?

(c) What are the conditions of optimal economic growth of a certain region within a system of regions, subject to certain requirements regarding the growth objectives of the rest of the regions in the system?

In general what is needed to answer these questions is information on the formal structure of, and the variables included in, the regional welfare functions, the regional production functions, the conditions prevailing on product and factor markets, as well as information on the economic and policy variables relating the different regions in the national economic system to each other. In order to provide answers to question (a) above, that is to describe the process of economic growth in a system of regions, mainly dynamic interregional input–output systems are being used. A recent version, which in its final stage will allow projections of the production and demand variables indicated in the respective dotted areas in figure 1, is currently being prepared by a group of research teams for the Federal Republic of Germany. For this purpose, the German economy has been disaggregated into 79 regions and 14 sectors. The relationships between the variables, and their natural and economic determinants, for one region have been outlined as a flow chart in figure 1. The regions have been defined, and the system of equations is being formulated, in such a way as to allow the use of the model for the developing of strategies of regional economic policy on a national level (see Kirner, 1971).

Contributions to the discussion of question (b) on the significance of policy objectives with respect to regional economic growth have been made, among others, by Hansmeyer (1968), Funck (1968), and Siebert (1969), who extensively deals with goal relations in regional economic growth policies.

Among the few authors[1] who have dealt with theoretical aspects of regional economic growth, and thus contributed to a solution of problem (c), Siebert (1967) has presented the most comprehensive study. Along with more general methodological considerations, he presents a general dynamic system for an open region, and a specific two-region model concentrating on the changes in productive capacities, including

(1) The following brief review is not complete. For a more extensive bibliography see Siebert (1967).

interregional factor movements. The implications of the model are stated in a number of theorems. In their book on economic growth models, Tinbergen and Bos (1962) devote a short chapter to the problem of regional growth. They construct an input–output model for development planning, dealing with several regions and several sectors, and considering the transport sector explicitly. Mera (1968), in a very rigorously formulated model, extends the competitive general equilibrium for a static

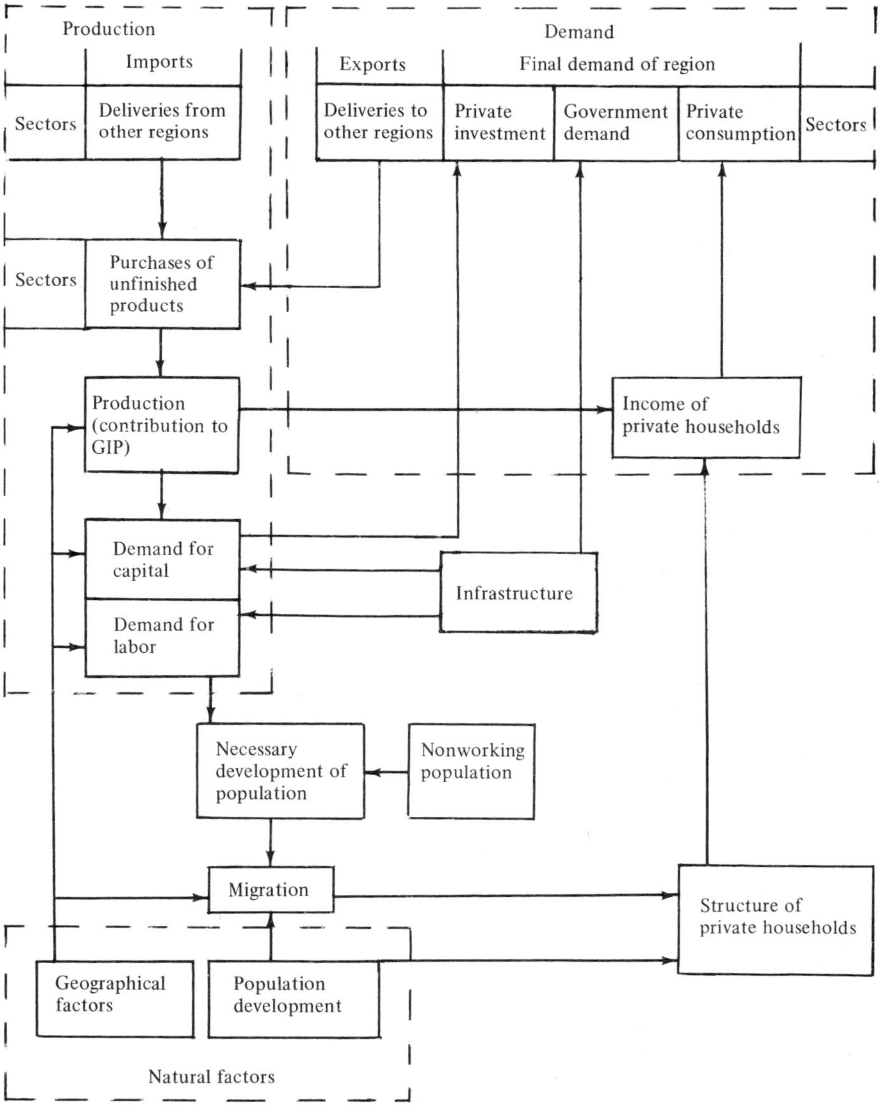

Figure 1. Interregional projection model for the Federal Republic of Germany. Variables and their relationships for one region (see Kirner, 1971, p.151).

system to the intertemporal framework. Furthermore, he presents a computational algorithm which makes it possible to solve the system through the use of a computer.

In the following sections of this paper a further attempt will be made to come closer to an answer to question (c).

2 The basic model

Let the notation $\dot{V}$ indicate, in the usual way, the change of any variable V over time $\mathrm{d}V/\mathrm{d}t$. A second possible interpretation would then be $\dot{V} = \Delta V$, where $\Delta t = 1$ in $\Delta V/\Delta t$ and represents a sufficiently short unit period of time to allow for the approximation $\Delta V/\Delta t = \mathrm{d}V/\mathrm{d}t$.

Assume that m goods other than transport services are being produced in z regions, and that transport services which are of one unified type are necessary only for interregional shipments. The following system of $[(m+3)z^2+4mz+9z]$ equations, determining the same number of internal variables (see appendix 2), may then describe the equilibrium growth of the system (for notation of variables, constants, and parameters, see appendix 1).

The regional welfare function,

$$\dot{W}^r = \mathrm{F}^r(\dot{Y}^r, \omega^r) \qquad r \in \{1, ...r, ..., s, ..., z\}, \quad \omega^r = \mathrm{aut}\forall r, \tag{1}$$

determining the period change[(2)] of regional welfare as a function of the change in regional income and of the intraregional income distribution, is really but a token welfare function. In order to avoid the complications of regional welfare functions based on individual preference patterns (see Funck, 1970), the income distribution has been introduced as an independent variable instead. Changes in the intraregional distribution of income, however, are considered as either negligible (ω^r = const) or manageable through actions of regional policy authorities (ω^r = aut). Changes in regional welfare other than results from policy action are, therefore, identical with changes in regional income,

$$\dot{Y}^r = \sum_s \sum_i [(\dot{x}_i^{rr} + \dot{x}_i^{rs})(p_i^r + \dot{p}_i^r) + \dot{x}_n^{rs}(p_n^r + \dot{p}_n^r)], \tag{2}$$

$$i \in \{1, ..., i, ..., m\};\ r, s \in \{1, ..., z\};\ r \neq s$$
$$p_i^r = \mathrm{const}\forall i, r, \quad p_n^r = \mathrm{const}\forall r.$$

Obviously the consistency of the regional balances of payments then requires that

$$\sum_r \sum_s \sum_i \dot{x}_i^{rs}(p_i^r + \dot{p}_i^r) + \sum_r \sum_s \dot{x}_n^{rs}(p_n^r + \dot{p}_n^r) = 0 \qquad r \neq s.$$

(2) The terms welfare function, demand function, etc. will be used for simplicity of expression, although the respective functions in the system determine the *change* in welfare, the *change* in demand etc.

The deliveries are determined through demand and supply functions. Of these the period changes in demand for finished goods, as a function of respective price and income changes, read

$$\dot{x}_i^{r\rho} = \mathrm{h}_i^{r\rho}(\dot{p}_i^r, \dot{Y}^\rho) \qquad \rho = r,s \in \{1,...,z\};\ i \in \{1,...,m\}. \tag{3.1}$$

The change in demand for transport services, however, depends not only on transport prices but also on the volume of shipments and the distances between the regions of origin and destination:

$$\dot{x}_n^{rs} = \mathrm{h}_n^{rs}(\dot{p}_n^r, \sum_i \dot{x}_i^{rs}, d^{rs}) \qquad r \neq s, \quad d^{rs} = \mathrm{const} \forall rs. \tag{3.2}$$

The supply of goods and transport services is included in market functions, determining the changes of the respective prices as functions of the respective domestic market conditions, that is the changes in domestic production and total demand:

$$\dot{p}_i^r = \mathrm{g}_i^r(\dot{X}_i^r - \sum_\rho \dot{x}_i^{r\rho}) \qquad \rho = r,s \in \{1,...,z\};\ i \in \{1,...,m\}, \tag{4.1}$$

$$\dot{p}_n^r = \mathrm{g}_n^r(\dot{X}_n^r - \sum_s \dot{x}_n^{rs}) \qquad r \neq s. \tag{4.2}$$

Production functions describe the technological relations between changes in output of all goods and services, and the respective inputs of labor and capital,

$$\dot{X}_j^r = \mathrm{f}_j^r(\dot{L}_j^r, \dot{K}_j^r, \dot{\tau}_j^r) \qquad r \in \{1,...,z\};\ j \in \{1,...,m,n\}, \quad \dot{\tau}_j^r = \mathrm{aut} \forall r,j, \tag{5}$$

with technological change as an exogenous variable. Equations (6.1) to (6.5) then determine the situation in the labor market, and equations (7.1) to (7.5) determine that in the capital market.

The sectoral changes in demand for labor inputs are assumed to be a function of profit developments which in equation (6.1) are implicitly described through prices, wages, and costs of capital use:

$$\dot{L}_j^r = \mathrm{l}_j^r(\dot{p}_j^r, \dot{w}^r, \dot{q}^r) \qquad r \in \{1,...,z\};\ j \in \{1,...,m,n\}. \tag{6.1}$$

The total supply of labor in a region stems from domestic sources and from net migration of labor to or from this region, so that

$$\dot{L}^r = \dot{L}^{rr} + \sum_s \dot{L}^{sr} \qquad r \neq s, \tag{6.2}$$

with $\sum_s \sum_r \dot{L}^{sr} = 0$ for consistency.

It may be assumed that the change of the labor supply from domestic sources can be determined as the product of the volume of the labor force at the beginning of the period, measured in units of labor input, and an autonomous growth rate,

$$\dot{L}^{rr} = \lambda^r L^r \qquad \lambda^r = \mathrm{aut} \forall r \in \{1,...,z\}, \quad L^r = \mathrm{const} \forall r \in \{1,...,z\}. \tag{6.3}$$

The changes in labor migration may be regarded as a function of relative wage developments in the regions of in- and out-migration [3]

$$\dot{L}^{sr} = 1_*^{sr}\left(\frac{\dot{w}^r}{\dot{w}^s}\right) \qquad r \neq s \,. \tag{6.4}$$

The period changes of regional wage rates are assumed to be depending on the situation on the domestic labor market,

$$\dot{w}^r = \Phi^r(\dot{L}^{rr} - \sum_j \dot{L}_j^r) \,. \tag{6.5}$$

Similar to equation (6.1), equation (7.1) explains the sectoral changes in demand for capital inputs as an implicit function of profits,

$$\dot{K}_j^r = \mathrm{k}_j^r(\dot{p}_j^r, \dot{w}^r, \dot{q}^r) \qquad r \in \{1, ..., z\};\ j \in \{1, ..., m, n\} \,. \tag{7.1}$$

The changes in total regional capital supply may result from domestic capital creation or from net interregional capital movements,

$$\dot{K}^r = \dot{K}^{rr} + \sum_s \dot{K}^{sr} \qquad r \neq s \,, \tag{7.2}$$

with $\sum_s \sum_r \dot{K}^{sr} = 0$ as a consistency condition.

Let the changes in domestic capital supply be determined by the regional saving behavior

$$\dot{K}^{rr} = \sigma^r \dot{Y}^r \qquad \sigma^r = \mathrm{aut} \forall r \in \{1, ..., z\} \,, \tag{7.3}$$

and let the changes in capital flows between regions reflect the relative variations of interest rates

$$\dot{K}^{sr} = \mathrm{k}_*^{sr}\left(\frac{\dot{q}^r}{\dot{q}^s}\right) \qquad r \neq s \,. \tag{7.4}$$

The assumption that the changes in regional interest rates depend on the developments of the domestic capital market,

$$\dot{q}^r = \psi^r(\dot{K}^{rr} - \sum_j \dot{K}_j^r) \,, \tag{7.5}$$

then completes the system.

The theoretical implications and basic properties of the model (explicit formulation of all functions, equilibrium solution, examination of existence and stability) will be subject to further examination elsewhere (Brand and Funck, to be published). The following analysis will instead be devoted to the question of how the model can be used in the preparation of decision making in the context of regional growth policy.

3 Applications in regional growth planning

The planning goal for a particular region may be formulated by introducing a political constraint into the basic model, that is by relating one or

(3) The function may include an autonomous element designed to reflect the non-wage related determinants.

several out of the number of economically relevant variables for the region to the same variables for a reference region (see Funck, 1970). Let the economy as a whole be chosen as a reference region, and let the planning goal for a certain region r in the system of regions $\{1, ..., z\}$ be the achievement of a period growth in regional income which is $(\gamma^r \times 100)$ percent of the average income growth in the economy. From the equation

$$\dot{Y}^r = \gamma^r \frac{\dot{Y}^1 + ... + \dot{Y}^r + ... + \dot{Y}^z}{z} \tag{8}$$

this goal can be formulated as a political constraint, with

$$\frac{\gamma^1 + ... + \gamma^r + ... + \gamma^z}{z} = 1$$

as a consistency condition, and γ^r = aut for at least one and not more than $(z-1)$ regions r.

A regional planning problem arises only if the value of $\dot{Y}^r$, as determined by expression (8) from the result of an autonomous choice of γ^r by the regional planning authorities, differs from the value of $\dot{Y}^r$ as determined by the system of equations (1) to (7.5). More specifically that is: if the required income growth falls short of the actual income growth (4). In this case the question arises as to which policy measures can be taken to increase the actual value of $\dot{Y}^r$.

In the basic model there are four kinds of parameters available to be used as levers for possible actions:

1 the income distribution ω^r;
2 the rates of technological change in the different sectors $\dot{\tau}_j^r$;
3 the growth rate of the labor force λ^r; and
4 the marginal quota of saving out of the regional income σ^r.

In order to discuss the impact and implications of autonomous changes in these parameters, and at the same time supply a larger choice of operational parameters, a selected number of functions may be formulated explicitly.

Thus, in equation (3.1) let the demand changes be in negative proportion to price changes in the region of origin, and in positive relation to changes of the income in the region of destination of the delivery, as indicated by the equation

$$\dot{x}_i^{r\rho} = \alpha_i^{r\rho} \dot{p}_i^r + \mu_i^{r\rho} \dot{Y}^\rho \qquad 0 > \alpha_i^{r\rho}, \; \mu_i^{r\rho} > 0, \tag{3.1.1}$$

where,

5 $\alpha_i^{r\rho}$ is the coefficient of reaction of demand in region ρ for good i, produced in region r, to changes in price;
6 $\mu_i^{r\rho}$ is region ρ's marginal propensity to spend on product i of region r.

(4) It might be assumed that in case of a growth surplus the regional authorities would adjust their planning goal to the actual situation by assigning the adequate value to the parameter γ^r.

Similarly the changes in demand for transport services, given in equation (3.2), may be in negative proportion to changes in transport prices, and in positive proportion to changes in total deliveries between two regions as well as their (constant) distance. This assumption gives us the equation

$$\dot{x}_n^{rs} = \alpha_n^{rs}\dot{p}_n^r + {}^r\nu^{rs} d^{rs} \sum_i \dot{x}_i^{rs} \qquad 0 > \alpha_n^{rs}\ ,\ {}^r\nu^{rs} > 0 \tag{3.2.1}$$

where

7 α_n^{rs} is the coefficient of reaction of demand for transport services between regions r and s, to changes in the price of this service;

8 ${}^r\nu^{rs}$ is the coefficient of reaction of the demand for transport services between regions r and s, produced by the transport sectors in region r, to changes in deliveries from region r to region s.

Furthermore, let the price functions (4.1) and (4.2) read as follows:

$$\dot{p}_i^r = \dot{\pi}_i^r - \frac{1}{\beta_i^r}(\dot{X}_i^r - \sum_\rho \dot{x}_i^{r\rho}) \qquad \dot{\pi}_i^r = \text{aut}\ ,\ \beta_i^r > 0\ , \tag{4.1.1}$$

and

$$\dot{p}_n^r = \dot{\pi}_n^r - \frac{1}{\beta_n^r}(\dot{X}_n^r - \sum_s \dot{x}_n^{rs}) \qquad \dot{\pi}_n^r = \text{aut},\ \beta_n^r > 0 \tag{4.2.1}$$

where

9 $\dot{\pi}_i^r$ is an autonomously determined variable, specific to good i in region r;

10 $\dot{\pi}_n^r$ is an autonomous variable, specific to the transport sector in region r,

11 $1/\beta_i^r$ is the coefficient of price reaction to changes in market situation, referring to good i in region r.

12 $1/\beta_n^r$ is the coefficient of price reaction to changes in situation on the transport market in region r;

Using the expressions (4.1.1) and (4.2.1), one can reformulate equations (3.1.1) and (3.2.1), which gives us the expressions

$$\dot{x}_i^{r\rho} = \alpha_i^{r\rho}\dot{\pi}_i^r - \frac{\alpha_i^{r\rho}}{\beta_i^r}(\dot{X}_i^r - \sum_\rho \dot{x}_i^{r\rho}) + \mu_i^{r\rho}\dot{Y}^\rho \quad ^{(5)}\ , \tag{3.1.2}$$

and

$$\dot{x}_n^{rs} = \alpha_n^{rs}\dot{\pi}_n^r - \frac{\alpha_n^{rs}}{\beta_n^r}(\dot{X}_n^r - \sum_s \dot{x}_n^{rs}) + {}^r\nu^{rs} d^{rs} \sum_i \dot{x}_i^{rs}\ . \tag{3.2.2}$$

Finally let equation (7.4), which determines the interregional capital flows, take the explicit form

$$\dot{K}^{sr} = \kappa^{sr} + \xi^{sr}\frac{\dot{q}^r}{\dot{q}^s} \qquad \dot{\kappa}^{sr} = \text{aut}\ ;\ \xi^{sr} > 0\ , \tag{7.4.1}$$

(5) If the deliveries from region r to one specific region, say region z, are being considered, equation (3.1.2) after several rearrangements takes the following form:

$$\dot{x}_i^{rz} = \frac{1}{(1/\alpha_i^{rz}) - (1/\beta_i^r)}\dot{\pi}_i^r - \frac{1}{(\beta_i^r/\alpha_i^{rz}) - 1}\left(\dot{X}_i^r - \sum_{\rho=1}^{z-1} \dot{x}_i^{r\rho}\right) + \frac{\mu^{rz}}{1 - (\alpha_i^{rz}/\beta_i^r)}\dot{Y}^z\ .$$

where
13 $\dot{\kappa}^{sr}$ is the autonomous capital flows between regions s and r;
14 ξ^{sr} is the coefficient of reaction of induced capital flows between regions s and r to changes in relative interest rates.

In this equation the net change of the interest rate, as given by equation (7.5), may read

$$\dot{q}^r = \dot{\chi}^r - \frac{1}{\zeta^r}(\dot{K}^{rr} - \sum_j \dot{K}_j^r) \qquad \dot{\chi}^r = \text{aut}\ ,\ \zeta^r > 0\ , \tag{7.5.1}$$

with
15 $\dot{\chi}^r$ the autonomous change of interest rate in region r;
16 $1/\zeta^r$ the coefficient of reaction of interest rate to changes in the domestic capital market of region r.

The assumption that the policy-oriented model as well as the basic model includes a number of constant parameters, does not of course imply that no variables exist which determine the period values of the parameters. It means that the parameters are to be regarded as autonomous variables whose determination and interrelationships to other parameters are not considered within the model. This in principle makes the parameters usable for autonomous actions of economic policy. The following two questions are now considered with reference to the 16 types of parameters developed above: is the assumption realistic and what are the implications of such policy actions with respect to other parameters, as well as their impacts on the variables in the system?

(1) An autonomous change of the regional interpersonal income distribution ω^r would have direct effects on regional welfare only, as equation (1) shows. However, indirect influences on regional income may result if the distributional change sets in motion one or several determinants of $\dot{Y}^r$. Let us assume for instance that variations in distribution affect the saving (and consumption) behavior of the regional population[6] by changing the marginal propensity to save σ^r, which is to be regarded as the weighted regional average of the various saving ratios prevailing in different income brackets.

An increase in the marginal saving ratio effectuates a higher domestic capital supply [equation (7.3)] and will lead to an increased demand for capital if the interest rate is being depressed in the course of the adjustment process [equation (7.1)]. Whether, in the new equilibrium situation, the interest rate will have risen, fallen, or remained constant [equation (7.5)] depends on the values of the partial coefficients of

[6] The question, whether this assumption reflects reality, and if so in which direction the influence goes has been extensively discussed in the literature on consumer behavior, especially referring to Duesenberry's (1949) arguments. In a given situation, the relationship between ω^r and σ^r for a particular region should be determined through empirical study.

reaction $\partial \dot{K}_j^r / \partial \dot{q}^r$ in the explicit form[7] of equation (7.1), relative to the value of σ^r. It should be borne in mind, however, that a positive net change of the interest rate, $\dot{q}^r > 0$, if not desirable because of its effects on the regional policy goal, can be prevented by an adequate reduction of the autonomous element in the interest function $\dot{\chi}^r$.

According to equation (5), as a result of these developments total production of goods and transport services will rise but, as prices tend to fall—or as an exogenous tendency for price increases, which may prevail in various markets [$\dot{\pi}_i^r, \dot{\pi}_n^r > 0$ in equations (4.1.1) and (4.2.1)], will be at least partly offset by the reactions of these markets to the increased production—domestic and out-of-region demand [equations (3.1.2) and (3.2.2)] will be able to absorb this additional supply. Regional income will, therefore, be affected positively. These results are not affected by the fact that, as σ^r rises, the marginal propensity to consume out of the regional income, $1-\sigma^r$, which is not explicitly included in the system, is reduced by definition. The system contains a built-in equilibrator based on the assumption that the total marginal propensity to spend out of the income of region r, that is $\sum_\rho \mu^{r\rho}$ according to definition 6, is autonomously determined in its elements and is independent of σ^r. This means that as marginal consumption declines with a rise in marginal saving, the equilibrium is reestablished through a parallel rise in marginal spending for nonconsumptive purposes.

The question remaining to be answered is by what actions of the regional authority can the intraregional income distribution be appropriately influenced. In most cases the easiest way of doing this would be to change regional, that is state or local, tax rates in the required direction. Assuming that sales taxes are being increased in order to reduce consumer spending relative to total regional spending, the additional tax revenues might then be used in such a way as to provide direct stimuli on saving[8].

(2) An improvement in the technology used in one or several sectors of the region, $\dot{\tau}_j^r > 0$, will directly increase the regional income level, assuming that the additional supply of goods, which is made possible through technological progress, is met by an increase in demand [equations (5), (3.1.1), (3.2.1), (2)]. Usually, as the rates of technological change differ in the various sectors of the region (see Funck, 1964), the adjustment of demand will be eased by price variations relative to the average development of the regional price level. The extent of these price movements, and their influence on sectoral demand according to equations

(7) Not included in this paper.

(8) In West Germany, for instance, premium payments in the range of 20 to 35 percent of the annual savings, up to a certain maximum figure, are being used on a national scale to stimulate saving of low- and medium-income households.

(4.1.1) and (3.1.1)[9], will depend on the volume of the change of output $\dot{X}_i^r$ initiated by the change in technology, and on the respective values of the reaction coefficients $1/\beta_i^r$ and $\alpha_i^{r\rho}$. It may, however, be rather difficult for a regional development authority to effectuate technological changes, especially on a short term basis. In order to make available to the region's producers organizational methods or production techniques already available elsewhere, the regional capital supply would have to be expanded either by increasing domestic saving (see sections 1 and 4) or by shifting the curve of net capital inflows upward (see sections 13 ff). Long term effects on the regional level of technology would be made possible through increased public or private spending on research, development, and education, with private spending possibly being open for instance to tax incentives given by the regional planning authority.

(3) Assuming that the natural rate of growth of the regional population is a demographic constant, not very much can be done to influence the growth rate of the domestic labor force λ^r, especially in countries like the Federal Republic of Germany, where most of the nondemographic determinants of this rate are subject to law or business-union agreement on the supraregional level. One possibility, however, might be to increase the amount of female labor, especially on a part-time basis, not only through the supply of the necessary information but also through encouraging complementary social activities like nursery schools, kindergartens, etc. These latter activities again raise the question of the availability of the necessary capital. Since, however, to a certain degree an increasing labor supply would stimulate substitution of capital through labor—assuming that the regional production functions (5) are nonlimitational—the financing of such projects might not have to rely exclusively on additional saving or capital inflows into the region. At any rate a direct, though perhaps only slight, effect on the level of regional income may be expected [equations (6.3), (6.5), (7.1), (5)].

(4) The marginal propensity to save out of the regional income σ^r has already been dealt with in its relationship to the regional income distribution (see section 1). In general it is possible to pursue the goal of increasing σ^r without relating to the question of income distribution. However, since the marginal saving ratio is basically a behavioral constant, there are not many ways available to change the value of this constant; except by changing the structure of the variable governing the interpersonal average of σ^r, that is the income distribution, or by providing incentives in order to change the personal saving behavior. One such possibility has been mentioned in section 1, note 8.

[9] For the transport sector, see equations (4.2.1) and (3.2.1).

(5) The reaction coefficient $\alpha_i^{r\rho}$ is closely related to the direct price elasticity of demand in region ρ for good i, produced in region r[(10)]. This coefficient may be regarded as a behavioral constant which is not accessible to actions of the regional policy authority.

(6) Out of the mz coefficients $\mu_i^{r\rho}$, denoting region ρ's marginal propensity to spend on product i produced in region r, only the μ_i^{rr} figures, the marginal propensities to spend domestically, are directly accessible to the policy actions of this region's planning authority. Since the imposing of quantitative barriers to imports from other regions is not in general a measure of regional economic policy, the exertion of moral persuasion through a 'buy domestic' campaign will probably be the easiest way to increase domestic spending relative to total regional spending in the short run. It should, however, be noted that, in regional policy as in similar situations in international economic policy, artificial efforts to reduce imports from other regions (countries) will eventually create retroactive efforts on the part of the regions (countries) discriminated against, and thus lead to a cumulative contraction of interregional (international) trade. Consequently, a policy directed toward qualitative improvements of domestically supplied commodities and services may well be the most effective medium and long run policy to increase intraregional spending, and the spending of customers located in other regions on regional products at the same time. Measures aiming in this direction are closely related to those discussed in section 2 above. [See equations (3.1.1), (2).]

(7) The coefficient α_n^{rs}, which determines the reaction to price changes of the demand for transport services from region r to region s, must be regarded as a behavioral constant which cannot be changed by regional policy (see the analogous argument in section 5).

(8) The coefficient of reaction of the demand for those transport services between regions r and s, which are produced by the transport sector in region r, to a change in total deliveries between these two regions, ${}^r\nu^{rs}$, has a certain similarity to the parameter $\mu_i^{r\rho}$, region ρ's marginal propensity to spend in region r on good i (see section 6). Except by means of a policy directed towards an improvement in the quality of transportation, it may be impossible to influence the value of this parameter.

(9) Autonomous changes of the price of good i in region r, $\dot{\pi}_i^r$, will, as a rule[(11)], directly affect the respective demand. Since [in equation (3.1.2)]

(10) Let $\eta_i^{r\rho}$ denote this elasticity. Then

$$\eta_i^{r\rho} = \alpha_i^{r\rho} \frac{p_i^r}{x_i^{r\rho}} ,$$

where $x_i^{r\rho}$ is the deliveries of i, produced in r, to region ρ in the previous period when p_i^r was valid.

(11) It has been assumed [see equation (3.1.1)] that in the model this is always so: the case $\alpha_i^{r\rho} = 0$ has been excluded.

$\alpha_i^{r\rho}$ is always negative, autonomous price reductions will induce an increase in demand, and thereby [see equation (2)] a positive change in the respective deliveries which constitute the real regional income. The effect on regional income in monetary terms will then depend on the relation between price and quantity effects, and that means on the actual value of the reaction coefficient $\alpha_i^{r\rho}$.

In principle, regional authorities have at their disposal a variety of possibilities to influence prices, or at least the production costs of goods produced in the region as one determinant of prices. This is most obvious where the prices of products of such companies are concerned as are owned by the regional government (12). Utility producing companies probably represent the best known example. Utility prices must be considered as an especially efficient lever for autonomous price changes, since they represent cost items in virtually all branches of regional production. A second possibility is the reduction of regional indirect taxes, that is sales taxes or certain property taxes, etc., depending on the actual tax system (13). In order to make sure that tax or price reductions of this kind are going to be reflected in price effects in the private business sectors of the region, the planning authority might require such price reactions as a precondition of yielding the cost reduction. In any case, however, the planning authority would have to consider the combined effects of autonomous price reductions on regional demand, and of decrease in tax revenues or in the surplus of public enterprises on the financing of regional development projects.

(10) Autonomous reductions in region r's transport prices, $\dot{\pi}_n^r < 0$, may be brought about in the same way as price changes of goods other than transport services (see section 9). This includes the possibility of direct changes in transport prices, if the haulage company is owned by the regional government. In many cases in reality this applies to urban transportation systems; intraregional transportation is, however, not a part of the model [see equation (3.2.2)].

(11) and (12) The coefficients $1/\beta_i^r$ and $1/\beta_n^r$, denoting the price reactions to changes in the demand–supply relationships in the respective markets, are related to price elasticities of supply (14). Thus these coefficients must be regarded as constants which depend largely on the technological conditions of production in the particular sector, and on the absolute and relative values of factor prices in the region. They can, therefore, only be

(12) Throughout this paper, the assumption is made that regions have been defined in such a way that the regional government or the regional planning or regional policy authority represents the lowest territorial level of government activity.

(13) According to the national accounting definitions, if indirect taxes are included as cost items in the calculating of market prices, the term Y^r [equation (2)] would have to be redefined as: change in net regional product at market prices.

(14) In equation (4.1.1): $\beta_i^r = \dot{X}_i^r/\dot{p}_i^r$ for $\dot{\pi}_i^r = \sum_\rho \dot{x}_i^{r\rho} = 0$.

influenced through changes in technology (see section 2) or autonomous changes in factor prices (see section 15). It is unlikely that indirect effects like these could be adequately controlled by the regional planning authority.

(13) An additional autonomous net inflow of capital into region r, $\dot{\kappa}^{sr} > 0$, is probably the most important instrument of regional growth and development policy. As far as funds from supraregional government sources are concerned, that is development aid which may be available on the state, federal, or even supranational[(15)] level, the soliciting of such funds may be regarded as one of the major functions of the regional planning authority. Usually the preparation of a consistent regional development plan will be a necessary condition for success of these efforts.

Three types of effects can be attributed to an autonomous inflow of supraregional government capital: (a) The short-run *spending effect* which directly increases demand for certain goods produced in region r or elsewhere. (b) The *capacity effect* which is of longer duration, especially if the capital is used for an expansion of the infrastructure supply of the region; in this case the capacity effect applies to a quantitative or qualitative increase in the region's possibilities to offer transportation, educational, health, or other public services. (c) The *attractiveness effect* which is a result of the capacity effect; an improved and more diversified infrastructure system increases the region's attraction to private capital inflows and labor immigration. In cases where the capacity effect is concentrated on pollution intensive industries, the attractiveness effect may be negative.

Autonomous capital inflows, however, need not necessarily consist of government funds. Private capital may find it profitable to move into a certain region for reasons other than interest rate differentials [equation (7.5.1)]. Whereas some of these reasons—for instance climatic conditions attractive to scarce highly skilled labor—are beyond the control of planning authorities, others are instrumental. Among these are the attractiveness effects of a high level of infrastructure, which has just been mentioned, the providing of government owned land at prices below the market level, and the granting of tax and cost reductions in the long run or for an initial period (see sections 9, 10).

(14), (15), and (16) The coefficient of reaction of capital flows, from region s to region r, to changes in the relative level of interest rates, ξ^{sr}, must be regarded as a noninstrumental behavioral constant. The volume of induced capital inflows into region r then depends on the development of the domestic interest rate as compared with the interest level in other regions. The variable $\dot{q}^{r}$, and thus the induced capital flows, can be influenced by the regional economic policy authority basically in two ways. Autonomous changes of the interest rate in region r, denoted by

(15) For example, World bank loans.

the symbol $\dot{\chi}^r$ [equation (7.5.1)] may be effectuated by the pursuing of a direct interest policy through savings banks or other financial institutions owned by the regional government. Since $1/\zeta^r$, the coefficient of reaction of the interest rate to developments in the regional capital market, has to be regarded as a behavioral constant, the second way of maneuvering the interest rate would be to influence the domestic capital supply by bringing about autonomous changes in the marginal saving ratio σ^r (see sections 1 and 4). All actions affecting the interest rate in the region are, however, secondary to monetary policy measures which may be taken to control total demand on the national level. Anyway, the main objective of a regional interest policy may be directed towards an increase in demand for capital [equation (7.1)] in order to achieve effects on regional employment and productivity, rather than towards an increase of capital inflows. These effects may be pursued by other measures (see section 13) more easily, and without undesired side effects to the level of achievement of other goals of regional economic policy.

References

Brand, D., Funck, R., 1972, *Equilibrium Growth in a System of Regions* (forthcoming).

Duesenberry, J. S., 1949, *Income, Saving, and the Theory of Consumer Behavior* (Harvard University Press, Cambridge, Mass.).

Funck, R., 1964, "Möglichkeiten einer verteilungsaktiven Lohnpolitik", in *Gestaltungsprobleme der Weltwirtschaft, Festschrift für Andreas Predöhl* (Jahrbuch für Sozialwissenschaft, **14**, No.3) (Vandenhoeck & Ruprecht, Göttingen).

Funck, R., 1968, "Instrumente der Regionalpolitik", in *Beiträge zur Regionalpolitik, Schriften des Vereins für Socialpolitik,* N. S. 41 (Duncker und Humblot, Berlin).

Funck, R., 1970, "Welfare solutions and regional policy decisions", *Papers Regional Science Association,* **24** (Copenhagen Conference, 1969).

Hansmeyer, K. H., 1968, "Ziele und Träger regionaler Wirtschaftspolitik", in *Beiträge zur Regionalpolitik, Schriften des Vereins für Socialpolitik,* N. S. 41 (Duncker und Humblot, Berlin).

Kirner, W., 1971, "Ein interregionales Gesamtmodell für die BRD Konzept eines Forschungsprojekts", in *Vierteljahrshefte zur Wirtschaftsforschung,* H. 2, 148-156.

Mera, K., 1968, "A multi-region multi-sector model of equilibrium growth", *Papers Regional Science Association,* **21** (Cambridge, Mass. Conference, 1967).

Morishima, M., 1969, *Theory of Economic Growth* (Clarendon Press, Oxford).

von Neumann, J., 1937, "Über ein ökonomisches Gleichungssystem und eine Verallgemeinerung des Brouwerschen Fixpunktsatzes", in *Ergebnisse eines mathematischen Kolloquiums* (Ed. K. Menger, Wien). English translation, 1945-46, "A model of general economic equilibrium", *Review of Economic Studies,* **13**, 1-9.

Siebert, H., 1967, *Zur Theorie des Regionalen Wirtschaftswachstums*, J. C. B. Mohr (Paul Siebeck, Tübingen) (2nd ed. under the title *Regionales Wirtschaftswachstum und Interregionale Mobilität*, 1970). English translation, 1969, *Regional Economic Growth: Theory and Policy* (International Textbook Co., Scranton, Pennsylvania).

Tinbergen, J., Bos, H. C., 1962, *Mathematical Models of Economic Growth* (McGraw-Hill, New York).

Uzawa, H., 1962, 1963, "On a two-sector model of economic growth", *Review of Economic Studies,* **29**, 40-47; **30**, 105-118.

APPENDIX

1 Notations

Symbol	Meaning
Variables	
$\dot{W}^r$	period change of welfare in region r
$\dot{Y}^r, \dot{Y}^s, \dot{Y}^\rho$	period change of income in region r, s, or ρ $(= r, s)$ respectively
$\dot{x}_i^{rr}, \dot{x}_i^{rs}, \dot{x}_i^{r\rho}$	period change in volume of deliveries of finished product i, produced in region r, to customers in region r, s, or ρ $(= r, s)$ respectively
$\dot{x}_n^{rs}$	period change in ton-mile volume of transport service n from region r to region s
$\dot{p}_i^r$	period change in unit price of good i in region r
$\dot{p}_n^r$	period change in unit (ton-mile) price of transport service n originating in region r
$\dot{X}_i^r$	period change in total production of good i in region r
$\dot{X}_n^r$	period change in total production of transport service n originating in region r
$\dot{X}_j^r$	$\dot{X}_i^r$ and $\dot{X}_n^r$
$\dot{L}_i^r, \dot{L}_j^r$	period change in labor input in production of good i in region r, or of good or transport service j in region r, respectively
$\dot{K}_i^r, \dot{K}_j^r$	period change in capital goods' input in production of good i in region r, or of good or transport service j in region r, respectively
$\dot{L}^r$	period change in total supply of labor in region r
$\dot{L}^{rr}$	period change in domestic labor supply in region r
$\dot{L}^{sr}$	period change in net labor migration from region s to region r
$\dot{w}^r, \dot{w}^s$	period change in wages per unit of labor input in regions r or s, respectively
$\dot{q}^r, \dot{q}^s$	period change in interest per unit of capital input in regions r or s, respectively
$\dot{K}^r$	period change in total supply of capital inputs in region r
$\dot{K}^{rr}$	period change in domestic capital supply in region r
$\dot{K}^{sr}$	period change in net capital flows from region s to region r
Constants	
p_i^r	price of unit of good i in region r at beginning of period
p_n^r	price of unit (ton-mile) of transport service n originating in region r at beginning of period
d^{rs}	distance between regions r and s
L^r	total labor force (in units of labor input) in region r at beginning of period

Parameters (autonomously determined variables)

ω^r	income distribution in region r
$\dot{\tau}_j^r$	period change of technology applied in production of good or transport service j in region r
λ^r	growth rate of total labor force in region r
σ^r	marginal propensity to save out of regional income in region r

2 Number of equations and variables

Expression	Number of equations	Variables		
		Indication	Number	Total number
(1)	z	$\dot{W}^r$	z	
		$\dot{Y}^r$	z	$2z$
(2)	z	$\dot{x}_i^{rr}$	mz	
		$\dot{x}_i^{rs}$	$mz(z-1)$	
		$\dot{p}_i^r$	mz	
		$\dot{x}_n^{rs}$	$z(z-1)$	
		$\dot{p}_n^r$	z	$(m+1)z^2+mz$
(3.1)	mz^2	–	0	0
(3.2)	$z(z-1)$	–	0	0
(4.1)	mz	$\dot{X}_i^r$	mz	mz
(4.2)	z	$\dot{X}_n^r$	z	z
(5)	$(m+1)z$	$\dot{L}_j^r$	$z(m+1)$	
		$\dot{K}_j^r$	$z(m+1)$	$2z(m+1)$
(6.1)	$(m+1)z$	$\dot{w}^r$	z	
		$\dot{q}^r$	z	$2z$
(6.2)	z	$\dot{L}^r$	z	
		$\dot{L}^{rr}$	z	
		$\dot{L}^{sr}$	$z(z-1)$	$z(z+1)$
(6.3)	z	–	0	0
(6.4)	$z(z-1)$	–	0	0
(6.5)	z	–	0	0
(7.1)	$(m+1)z$	–	0	0
(7.2)	z	$\dot{K}^r$	z	
		$\dot{K}^{rr}$	z	
		$\dot{K}^{sr}$	$z(z-1)$	$z(z+1)$
(7.3)	z	–	0	0
(7.4)	$z(z-1)$	–	0	0
(7.5)	z	–	0	0
	$(m+3)z^2+4mz+9z$			$(m+3)z^2+4mz+9z$

Sensitivity Analysis of the Industrial Demand for Water Resources†

J.De ROOY
Lehigh University

Introduction

Two issues faced by regional planners in the design and administration of pollution abatement programs are the impact of regulation on the pattern and level of water use, and the economic efficiency of resulting redistributions of supplies among various sectors. This paper proposes the application of demand analysis to the first of these issues, and provides new evidence on the behavior of firms using water as a productive service —in highly industrialized areas manufacturing may account for more than 80% of the total withdrawal. While the present study is concerned only with manufacturing, the approach can be used for other sectors as well.

Agencies responsible for pollution control generally seek to affect quality by restricting the discharge of wastes into a stream or other water body. This may be accomplished in several ways; by a permit system which restricts withdrawals by individual users; effluent charges which vary with the volume and type of waste discharged; absolute restrictions on effluent with undesirable concentrations (such as phenols); or tax incentives for the acquisition of waste treatment facilities. Whatever the system, satisfying water quality standards represents a cost to the firm. Demand functions provide information on changes in total withdrawals which would be made once such a cost is incurred and, in addition, on changes in patterns of use within the plant. This is important in ascertaining shifts in usage among sectors, and in judging how successfully a program achieves the best utilization of a stream's assimilative capacity. Of course, it is also of importance to know how the impact of a program may be modified by changes in total production and/or the technology of water use. These can also be determined from a properly specified set of demand functions.

† Initial research and field work for this study was provided by a grant from the US Department of the Interior to the Water Resources Research Institute at Rutgers University for OWRR Project No. A-010-NJ. Computational work and final research was made possible by the Office of Research and the Center for Business Economics and Urban Studies at Lehigh University.

With respect to the second issue mentioned above, demand functions of different users provide a means for measuring the extent to which private costs incurred in one sector are offset by gains enjoyed by beneficiaries of improved water quality in other sectors, thereby facilitating selection of programs which are optimal ('efficient') in the sense of maximizing regional product. This use of demand functions is an extension of the analysis presented here, but will not be explicitly considered in this paper.

The following section will contain a brief description of the way water is used in manufacturing, after which, in the third section, a theory of derived demand for water will be developed following the neoclassical model. The next section will then contain an examination of the theory using data collected for this study from the chemical industry in northeastern New Jersey. Finally, the analysis of specific demand parameters will be extended to allow some implications to be drawn about the effect of technology in the design of pollution abatement programs.

Water use in industry

Costs are incurred at four stages of water handling: purchase from a public utility or procurement directly from a natural source, treatment prior to use, treatment prior to reuse, and waste treatment and discharge. The costs of pre-treatment depend both upon the function to be performed by the intake, and on external effects of previous users of the water source. Expenses relating to disposal are determined by the legal or extra-legal (social consciousness) requirements incumbent upon the user.

The four major categories of water use common in manufacturing are: (1) cooling, for controlling temperatures of machinery; (2) generation of steam power in boilers; (3) processing of final products; (4) sanitation, including plant maintenance and service of personnel.

Users of cooling water have wide tolerances for quality, aside from temperature, so that pre-treatment is minimal. Similarly discharges may require little or no treatment, although heat pollution of streams and lakes may impair their subsequent use as a water source. Input quality is clearly more important for processing water which either comes into contact with the final product (for example, in washing), or is an ingredient in it, making prior treatment necessary in most cases. Processing water used to convey impurities out of the plant may also require costly discharge treatment if serious external effects are to be minimized. Feed water of great purity is required for high pressure boilers, so that steam power water is normally, per unit, the most expensive intake used.

These first three functions relate directly to production. Sanitation water is used primarily by workers in the plant, so its volume may fluctuate more with employment than output. Its disposal is similar to that for household sewage: that is, through municipal sewage plants.

Since only a small percentage of industrial withdrawals are consumed in use, recycling of water is a viable means of in-plant conservation, and reused intake is the closest substitute for new withdrawals. Use of recycled intake for cooling water is becoming a frequent practice in manufacturing, due both to the large volume and low cost involved in the pre-treatment of water for this function.

Water sellers primarily serve households, since the high quality and cost of their product, as well as limited capacities, make them an uneconomical supply source for large plants, except for sanitation and steam power needs. Thus, 90% of all industrial withdrawals are self-supplied directly from ground or surface sources (US Department of Commerce, 1966), which presents a problem in measurement of both volume and cost of water used.

A theory of derived demand for water resources

Let the production function for output X of the tth firm be

$$X_t = \Phi_{xt}(g_1, ..., g_w) , \tag{1}$$

where g_i ($i = 1, ..., w$) are quantities of inputs, including water. Assume that the marginal products of all factors are non-negative, and that the firm is a competitive buyer in the factor markets where it can purchase unlimited quantities at given prices $p_1, ..., p_w$. The objective of the entrepreneur is to minimize costs for any given level of output X_t. It has been shown (Baxter and Rees, 1968; Samuelson, 1947) that the optimal quantity of any input under these conditions can be represented by the function

$$g_{wt} = \theta(p_1, ..., p_w, X_t) , \tag{2}$$

that is, the desired quantity of an input depends upon factor prices and output. Equation (2) is the neoclassical derived demand model.

The properties of this function are easily derived (for example, see De Rooy, 1969) and are well known. They may be summarized by the following inequalities,

$$\frac{\partial g_{wt}}{\partial X_t} > 0 , \quad (3') \qquad \frac{\partial g_{wt}}{\partial p_w} < 0 , \quad (3'') \qquad \frac{\partial g_{wt}}{\partial p_j} > 0 , \quad (3''')$$

where $w \neq j$.

Condition (3′) indicates that the output elasticity of demand for the wth factor (that is, water) will be positive,

$$\frac{\partial g_{wt}}{\partial X_t}\frac{X_t}{g_{wt}} = \frac{\partial \lg g_{wt}}{\partial \lg X_t} > 0 . \tag{4'}$$

Condition (3″) shows that the price elasticity of demand will be negative,

$$\frac{\partial g_{wt}}{\partial p_{wt}}\frac{P_{wt}}{g_{wt}} = \frac{\partial \lg g_{wt}}{\partial \lg p_{wt}} < 0 . \tag{4''}$$

Finally, it is implied by condition (3‴) that the marginal rate of substitution of factor w for j, and so too the cross-elasticity of demand, will have a positive value,

$$\frac{\partial g_{wt}}{\partial p_{jt}}\frac{p_{jt}}{g_{wt}} = \frac{\partial \lg g_{wt}}{\partial \lg p_{jt}} > 0 . \tag{4‴}$$

Because the demand equation (2) is derived from the production function, its mathematical form will depend upon that of equation (1). It follows that if the latter is approximated by a function of the Cobb–Douglas type, which has been found applicable to a wide range of industries, then equation (2) will also be exponential (Baxter and Rees, 1968). When only the closest substitute is considered, *in lieu* of the entire class of possible substitutes, the general demand equation may be represented by

$$g_{wft} = F_{wft} X_t^{b_1} P_{wft}^{b_2} P_{Rft}^{b_3} , \tag{5}$$

where f (= 1, 2, 3) represents the three output-related usages (cooling, processing, and steam power), F_{wft} is the constant quantity demanded over the short-run (fixed plant), P_{wft} is the unit price of water withdrawals, and P_{Rft} is the unit price of the substitute. The parameters b_1, b_2, and b_3 are the elasticities given by equations (4′), (4″), and (4‴), respectively.

Demand for sanitation water is expressed as a function of total employment within the plant, rather than as output and prices,

$$g_{wst} = c_1 N_t , \tag{6}$$

where N_t is the number of workers. Since this intake is used exclusively by, and for, personnel the constant term is suppressed.

The three equations represented by (5) together with (6) cover all water uses, so that total demand by the individual plant is given by the identity,

$$g_{wt} \equiv \sum_f g_{wft} + g_{wst} , \tag{7}$$

which closes the model.

In general, the existence of a substitution effect in the demand for inputs would require measurement of interaction between factor price and output. Such interaction was not allowed for in this model for two reasons. Firstly, it is not probable that competitive producers would pass on changes in water costs to consumers since such changes are not likely to be uniform for all firms in an industry, even within the same region. Self-supplied water costs are unique to the location and productive requirements of the user. Rate structures for purchased water are similarly variable since public utilities, which are not competitive, typically serve limited markets such as a single municipality. As a result, geographical cost patterns tend to be constant over time[1]. Secondly, as a finely classified input, g_{wt} accounts for a small proportion of total costs of production. Consequently, even large changes in unit cost would not alter the price of output sufficiently to change demand if fully passed on by a producer enjoying a less than perfectly competitive market.

But these reasons do not diminish the importance of price as a determinant of demand for water. Price-elasticity depends on the rigidity of the production function, and the desire of the entrepreneur to minimize costs will induce input substitutions. Indeed, the greater the disaggregation of inputs the wider is the range of substitutes and the greater is the sensitivity to price changes (Stigler, 1957).

It should also be recognized that the relationship of demand to output and price depends upon the specific production function employed, as well as the quality of complimentary inputs. Since firms in a given industry and region may utilize dissimilar technologies (or production functions) at one point in time, the effect of these differences should be explicitly introduced. One method of doing this is to introduce a technological shift parameter, π_t, which assumes that differences in technology have a multiplicative effect on derived demand. A re-specification of equation (5) could thus be written,

$$g_{wft} = F_{wft} X_t^{b_1} P_{wft}^{b_2} P_{Rft}^{b_3} \pi_t \ . \tag{5'}$$

Alternatively, technology may be considered as affecting the individual elasticities b_i, in which case parameters should be estimated separately for different groups of firms. This re-specification may be written by introducing additional subscripts for the exponents in equation (5′). Both methods will be considered in subsequent sections.

Data and measurement

For the purpose of testing this model, data were collected from a sample of large chemical manufacturing firms in northeastern New Jersey, which is a part of the New York metropolitan area. The information obtained covered water use during the calendar year of 1965. A full report of the survey is given elsewhere (Granstrom *et al.*, 1969).

Conventionally analysis of industrial demand involves disaggregation by final product. Development of the model in the previous section proceeded on the assumption that greater variation exists in water quality and costs between uses, than between output categories so that disaggregation was on the basis of function. However some firms in the

[1] A similar observation has been made in the case of electricity, which is also self-supplied by larger industrial users as well as purchased from public utilities. Because of these constant differences there may be a high correlation between capacity output and unit price or cost. Firms using water-intensive techniques will locate in areas where this resource is relatively cheap (Fisher, 1962).

sample diverted such a small proportion of their withdrawals, or even none at all, to certain of the functions, that plant records did not always permit a breakdown of all four uses. Consequently sets of observations used to estimate each equation were distinct although not mutually exclusive.

Value added was used as an index of production for the three output-related demand equations since the model was designed to permit aggregation within multi-product firms and within industries having a heterogeneous product mix [2].

Factor price presented a more difficult measurement problem since the bulk of withdrawals were obtained outside the market. Hence unit cost was used as a proxy of the market price of self-supplied water. This cost is the sum of capital charges for the year and current costs (operation and maintenance), divided by intake, incurred at each stage of handling during a single use cycle: intake, prior treatment, and discharge. To circumvent differences in accounting practices of firms a uniform approximation of capital charges was made by dividing original life expectancy L into purchase cost K. The cost of purchased supplies C_u was considered analogous to the intake component of the total outlays for self-supplied water. Thus

$$P_{wft} = \frac{1}{g_{wft}} \left\{ \sum_h \sum_j \left[\frac{K_{hj}}{I_{y_{hj}}} \bigg/ \frac{i}{(1-v)L_{hj}} \right] + E_{hj} + C_u \right\} , \qquad (8)$$

where I_y is the value of the cost index, with 1965 base, in the year of acquisition of the hth piece of stock used in the jth ($j = 1, 2, 3$) stage of handling which has current cost E, and i is the rate of discount so that $v = (1+i)^{-1}$.

The average cost of reused water P_{Rft} was calculated by dividing the sum of relevant capital charges and current expenses (for example, for cooling towers) by the quantity of intake conserved by recycling [3].

Three variables were employed to measure the state of technology of plants. Two of these were the vintage of capital stock and capital intensity, which represented the quality and quantity of water-using equipment. The third was a simple categorization of final output, which served as a rough classification of production methods.

Because of the difficulty of constructing an index including all capital inputs, age of plant A_t was used to measure vintage. The labor–output ratio $(W/X)_t$, calculated by dividing value added into wage bill, was employed as a convenient measure of intensity. The triad was completed with a dummy variable S, where $S = 0$ for producers' goods and $S = 1$

(2) Thus, it was not necessary to confine analysis to a single industry, although in this study it was convenient to do so. The model could be also applied to a sample representing all major industrial users in a region.

(3) The divisor was found by determining the quantity of intake necessary, *ceteris paribus*, if none was reused, and subtracting from this the actual withdrawals made during the year. This former quantity is referred to as 'gross water use'.

for consumers' goods. Multi-product plants were classified according to the product group representing the largest share of value added.

The technological shift parameter introduced in equation (5′) was defined as a linear combination of these three variables,

$$\pi_t = b_4 A_t + b_5 \left(\frac{W}{X}\right)_t + b_6 S_t \ . \tag{9}$$

Upon examining the sample data it was found that there were too few firms recirculating processing and steam power water to permit efficient estimation of their respective cross-elasticities b_3, perhaps due to the high costs of treating processing wastes and recapturing boiler feed water. Since total water use would be understated by ignoring recycled intake, a new dependent variable was formed by aggregating actual intake and the additional intake which would be required if none were reused. This variable was called gross water demand, G_{wft} (see footnote 3). The average cost of gross water use is a weighted average of P_{wft} and P_{Rft} (4),

$$P_{Gft} = \frac{(G_{wft} - g_{wft})P_{Rft} + (g_{wft})P_{wft}}{G_{wft}} \ . \tag{10}$$

Consequently, equation (5′) was re-written as,

$$G_{ft} = F_{Gft} X_t^{b_1} P_{Gft}^{b_2} \pi_t \ , \tag{5''}$$

and the closing identity (7) became,

$$g_{wt} \equiv \sum G_{wft}\left(\frac{g_{wft}}{G_{wft}}\right) + g_{wst} \ . \tag{7'}$$

Here the parenthetical term is the inverse of the reuse ratio and is exogenous to the model.

Descriptive measures of the principal variables are given in table 1.

Table 1. Arithmetic means and coefficient of variation of principal variables.

Variable	Use Cooling		Steam power		Processing		Sanitation	
	mean	cf	mean	cf	mean	cf	mean	cf
g_{wft} (1000 gal)	1462070	2·75	66571	1·56	154425	1·99	1552	1·56
G_{ft} (1000 gal)	2714351	1·90	66571	1·56	154425	1·99	1552	1·56
X_t ($1000)	22772	1·27	22869	1·27	24497	1·24		
P_{Gft} ($)*	0·217	1·03	0·475	0·83	0·855	1·48		
N_t							807	1·14

* Average cost equals average operating cost plus average capital charges calculated as straight-line depreciation.

(4) The practice of recirculation reduces the unit cost of gross use as long as $P_{rft} < P_{wtf}$. Note that if water were not reused P_{Gwft} would reduce to P_{wft} and G_{wft} to g_{wft}, since the reuse ratio would be unity.

Estimates of demand parameters

Ordinary least squares estimates were obtained for the log–linear form of equation (5″), and restricted least squares estimates for the linear sanitation equation (6)[5]. An incidental advantage of the log–linear form is that the regression coefficients can be interpreted as the demand elasticities defined by equation (4).

For convenience in experimenting, the model capital charges, which were added to current expenses to find total water costs, were calculated using a straight-line depreciation method[6].

Seven specifications of each output-related equation were formed, and tested, by varying the combination of variables used to derive the technological measure π_t [see equation (9)]. The best equations were selected on the basis of goodness-of-fit and efficiency of coefficient estimates (hence combinations involving multicollinearity were eliminated). These best equations in each usage category appear in table 2.

Of particular interest is the importance of the price-elasticities for cooling and steam power demand as indicated by their size, statistical significance, and the magnitude of their corresponding partial correlation coefficients. Together cooling and steam power uses account for about 90% of all manufacturing withdrawals, so these results demonstrate that pollution abatement programs which have an impact on private costs may be expected to alter significantly total demand and water-use intensities.

To illustrate this point, consider the imposition of a 'tough' anti-pollution policy which requires firms to process wastes through an additional treatment stage[7]. On the basis of data provided by the sample firms, waste treatment costs constitute an average of one-third of the total cost of cooling water and a slightly smaller proportion of the cost of steam power water. Consequently, this policy would increase average cost of these two uses combined by approximately 30% and,

(5) Linear and semi-logarithmic forms were also tested but all displayed much poorer fit.

(6) Selection of a discount rate for calculating average cost by equation (8) is, at best, arbitrary since the appropriate, but unknown, rate may be expected to vary from firm to firm. Differences in cost due to varying the rate are directly related to capital intensity of the plant's water system. One version of each of the three functions in equation (5″) was run using $i = 0, 0{\cdot}04$, and $0{\cdot}08$, but the differences in coefficient estimates were found to be very small (De Rooy, 1969).

The value of average cost was therefore approximated by,

$$P_{wft} = \frac{1}{g_{wft}}\left[\sum_h \sum_j \left(\frac{K_{hj}}{I_{y_{hj}}}\bigg/ L_{hj}\right) + E_{hj} + C_u\right] . \tag{8'}$$

(7) An important measure of waste water quality is biochemical oxygen demand (BOD) created by the decomposition of organic matter. Primary treatment (filters, screening, or settlement) generally reduces BOD by one-third. Secondary treatment (activated sludge, coagulation, etc.) may further reduce BOD by one-third. The costs of both treatments are about equal.

Table 2. Regression equations and coefficient estimates.

Use	SE/SD	R^2	F_t	X_t	P_{Gft}	A_t	S_t	$(W/X)_t$	N_t
Cooling†	0·187	0·840	−0·579	1·295	−0·916			4·704	
				(5·71)**	(4·94)**			(6·11)**	
				[0·759]	[0·710]			[0·780]	
Steam power†	0·335	0·783	−4·423	1·446	−0·683		−2·195	2·729	
				(5·59)**	(2·92)**		(3·40)**	(2·37)*	
				[0·788]	[0·557]		[0·615]	[0·477]	
Processing†	0·489	0·595	−6·021	0·877	0·192	1·099			
				(3·23)**	(0·64)	(3·39)**			
				[0·586]	[0·142]	[0·604]			
Sanitation††	0·336	0·890	0·000						0·171
									(12·56)**

Notes: Figures in parentheses are t-ratios; figures in brackets are partial correlation coefficients.
SE/SD = standard error of the regression estimate divided by standard deviation of the dependent variable
† Log-linear equation
†† Linear equation
* Coefficient significant at 0·05 level
** Coefficient significant at 0·01 level

Sample sizes: Cooling 28; Processing 24; Steam power 24; Sanitation 20

ceteris paribus, decrease total demand of the firm by at least one-quarter. If anticipated increases in non-industrial uses do not take up the slack, discharges into the watercourse may be well below the level the stream is capable of safely assimilating, thereby underutilizing this resource and imposing unnecessary costs on production in the region.

On the other hand, construction of a municipal treatment plant might have the effect of reducing private costs by eliminating some of the need for in-plant treatment. This would give an increase in demand for water and in the joint demand for the services of the stream as waste receiver. If the new treatment plant were designed to handle a capacity only equal to the volume formerly treated by users, the quality of the stream would be impaired.

The sign of the estimate of price-elasticity of processing demand appears to be an anomaly, although the estimate is not statistically significant and this result may be attributable to sampling error. It is suggested, however, that the price variable be retained on *a priori* grounds. The true elasticity may in fact be negative but small, in which case it should be recognized that the power of the t-test decreases with effect size (here, the absolute value of the true parameter) as well as with sample size.

Estimates of output-elasticity are also of interest in regional planning of water resources. Cooling and steam power elasticities, which are greater than unity, imply that water-intensity, on average, varies directly with firm size. This may be attributable in part to the fact that larger establishments tend to have higher capital–labor ratios than smaller ones, and their bigger stocks of capital create a greater need for cooling and power. Thus, an area where growth in output is due primarily to expansion of existing firms may anticipate a greater relative change in demand than an area in which the same growth comes about as a result of the establishment of new plants.

Although increases in price and output have opposing effects on demand, it is important to compare the relative sizes of their respective elasticities. Administrators of abatement programs who wish to maintain stable, or moderately increasing, demand will find it advisable to permit a rate of increase in real costs which exceeds the rate of growth in production. The proper extent of this differential depends upon the type of program. One which is intended to control thermal pollution should take into account the parameters of the cooling and steam power demand functions, while the elasticities of processing demand are relevant for programs aimed at regulating processing wastes. For example a thermal pollution abatement plan, implemented in an area where the population of firms is somewhat stationary, should specify gradual improvements in effluent quality to the extent that the rate of increase in real average cost of cooling water is about 40% greater (that is, $1\cdot295\Delta X_t/{-0\cdot916}\Delta P_{Gft}$) than the rate of growth of output, *ceteris paribus*, if it is desired to avoid increases in the quantities demanded.

Where price and output levels are given, the study revealed that a substantial portion of remaining differences in demand can be attributed to dissimilarities in technology. One reason why the labor–output ratio performed well as a measure of technology is that older plants, on average, used less capital per worker and also tended to use production methods and machinery which were not designed to conserve water. In-plant water conservation is largely a new phenomenon since it is only during recent years that users have realized that water is not a free good. In support of this reasoning, it is interesting to note that specifications using age of plant performed almost as well as those using the labor–output ratio (De Rooy, 1969). The age variable was found to be the best surrogate for technology in the processing demand equation. An additional technological measure in the steam power equation was the product classification dummy variable, which was appropriate because consumer goods in the chemical industry (for example, toiletries and paints) require less of a power input than do industrial goods. However, it would be difficult to generalize this reasoning to cover consumer goods in many other industries.

An alternate specification of the output-related demand equations was made by employing principal components of the technological measures, thereby permitting identification of common causal constituents but avoiding multicollinearity among the variables[(8)]. The performance of this alternative, however, did not warrant use of the principal components as

[(8)] Principal components were formed from four variables: labor–output ratio, age of plant, product group, and output per worker. The last was dropped from the original model primarily due to a high correlation with W/X. For so few variables, the principal components provided a minor saving of degrees of freedom.

replacements for the original variables, although they did prove helpful at a later stage of the study.

The analysis of technological effects did demonstrate the necessity of adjusting calculation of demand quantities in proportion to the labor-intensity, or the age of firms. This implies that if the manufacturing sector consists, on average, of plants with less efficient water use in their production methods, regulation is harder than in areas with more modern firms, so that objectives may have to be modified to conform with such circumstances. Otherwise the higher levels of treatment, which would be required to offset adverse technological effects, would involve such high private costs that firms might curtail expansion or even migrate from the region, which would lower the rate of growth of industrial activity and employment.

Technology and demand elasticities

The specifications in table 2 imply that price and output elasticities are independent of the state of technology of a firm. However, it is of interest to examine a model which permits interaction between π_t and the values of b_1 and b_2. If technological improvements enhance the ability of firms to alter the complex of inputs in response to variations in (factor) market conditions and output, the elasticities of firms with modern processes should be greater than those of firms with older equipment and techniques.

The principal components mentioned in the preceding section provided a convenient means of partitioning observations and thereby testing this hypothesis. Firms used in estimating the demand functions in each output-related category were divided into two groups depending upon the sign of the first principal component. This represented an average of 63% of the variation among the technological variables and was highly correlated with W/X. Thus, positive values (generally associated with above average values of original measures) identified relatively 'high technology' firms, and negative values identified 'low technology' firms. Demand quantities were separately regressed on output and price for each group in the three categories. These results are shown in table 3.

An analysis of covariance was made to test the significance of the differences between the sets of coefficients, or elasticities. The null hypothesis of this test implied an independence between marginal rates of substitution for water and sophistication of the production processes, as characterized chiefly by capital intensity, that is,

$$H_0: \begin{vmatrix} b_{1+} \\ \\ b_{2+} \end{vmatrix} = \begin{vmatrix} b_{1-} \\ \\ b_{2-} \end{vmatrix}, \qquad (11)$$

where the sign of the first principal component is indicated by the second subscript. The procedure was to find (1) the mean squared residuals of

Table 3. Regression equations and coefficient estimates of sub-samples of firms grouped by the value of the first principal component of technological variables.

Category	Value of principal component 1†	R^2	Sub-sample size	F_t	X_t	P_{Gft}
Cooling	positive	0·914	11	−16·833	2·068 (4·40)**	−1·257 (3·91)**
Cooling	negative	0·622	17	−1·561	0·930 (3·03)**	−0·759 (3·20)**
Processing	positive	0·791	11	−14·710	2·00 (5·16)**	0·403 (1·01)
Processing	negative	0·598	13	−5·723	1·332 (3·60)**	0·022 (0·06)
Steam power	positive	0·432	14	−7·033	1·386 (2·50)*	−0·696 (2·01)
Steam power	negative	0·857	10	−7·919	1·067 (2·53)*	−1·804 (3·96)**

Note: Figures in parentheses are *t*-ratios.
† Positive values of principal component are associated with 'high technology' firms and negative values are associated with 'low technology' firms.
* Significant at 0·05 level
** Significant at 0·01 level

the two regressions in each category which had unequal elasticities but equal intercepts, and (2) the mean squared residuals of the same regressions wherein all parameters were allowed to vary. The ratio of these quantities is known to follow the F-distribution. The analysis is reported in table 4.

Differentials in cooling and steam power elasticities due to technology were highly significant. As revealed in table 3, high technology firms had more elastic demand with respect to output, suggesting that such firms tend to conserve more as they grow in size [9]. In addition, modern techniques seemed to provide cooling users with greater flexibility in responding to changes in price. However, the relatively higher price elasticity of low technology firms for steam power water may be indicative of a more limited choice of power source for large scale operations.

Elasticities of processing demand were not significantly different in this test, perhaps due to the high variance of the price coefficient estimates. However, assuming this result was not attributable to sampling error, the next step was to examine the equations for homogeneity of the intercepts [10]. In this test the null hypothesis was safely rejected, so that

[9] It is doubtful whether the greater water input-output ratios of larger firms can be attributed to capital intensity alone, since a finer examination of the data revealed no highly significant correlation between output and the labor-output ratio.

[10] This corresponds to a simple test of the difference between sample means, where the mean quantities demanded have been adjusted by the price and output coefficients.

there appeared to exist a constant shift in quantity demanded as a consequence of technological change. But the fact that the three major determinants of processing demand act independently favors the original specification in table 2, which postulates a continuous rather than a discrete relationship between technology and demand and which, therefore, affords greater precision.

The model demonstrates that the demand for cooling and steam power water increases rapidly in relation to growth in output in areas where firms employ advanced production techniques. Since differences between price and output elasticities are large, cost increases resulting from pollution controls will only moderately temper an upward trend in derived demand. On the other hand, if an industrial sector is composed primarily of older (or of labor-intensive) firms, programs permitting a rate of increase in private costs equivalent to the rate of growth of output will succeed in stabilizing cooling and steam power demands.

Table 4. Analysis of covariance of regressions on sub-samples†.

Source of variation	Cooling			Steam power			Processing		
	SS	*df*	*MS*	*SS*	*df*	*MS*	*SS*	*df*	*MS*
Residual *w*-in groups with unequal constants and elasticities	35·737	22	1·624	34·114	18	1·895	31·664	18	1·759
Differences due only to unequal elasticities	14·674	2	7·337	48·950	2	24·475	4·991	2	2·496
Residual *w*-in groups with unequal constants	50·410	24	2·101	83·065	20	4·153	36·655	20	1·833
Differences due to unequal constants	0·834	1	0·834	3·847	1	3·847	35·683	1	35·683
Total residual (equal elasticities and constants)	51·245	25		86·912	21		72·338	21	
Test of elasticities	$F(2,22) = 4 \cdot 517$*			$F(2,18) = 12 \cdot 914$**			$F(2,18) = 1 \cdot 419$		
Test of intercepts							$F(1,20) = 19 \cdot 470$**		

† See table 3
* Significant at 0·05 level
** Significant at 0·01 level

SS = unexplained sum of squares
MS = mean squared error
df = degrees of freedom

The models reported in this and the previous section differ in their implications for the design of programs. In the original model technological improvements lessened demand, independently of price and output, so that 'market-oriented' programs which affect private costs could be expected to successfully regulate withdrawals (and, consequently, waste loads). However, more direct controls, such as use of withdrawal permits, would be called for if the revised model constituted a more accurate representation of behavior of the firm.

Conclusions

Given the present data, the original model was on the whole more successful in explaining variations in demand. The revised model did, however, serve to underscore the importance of refining programs to take account of the degree of modernization of manufacturing units in a region, while working toward some target stream quality. Overambitious standards might seriously jeopardize the prospects for industrial development, particularly among 'low-technology' firms. The fact that standards in many areas are now set by public health agencies, without knowledge of the value of water as a productive service, may obscure the economic realities of regulation.

The work reported here is only the first step in developing a complete model for evaluating the economic effects of pollution abatement programs. Equations must be added to explain demand not only in other industries but also for all other major uses: recreation, agriculture, and household. With such a system it would be possible to design programs which are intended to maximize a region's total product, as suggested in the opening section of the paper.

Economic analysis cannot be used alone in managing the quality of water resources. Ecological consequences of different stream standards are also important; but even those which are known cannot always be assigned an economic value. But once such standards are set in accordance with ecological priorities, demand functions will prove helpful in explaining the effect of these preferences on water users.

References

References which have not been cited in this paper are marked with the symbol •

Baxter, R. E., Rees, R., 1968, "An analysis of the industrial demand for electricity", *The Economic Journal,* **77**, 310.

•Beckman, M. J., Sato, R., 1969, "Aggregate production functions and types of technological progress: a statistical analysis", *American Economic Review,* **59**, 1.

De Rooy, J., 1969, "The industrial demand for water resources: an econometric analysis", unpublished Ph. D. Dissertation, Rutgers University, New Brunswick, New Jersey.

Fisher, F. M., 1962, *A Study in Econometrics: The Demand for Electricity in the United States* (North-Holland, Amsterdam).

Granstrom, M. L., Dutta, M., De Rooy, J., 1969, *Water Use in the Chemical Industry in New Jersey: An Econometric and Engineering Analysis* (New Jersey Water Resources Research Institute, New Brunswick, New Jersey).

•Malinvaud, E., 1966, *Statistical Methods in Econometrics* (Rand-McNally, Chicago).

Samuelson, P., 1947, *Foundations of Economic Analysis* (Harvard University Press, Cambridge).

•Snedecor, G., 1965, *Statistical Methods in Research* (Iowa State University Press, Ames, Iowa).

Stigler, G. J., 1957, *The Theory of Price,* revised edition (University of Chicago Press, Chicago).

US Department of Commerce, Bureau of the Census, 1966, *Census of Manufactures, 1963. Subject Statistics: Water Use in Manufacturing,* MC63(1)-10, Washington.

Why is General Relativity Theory Relevant to Regional and Other Social Sciences?†

W.ISARD
University of Pennsylvania

In several other papers (Isard, 1971a, 1971b, 1971c) I have presented some initial exploratory findings on the possible use of new concepts and models in regional science that are suggested by general relativity physics. In this brief paper I wish to state why general relativity theory may provide some extremely useful insights into regional processes. I shall do so by listing a set of points which in part incorporate the rationale that general relativity theorists employ.

1 General relativity theorists are motivated to explain gravitational interaction among masses. So are regional scientists, when they deal with populations and other social masses.

2 Classical Newtonian and other physics do not provide adequate accounting for the empirical observations on the gravitational interactions among masses—such as the shift of the perihelion of Mercury, and according to some physicists, the bending of light. In social science, the inadequacies of the Newtonian-type gravity model are well-known.

3 A highly appealing feature associated with general relativity theory (though not exclusively with general relativity theory) is the statement of laws in a covariant fashion—that is, in a manner that holds for all observers in all frames of reference. There is no need for me to underscore the importance that such a feature would have for any social science theory in our world of sharply contrasting cultures.

4 One of the basic shortcomings of Newtonian and other physics is their failure to recognize that physical processes are determined by and help determine the geometry of space–time. That is, the properties of any mass present at any given point of space–time are affected by the geometry of that space–time and simultaneously affect that geometry. In regional science, we well know that the significance (employment-and income-generating capability) of an industry mass (say an integrated iron and steel works) is affected by the geometry of the space–time as

† These remarks are refinements of statements made in a lecture delivered at Karlsruhe, August 1970.

reflected at the point at which it is located, and in turn affects the geometry of social, economic, and political space–time. This is in keeping with that traditional agglomeration thinking of economics and regional science which we have never been able to incorporate in a satisfactory theory.

5 Einstein was motivated to overcome this shortcoming. However, since Newtonian physics was found to be valid in a limited domain of phenomena, he required that his theory reduce to Newtonian mechanics in this limited domain. In regional science, we too seek for such a theory which would reduce to the Newtonian-type gravity model in the limited domain in which it has been found quite adequate.

6 Further, Einstein found it necessary to abandon the notion of space and time as separate and absolute entities, as in the Newtonian framework of physics. Likewise, for regional science I have begun to present the case for the hypothesis that space and time cannot be viewed as separate and absolute entities for a proper understanding of the dynamics of society. See Isard (1970, 1971a, 1971b)

7 In the place of a three-dimensional Euclidean space and a one-dimensional Euclidean time, Einstein introduced a four-dimensional space–time continuum, the history of any material object being a sequence of points in space–time, or what has come to be designated a *world-line.* Correspondingly, in regional science we must adopt a four-dimension space–time continuum and speak of world lines (world helices, etc.) of behaving units and institutions. The only time sequence which now remains absolute is the one recorded by a unit or institution on its own world line.

8 Einstein finally realized that flat space–time (of the Euclidean type) is inadequate for incorporating gravitational interaction among masses, and thus found it necessary to introduce a new type of space–time continuum. We, too, need to probe deeply the gravitational interaction among social masses, as well as the impact of accelerating masses upon other masses; therefore, we too must abandon flat space–time.

9 In searching for a type of space–time continuum which could be highly non-uniform, Einstein looked for the simplest general geometry, and found it in Riemannian space–time. We, too, do not wish to adopt a general geometry which is any more complicated than is necessary. Therefore, following Einstein, we are currently exploring the usefulness of Riemannian space–time.

10 There are various classes of Riemannian space–time; Einstein adopted that class which yields *in any local area* a flat space–time of a Euclidean character, consistent with the requirement of point 5. So, too, with us.

11 To describe Riemannian space–time, the simple tensor of rank one—namely, the *vector*—is inadequate. We must use, instead, tensors of the second or higher rank. In other papers (Isard, 1971a, 1971c) I have tried to elucidate the significance of tensors of second rank, and to suggest their significance for regional science.

12 The metric of Riemannian space-time is described by a symmetric second-rank tensor, usually designated the metric tensor $g_{\mu\nu}$, which has ten independent components. So Einstein reasoned that he required ten independent equations to determine the ten independent components of the metric tensor $g_{\mu\nu}$, his interest being of course to incorporate in the geometry a complete description of the gravitational forces among masses. Correspondingly, it seems to me that if we are to treat agglomeration and other general-type forces, that we too should incorporate these forces in a complete manner into a geometry, hopefully one as simple as the Riemannian space-time used by Einstein.
13 Einstein field equations are given by

$$R_{\mu\nu} - \tfrac{1}{2} g_{\mu\nu} R = k T_{\mu\nu} .$$

These are ten in number, each being a second-order partial differential equation with respect to $g_{\mu\nu}$. Qualitatively these equations say:

the geometry of space-time = the distribution of masses and their motion.

For example, one of these equations explicitly states, in a qualitative manner, for any given point in the $x-t$ plane (x = the traditional x-dimension, t = time):

the curvature of the space-time at (x_0, t_0) = the flow (per unit of time) of mass or energy in the x-direction .

14 These equations, when properly differentiated, yield the laws of conservation of energy and momentum at any point (locally). For certain purposes of regional science, for example, the study of trade flows within a multi-region world, models which imply local conservation laws are absolutely essential.
15. With the Einstein equations, the amount of mass located at each point as well as the path of motion of every unit of mass are simultaneously determined together with the metric tensor. Such a simultaneous determination feature is highly appealing to regional scientists since the most satisfactory models in regional science are those that come closest to the simultaneous determination of location and trade (and other flows) of a general multi-region system.
16 Thus far, except in very limited situations, only approximate solutions to the Einstein equations have been obtained. These solutions, at their lowest approximations, involve a first term, which accounts for the force associated with the classical Newtonian effect, and a second term which may be interpreted as a correction to this force because of the relative acceleration of masses. Very roughly, the equation reads:

$$F_i = \sum_{j \neq i} G \frac{M_i M_j}{d_{ij}^2} e_{ij} + 4 \sum_{j \neq i} G \frac{M_i M_j}{c^2 d_{ij}} \alpha_j$$

where $\boldsymbol{F}_i$ = force on mass at i (in vector form),

M_i = mass at i,
M_j = mass at j,
d_{ij} = distance between i and j,
e_{ij} = the unit vector from i to j,
c = the speed of light,
α_j = the acceleration of j relative to i (in vector form).

I find this result most appealing of all, since elsewhere (Isard, 1971b) I have contended that (1) our social science models are anemic because they fail to embody basic dynamic processes, and (2) specifically, our models should, at the minimum, take into account the effect upon the behavior of individuals, organizations, and regional societies of the acceleration of other units and societies with which they are interacting.

17 Finally, I should state that higher approximations to the solution to the Einstein field equations involve the velocities of the masses, as well as accelerations. This property of these approximations is also appealing at first blush. However, I have not yet found the velocity-dependencies in these approximations to be consistent with the type of hypotheses that social scientists in general and that I, in particular, find reasonable to advance for a multi-region society.

Acknowledgement. The author is deeply indebted to Panos Liossatos for invaluable assistance in reformulating and restructuring his ideas in a more rigorous manner. The author, however, is fully responsible for any shortcomings of the manuscript.

References

Isard, W., 1970, "On notions and models of time", *Papers Regional Science Association*, **25**, 7-31.

Isard, W., 1971a, "On relativity theory and space-time models", *Papers Regional Science Association*, **26**.

Isard, W., 1971b, "Multi-nation interaction models: some useful insights from general relativity theory", *Papers, Peace Research Society (International)*, **XVII.**

Isard, W., 1971c, "Spatial interaction analysis: some suggestive thoughts for general relativity physics", *Papers Regional Science Association*, **28**,